THE KOREAN MINJUNG IN CHRIST

The KOREAN MINJUNG in CHRIST

David Kwang-sun Suh

Wipf and Stock Publishers
150 West Broadway • Eugene OR 97401
2001

The Korean Minjung in Christ

The Korean Minjung in Christ

By Kwang-sun Suh, David
Copyright©1991 by The Christian Conference of Asia
ISBN: 1-57910-509-2

Reprinted by *Wipf and Stock Publishers*
150 West Broadway • Eugene OR 97401

Previously published by The Christian Conference of Asia, 1991.

TABLE OF CONTENTS

Preface
  Choan Seng Song   vii

Introduction   1

PART I. KOREAN CHURCH HISTORY FROM MINJUNG   9
              PERSPECTIVE

Chapter One/Faith, Praxis and Theology   11
1.   At the Interrogation Center: Summer, 1980   11
2.   First Protestant Missionaries in Korea (1884-1910) 17
3.   Christian Gospel for the Liberation of the Minjung 24
4.   Christian Suffering with the Korean Minjung   31

Chapter Two/The Minjung Movement   43
1.   Japanese and the Christians   43
2.   The Minjung and the Christians in Divided Korea   55
3.   Rediscovery of the Minjung   68

PART II. RELIGION AND CULTURE OF KOREAN MINJUNG   87

Chapter Three/Shamanism: The Religion of Han   89
1.   Korean Shamanism   89
2.   "Theology" of Korean Shamanism   95
3.   The Shaman Rituals   102
4.   Mudangs and Minjung   107
5.   The Shamanized Christians in Korea   111

Chapter Four/Minjung and Spirituality   119
1.   Spirituality Abounds   119
2.   Religion and Spirituality   121
3.   Religious Spirituality   122
4.   Characteristics of Religious Spirituality   123
5.   Paul and the Gifts of the Spirit   124
6.   The Spirituality of Jesus   125

7.   The Spirituality of the Feast   130

Chapter Five/Minjung and Buddhism in Korea   133
1.   Korean Buddhism   133
2.   Buddha, the Founder of a Minjung Religion   136
3.   Boddhisattva and the Minjung   139
4.   Wonhyo and Korean Minjung   144
5.   Buddhism in the Koryo and Yi Dynasties   148
6.   Amitabha and Maitreya Buddhism   151

Chapter Six/Mask Dance of Liberation   159
1.   CCA Assembly Logo: A Korean Dance Mask   159
2.   The Stage   160
3.   Act I: Religion and Minjung   160
4.   Act II: Maltugi, the Hero   170
5.   CCA Assembly Logo Again: The Cross on the Mask   172
     of Maltugi

Chapter Seven/The Theology of Reunification : A Korean   177
                Theology of the Cross and Resurrection
1.   Hanshik and Wandering Spirits   177
2.   The Cross of Division   178
3.   Resurrection and the Rice Community   181
4.   Resurrection and Eschatological Visions of Reunification   184

PREFACE

How can Christian theology begin with an account of oneself, one's family and one's society? What can a biography of oneself, experiences of one's family and the history of one's nation tell about God, traditionally the subject-matter of Christian theology? Should not Christian theology begin with God-talk—teaching about God, and end with God-talk—a doctrine of God? Is it not this God who tells us about what we are as human beings? Is not God the beginning, the middle and the conclusion of our pursuit of meaning and truth? Is this not what Christian theology means by revelation? In order for theology to be possible, God must first tell us about God's own self, about us human beings, and about the world in which we live. To begin Christian theology with ourselves instead of God—is this not to stand theology on its head? Is this not to turn theology as God-talk to theology as human-talk? But, then, this could not be theology. At most, it is anthropology, sociology, psychology, or what have you.

However, Third World theologians have, in recent years, learned that theology does not, and cannot, set itself apart from what is happening to ourselves and to the world. We have realized that theology has more to do with this world, this life, here and now, than with the other world or the life to come. We have also come to see that ironically the main concern of theology is not so much God as us, human beings. If God has to be present in our theological experience, it is not the God who remains in splendid isolation but the God who has chosen to be with us human beings, that is, God Immanuel, God with us and in us. Is there then anywhere else other than the human world in which to conduct the business of theology? Even when we talk about God, and talk we must, should it not be God with us and in us, and not God in, for, and by God's own self, that we must be talking about?

It is this kind of Christian theology that Professor David Kwangsun Suh has done in this book of his, entitled *The Korean Minjung in Christ*. In the theological reflections contained in this book, Professor Suh is preoccupied with himself, his parents and the minjung of Korea, people economically, socially, politically or sexually oppressed in the long history of Korea. Has he, then, dispensed with God in his theology? Has he done away with God in his theological exercise? Not in the least. The theology with which he is engaged in this book is full of God because it is full of himself. The theological exercise he has done in this volume discloses so much about God because it has disclosed so much about his parents and what they had to go through. And the theological reflections he shares with us in this work has everything to do with God because it has everything to do with the long suffering minjung of Korea. He puts it so well when he says: "The theology of Minjung is a socio-historical biography of myself, my father and my mother, under the Japanese occupation. At the same time, it is a theological story of the Korean Christians in the political struggle for freedom in the 1970's in Korea."

If this is what Christian theology must be, then it has to be a testimony to the ways in which God works in the personal life of individual persons. That is why Professor Suh begins his theological essay with his encounter with the powers that be at an interrogation center in Seoul, Korea, in the summer of 1980. He and a number of his theologian-colleagues had been arrested for involvement in the struggle for democracy and human rights. Theology for him and for his fellow theologians is not a second-step theology as Latin American liberation theologians call it, but a first-step and first-hand theology. What a privilege it is, then, for us to be allowed into the theological world in which some Korean theologians such as Professor Suh had a deep experience of God as God with and in us because they had a deep experience of the suffering minjung.

The Christian theology Professor Suh shares with us here is a theology of the first person pronoun, and not a theology of the second or third person pronoun. His is a theology conceived in the womb of passion (suffering) and given birth in the midst of the people struggling for freedom and democracy. He leads us back to the time when the Korean people underwent the turmoil of the Korean war. It was both a personal and a national tragedy. Korea has become divided between North and South for the past forty years. And it was an epic of hundreds of thousands of people fleeing to the South—an epic in which a large number of men, women and children either lost their lives or their families.

Professor Suh himself was involved in this national tragedy. Faith in God became an enormous project for Korean Christians such as Professor Suh. The theological reflections contained in this book are an outcome of that project called faith. Yes, faith is a life project and not a verbal consent. Theology which seeks to explicate faith is a commitment and not a mental gymnastic. Professor Suh's theology is a commitment to a project of faith. How could it, then, be anything other than a first person and first hand theology? "The Christian message," to quote Professor Suh, "came to life in the actual Korean experience of suffering for the cause of freedom and national independence." And again, "Christianity is for the poor and oppressed, and the history of Korean Christianity attests to that fact."

In this way, Professor Suh has given us in this book a theology that is unapologetically autobiographical. It is his autobiography. It is also the autobiography of the Korean minjung. And an autobiography of God? Is it not to be found in autobiographies such as one would read in the pages of this book? This may be a deviation from the traditional way of doing theology, but not from the way Jesus did his theology. Jesus did his theology in such a way that God was disclosed in what he was and in what he had to go through in life and death. Had not that Roman soldier at the foot of the cross been reported to have said: "Truly this man was the son of God" (Mt. 27:54)?

It must be for this reason that Professor Suh tells us in effect: "Jesus is the parable of Minjung and Minjung is the parable of Jesus." How true! I would like to add and say: Jesus is the parable of God and God is the parable of Jesus. The theological circle here is complete. It is from Jesus that we learn what theology must be and how to do it. And it has to do with ourselves as Christians and with minjung, people who suffer from injustice, oppression, discrimination, or poverty. In what you are about to read, Professor Suh has shown us an important theological insight: the heart of the Korean political theology of minjung is Jesus who was born, suffered, died and rose again in the company of countless suffering men, women and children in Korea and in other parts of the world through the centuries.

Choan-Seng Song
Berkeley
August 1990

INTRODUCTION

Korean Minjung theology has grown out of telling stories. The stories were mostly true—what the people have done, how they have struggled, and how badly they have been tortured and beaten up, how they have become poor and marginalized, and so on. Minjung theologians call these stories the "socio-biography" of minjung. One might as well call them "political biography" of minjung or life history of minjung. However you may call them, they are forgotten history; they are not recorded in the history of the kings and governments, nor in the history of wars and conquests. Furthermore, the stories of minjung are suppressed and censored. Although they are true, factual stories, they are suppressed and banned as "false rumors." And an oppressive government would decide that they could not be printed in the daily papers.

Minjung theologians gathered secretly with young workers, students, priests, and laborer-pastors and told the stories of the struggling minjung in Korea, in the mid-1970's. Secretly we met, but the "cover" was a dinner gathering, a fellowship, to exchange true stories which the censored Korean papers would not dare to print. The purpose of the gathering, so to speak, was to exchange "false rumors." The stories would be about recent student demonstrations, the number of participants, the number of persons arrested, issues and slogans, and the government reactions, etc. Sometimes the gathering would report the recent labor movements—workers who self-immolated as a form of protest against the severe labor oppression, and female workers who were beaten up by combat police. But at times the professors would talk about how they had been interrogated by the KCIA agents in their offices regarding their teaching materials, assigned books, and recent newspaper columns that they had written. The secret gathering would become saddened by the news of fellow Christian professors who had been taken in by the secret agents.

We hear news about indicted professors being court-martialed. The military tribunal has sentenced the professors to some ten years in prison, stripping them of their civil rights. Then we call for a meeting to organize protest movements against the emergency decrees which prohibit all kinds of political activities. We would issue protest statements and organize prayer meetings for the imprisoned students and professors. Some would preach, others would be assigned to pray for the political prisoners in the prayer meetings. And they would be taken in by the secret agents for investigation and harassment. But we would meet again to plan the next move against the oppressive government. In the process, some of us Christian professors were forced to leave our teaching posts. The announced reasons for dismissal would be "incompetency" or "loss of dignity as university professors." But everyone on and off the university campuses knew that all of us who were dismissed were highly respected by the students and well-educated, with highest academic degrees from international universities.

Minjung theology has grown out of these professors' political experiences in the 1970's under the very oppressive military dictatorship of President Park Chung-Hee. They first met for dinner parties and exchanged news and rumors and stories of the students and laborers who were struggling for human rights, justice and democracy. Then they came to stand on the side of the struggling people and to speak on behalf of the poor and oppressed. The Christian intellectuals themselves became involved in the struggle for academic freedom, social justice, human rights and democratic procedures of the government and politics. As they travelled in and out of jails, interrogation centers and political prisons, they were forced to reflect on their theology—why were they doing this; how come they had become involved in the struggles of the people; what were their theological bases for such political struggles with the students, laborers, the poor and oppressed?

Some of us began writing theological articles and a few of these were published, but some could not appear in print. Some of us began interpreting the Bible, the history of the Hebrews and the life and teachings of Jesus from the perspective of our struggles and suffering of the people. Others read the Korean history from the perspective of the struggles of the Korean people. And some began looking into the life-style of the poor and oppressed people of Korea out of which the relentless struggle for humanity has grown. We dug out the stories of the struggling minjung of Korea in their history, their socio-political biographies, their culture, songs, dances and dramas. We tried to make connections between the stories of the Bible and the stories of our people, between the socio-biography of the people in the Bible and that of the Korean minjung, between the stories of the past and the stories of the present and the future. In the process, we made connections between our stories and our actions. We reflected upon our own stories and our own action. Hence, our theological utterances are telling the stories of what we have done in the struggle for the kingdom of God with the people, and they are the faith reflections of our action on the struggle.

I was forced to reflect upon what I have done and the ways in which I lived. I was forced to think about my Christian faith and write, rather prematurely, my own socio-biography or politico-theological biography, in the summer of 1980 when I was taken into the military investigation torture chamber. It was a torture technique that forced you to write about yourself, your family, your education and why you have done what you had done. Day and night, page after page, you were forced to spell out your convictions and beliefs. The investigators would check out what you had written, event by event. They were the ones who decided whether you would stay in prison or not, with or without trial. Finally, at the end of the investigation I was forced to write a resignation paper from my teaching post in the university.

What follows in this book is what I had written in that torture chamber in the summer of 1980. I do not even imagine the Korean military government would return what I had written in that place, nor do I need them. In a sense, this is my life story, my socio-political and theological autobiography. But as I was writing my own life story under such circumstances, I realized that it was not just my own story, but it was a part of the whole story of the suffering and struggling people of Korea. I realized that this was the story of how and what God has been doing in our human history, in the history of the people of God, that is, minjung of Korea. If theology is to speak about God, then theology is to speak about the stories and history of the people of God in which God acts. And if theology is doing, then doing what the incarnate God has done in human history is precisely what doing theology is all about.

Thrown out of the university library and office, I was jobless. The Maryknoll Fathers and Brothers granted me the Welsh-Price Fellowship to write about the development of minjung in Korea. I was extremely grateful for the fellowship because it was the bread and life of my family for a year. It was a major financial resource for me so I could concentrate on my research and writing. I used the method of telling stories of my own life through which I wanted to tell the stories of the Korean minjung and the history of the mission of God in Korean history. I insisted on my way of writing theology and an abbreviated form of my manuscript was printed by the World Student Christian Federation Asia/Pacific Office in Hong Kong under the title of *Theology, Ideology and Culture* in 1983. What is included in that book are three lectures I gave to the Asian student leaders who met in Hong Kong for a conference in the summer of 1983.

The year 1984 was an eventful year for me because the government gave in to the public pressure to reinstate the dismissed professors back to their respective institutions without condition. Some eighty-five university professors returned to their original teaching positions that fall. That year, the Korean Christians celebrated 100 years of Protestant mission and 200 years of Catholic mission on the peninsula. Korean Christians were asked to talk about their stories, how they had received Christianity, the character of Korean churches, and how we had made Korean Christianity truly Christian and at the same time truly Korean. Some of the writings I included in this volume are pieces of my interpretation of Korean Christianity which grew out of our reflections about the history of Christian mission in Korea. I am no professional church historian, but I want to tell the stories of the Korean Christians in their struggles to make the Christian Gospel meaningful in their history—in their *han*-ridden history of foreign occupation, colonialism and national division.

As of 1990, Korea is the only country in the world that is still divided. In 1945 while the Korean people were celebrating the victory of the allied forces over Japan after the deadly atomic bombs were dropped over the Japanese cities of Hiroshima and Nagasaki, the Korean peninsula was divided into North and South. We thought we were liberated from Japan, but Soviet troops occupied the North and the US the South. In 1950, Koreans fought the war to try to unite the country by military means only to ruin the whole land , devastating the cities and villages, leaving homeless orphans, separated families, missing people and dead bodies over the mountains and river valleys. I lost my preacher-father in the North when I left the North Korean capital, Pyongyang; I was only 19 years old. I found my father's bullet-ridden body on the river bank of that Northern city and I buried him before I left for the South. I am now a gray-haired old man longing for the day when I could go back to that city of Pyongyang to find my father's graveyard. And I want to worship with Christian brothers and sisters in a church in Pyongyang.

Friends in the National Council of Churches in Korea organized meetings which would articulate the people's desire for peace and reunification of Korea. The planned meetings were interrupted and banned by the government authorities. According to the authorities, discussions of peace on the Korean peninsula, including disarmament, reduction of arms race, nuclear free zone, or withdrawal of foreign troops from the peninsula would be violations of the awesome national security laws. According to them, matters of reunification of the land were not to be discussed by the non-governmental civil organizations such as churches and councils of Christian churches. But we had insisted on organizing the meetings and we drafted the policy statement on peace and national reunification of the Korean peninsula. The policy statement was adopted unanimously at the General Assembly of NCCK in the spring of 1988.

Some of the writings I have included in this book came out of our common struggle for the reunification of Korea. We have identified the root cause of Korean minjung's suffering, political or otherwise, as the national division for nearly a half century. The Korean minjung suffered from Japanese colonialism for the first half of the 20th century, and for the last half from the division of the country. Minjung theology is to articulate the suffering of the Korean minjung resulting from the division and to organize struggles toward the establishment of peace and toward peaceful reunification of the nation and the people.

This book is not meant to be a coherent presentation and a neat argument to convince people on such theological questions as to who God is and what God is all about. For these writings were written in a situation of struggle and suffering, even with fear that you may be arrested at the end of your speech. In my theological training, no one told me that speaking of God and theological writing would become a subversive activity. But what I have realized in my public speaking and writing is that to talk about God is a mighty dangerous thing to do. With fear and trembling, our ancestors of Christian faith stood before God and spoke honestly about God and bore the Cross of suffering and death. Honest to God, I have tried to be faithful to the suffering and struggles of the Korean minjung in these writings.

I am grateful to my friend, Oh Jae Shik, who grabbed my papers and looked for ways to publish them and to introduce the public to Korean Christianity. Dr. Salvador T. Martinez, secretary for theological concerns of the Christian Conference of Asia, put much of his time and energy to the publication of this book. Without his encouragement and pressure, my speeches, notes and papers would still be stored in my steel cabinet. Marion Kim has always shown her comradeship by graciously consenting, despite time constraints, to do what sometimes was an almost impossible job of "Englishing" my writings. I am also indebted to Mr. Lee Chol-Su and Mr. Hong Song-Dam for the permission to use their beautiful and moving works of art for the cover and other illustrations in the book. I can go on writing about the friends and colleagues who helped me in formulating my ideas and thinking. They are numerous, and most of them are the Korean minjung struggling daily in their prison cells, factories and farms. I would like to dedicate this book to them—the Korean minjung in Christ.

stars
&
rain
tears

Rice is Heaven, Lee Chul-Su

Dream of Hercules, Lee Chul-Su

PART 1

KOREAN CHURCH HISTORY FROM MINJUNG PERSPECTIVE

1 FAITH, PRAXIS AND THEOLOGY

1. At the Interrogation Center: Summer, 1980

I t was one of those hot and humid July days in Seoul, almost two months since Martial Law had been declared. Many students had been arrested. Universities were shut down. Professor-friends had disappeared. No one seemed to know what was going to happen. It was certain the military would take over the country, but no one was sure how. Meanwhile, university business had to go on as usual, although students were not allowed on campus. All the university gates were heavily guarded by combat units in armored personnel carriers.

I was in the middle of a faculty committee meeting about the new science education building when a man from the Joint Investigation Headquarters called and asked me to meet him at a nearby tea house. I was supposed to be frightened by the call. His group was the one which took students and intellectuals and politicians to some unknown place for investigation and interrogation, sometimes for torture.

At the tea room I told them that I was right in the middle of a very important faculty committee meeting, and that I was the Dean of the College of Liberal Arts and Sciences—the largest college in the university. The plain clothesmen pointed out our Dean of the Faculty, who had just been called out of a meeting with the president of the university. They showed me a note which said I was to be taken to their Headquarters for investigation in connection with the Kim Dae-Jung incident. Kim had been court-martialed and sentenced to death for his political activities over a period of more than ten years as the opposition leader against the Park Chung Hee government. I knew immediately that they were investigating me for my political stance, and sensed that they were going to demand my resignation from the university at the conclusion of the investigation.

The military investigation center was rather clean and hushed. My room was about 8 by 12 feet, with a metal desk and two metal chairs, one on each side of the desk. Mattresses and blankets were neatly folded in the corner of the room. I was to have the room to myself. In no time, the man came into the room, and I had to take everything out of my pockets and take off my belt. It looked like I might have to stay quite a while. He asked me to sit down at the desk and gave me some government stationery and a ball point pen. He told me that I had a lot to write about.

The first thing I was to write was my autobiography. Not a brief one, or a summary of my life until now. No curriculum vitae, that is. I was supposed to write about my family, my father, my grandfather, my school, teachers, books, kind of education, kind of friends, and so forth, I was not to skip anything. In short, I was to write my autobiography. The man looked very tough and serious, and very business-like, but he did not tell me why I had to do this. That was not his business or mine. I was only to give him the complete story of my life.

I did not know where to begin. He said to begin with my birth. I thought that wouldn't be too interesting, and I told him so. He raised his voice a little and told me to follow his orders, saying something about this being no literature class. I was not to produce an autobiographical masterpiece. They were not interested in my writing skill, but rather in my life and thought—they were the thought police. It was 1980, only four years away from "1984"!

I began by writing my birth date and place of birth. The man, who so far had not introduced himself, left the room with a deep sigh, frowning. Maybe he didn't like me. What could he do even if he did like me?

I was born in 1931. I thought about whether there was any particular significance to the year. None. And I put down my birthplace: Kangkei, Korea. That is in North Korea, about thirty miles south of the Yalu River which divides Manchuria, northern China and North Korea. It was a very cold place during the winter with lots of snow, and beautiful skating rinks on the river, a clean and quiet town of some 30,000 people. I was born in a small house in the middle of the downtown section of the city—when I was a high school student in the city, my father showed me the house where I was born. The natives were quite proud of the clean water and beautiful mountain scenery surrounding their city, but when other people mentioned that most of the *kisaengs* (entertainment girls) in Pyongyang were from Kangkei, the people from Kangkei were embarrassed.

The interrogator came back to my cell (now it's mine), without knocking, to check on the progress of my literary work. He noticed my birth place, "Kangkei," and said exactly the same thing, stereotypical stuff about the people from Kangkei. For the first time he smiled. But then his face became stiff when he asked me when I had come to South Korea. This was important, for I was a refugee from Communist North Korea.

After he and I and another interrogation officer returned from a search of my house—our bedroom, the children's room, my study, the kitchen—and my office at the university, he pushed me to speed up the writing of my story. They had taken an armful of my office files. I was not allowed to tell my wife where I was going or for how long or for what purpose. Koreans are not supposed to ask such questions. That is the way we have been brought up. And moreover, it is good citizenship to cooperate with the authorities and not ask any questions. People's questions to the authorities are always stupid and dangerous. You can get in trouble if you have been asking too many questions.

My wife did not ask any questions about me. I thought she behaved very well while the men were going through our bedroom closet and chest of drawers. They did not seem too impressed by our small house. What they were looking for we didn't know. Maybe it was just a show to scare us or upset us, make us feel like criminals. I was surprised that my wife was rather calm about it, acting like she understood what was going on and what they were up to. They wanted my resignation from the university.

Back again in my room at the interrogation center, I resumed my writing. My father was minister of a small Presbyterian church in the southern part of Pyongyang, south of the Daedong River, until he was taken in by the North Korean thought police one early morning in 1950 during the Korean war. I was staying at home in Pyongyang not doing anything; the famous Pyongyang Presbyterian Theological Seminary I had attended for a brief period after high school had been virtually taken over by the Communists. At the time my father was taken in, I was hiding in the country to escape the communist draft for soldiers to fight the war against the Americans and South Koreans.

South Korean troops came into Pyongyang with MacArthur's American army in late October 1950, and we were temporarily liberated. My mother and I and my father's whole congregation went out to search for my father. Actually we were looking for my father's dead body. I encountered so many dead bodies in the mine shafts, public water wells, valleys and rivers—church leaders, old ladies, children and just plain people. We were lucky; we found my father lying on the bank of the Daedong River. His hands were tied behind his back . His was one of five bodies strung together,all Christian pastors and elders. I was able to recognize my father's face, though his whole body had been riddled with machine gun bullets. He was wearing his old gold pocket watch. After his funeral service, we left Pyongyang with the retreating American troops who were being pushed southward by Chinese forces. That was in the snowy and icy December of 1950. We do not know what happened to my father's grave site. Maybe it was later bulldozed down for a housing development, if there is any such thing in North Korea.

My father didn't have to die there in North Korea. Like many other Christians and ministers in the north, we all could have come to the south before the War, that is right after the liberation of Korea in 1945. We did not have to live under the Communists. Though our travel was closely regulated and watched, we could have risked our lives to cross the 38th parallel that divided the country into North and South . My father preached almost every Sunday about freedom and the democratic way of life. He couldn't speak about such topics openly, so he talked about Bible stories, and Exodus was the main text of his sermons. He was a conservative Presbyterian minister and he liked the Book of Revelation which described how the evil powers against God had fallen. People who do not believe in God, and a government that openly declares that there is no God or any supreme being will surely be destroyed. He refused to join the North Korean League of Christians, a government-inspired Church Council. He refused to send me to the communist National University, even before I told him that I would not be qualified because I was not the son of a communist party member. To fight the North Korean regime and communism in his own way—preaching the Gospel of freedom—was my father's commitment. And he stubbornly believed in his calling to tend his sheep, the Christians in the North. He thought that North Korean pastors ought to stay in the North to keep the Church going as long as possible. The local security police came around to our house every so often to have long conversations with my father. But usually he was called in to the police headquarters for questioning and intimidation We were always frightened by such close surveillance, but we were also emboldened by my father's courage and the people's loyalty and respect. He was taken in right after early morning service one Sunday, with only my mother watching him go.

I respected my father very much. I respected his courage. He was a typical Korean Puritan. He would not give in easily on matters of principle. He was a stern father. He raised me with whips. No cards, no dancing, no drinking, no smoking, and no girls. We were poor, and I was often hungry and had to endure it. I made good grades in Japanese schools and he was tremendously proud of my accomplishments.[1] I was told that I was born only to become a scholar preacher. No more, no less. My Japanese was better than his; he had almost none at all. I often helped him out reading the Japanese language Bible commentary for the preparation of his sermons. I was a precocious theologian. But he was a fundamentalist, and I was a bit to the left of his beliefs. We often had theological debates, and he always won with his "faith" against which, according to him, I should not argue.

When my police interrogator asked me to write down the name of the grade school I attended, I told him that I had to write down six of them at least. He thought it was a joke and ordered me to write down just one; that would be good enough. However, I actually attended six grade schools before finishing my elementary education. My father made the whole family move at least once a year. He could not stand church officers' going against his rules, so he often got into arguments with them. He would not give in. He would throw his resignation at the elders committee. And he would tell my mother to pack up for the move to a church in a nearby town, which would be at least 50 miles away in the deep north Korean mountains.

Finally, we lost our names—our Korean names. We were given Japanese names instead, and we were forced against our will to pay respect to Japanese Shinto shrines. My father joined the protest against this, and so was detained in the police station for about a month. We left for Manchuria in 1939, anti-Japanese political refugees. I guess I was a fourth grader then. My father was invited to serve a Korean congregation in a small Chinese town where many Korean farmers had settled. That was a place where you could see the horizon all around you, like in Texas. Once Red Skelton described on American TV a trip to Texas: "There were miles and miles, nothing but miles." Where we lived in Manchuria it was like that. Miles and miles, land and land, nothing but land.

Often my father and I walked to a nearby hill where you could see one of those gigantic sunsets over the horizon of the Manchurian hills. When the harvest was over, we looked beyond the empty rice paddies and corn fields. We watched a dark red sky over the land, the empty evening space. He told me about Korea. He told me about his father, his Christianity, and his love for his country. Many times he wept as I stood there holding his hand tight, weeping with him about Korea and the Japanese and American missionaries and my grandfather, without knowing what to think or how to feel. I had become a youthful exile theologian.

By now the man in my cell seemed quite happy about the progress of my autobiography, and he became interested in it. He asked me to tell him about my grandfather, though I did not have to write it all down. While he nervously chain-smoked, I told him about my grandfather. One of those Manchurian evenings as the sun set over the hill, my father told me about his father who had been an old Korean military general . When my father spoke about his father, he seemed to hold his head erect, as if saluting a general. My grandfather was a Yangban, a person belonging to one of two classes of the Korean aristocracy. One was the literati class and the other the military. Following the Chinese system of civil examinations, the two classes were formulated according to an individual's merit in Chinese classical learning and examinations. My grandfather passed the military class examinations, and he was placed in the north-eastern province guarding the Chinese border. In 1905, when the Japanese forced the Korean government to accept the Protectorate Treaty and thereby came to occupy Korea, they dismissed the Korean army. My grandfather and others led Korean soldiers fighting against the Japanese military. According to my father, my grandfather was a brave soldier. Armed only with his horse whip and sword, he single-handedly killed some 15 Japanese soldiers armed with rifles. What a brave soldier! But he was captured and thrown into prison.

My father was only five years old then. His mother thought life would not be worth living without her husband and under Japanese rule, so she poisoned my father's elder brothers and herself. She could not, apparently, give the poison to her five-year-old son. Her action was a virtuous thing for the wife of a patriot to do, and it was in the Korean women's tradition. It was a patriotic act on her part, according to my father. My father was soon taken in by a sister of his father who was married to a farmer in the northern mountain province near the town where I was born. My grandfather died soon after he came out of prison, according to my father.

My father was befriended by a Bible salesman who went around the countryside selling copies of the Bible in Korean. People who were interested would invite him in and listen to what he had to say about Christianity and the Bible and the world outside their village. When missionaries started evangelizing in Korea they established this system of itinerant Korean Bible salesmen. They traveled the whole country on foot. They didn't sell the whole book, for that would be too expensive for the country people. First they translated the book of Mark into Korean, and then the other Gospels. The people would buy the Bible piece by piece, one book this time around, and another book the next time the Bible salesman came around. My father learned Korean script by reading the Korean Bible while he was watching the cows and oxen in the field. The Bible salesman recommended that he go to the missionary school in Kangkei, where I was born. The name of the school was Yongsil School, and the principal was the Rev. Campbell. In 1968 at our apartment in Nashville, Tennessee, my wife and I had a chance to visit with the elder Rev. Campbell who was then long retired in a retirement home in Florida. He was so glad to see me. He could tell me very few things about my father except that he was such a poor lad that he had to work very hard in the missionary compound in Kangkei to support himself and earn his tuition.

My father never told me how he met my mother. Maybe church people arranged their marriage. My mother has never told me about her meeting with my father either. Perhaps they were never romantic. I have always considered my mother a strikingly beautiful Korean lady. She was always kind and smiling, though she had to endure much suffering—poverty, church work, children and a hardworking but troubled husband. It was a hard life for her. I never thought she was a happy woman. She obeyed my father and followed him wherever and whenever he wanted to move. She understood my father's religious and political position and took care of the family while he was away for police questioning. I knew she wept a lot because of her husband and because of her hardships as the wife of a country pastor, but she never showed me her tears. She was never a cheerful woman, but very considerate and kind. As many Koreans would say, she had a heart of fine silk. In Manchuria, after she gave birth to her fifth child she was striken by tuberculosis. In 1942, that was an incurable disease. My mother went back to her mother's home in Korea and passed away there. She died under the Japanese occupation, and so was not able to see the liberation of Korea in August 1945. I wept a lot at her burial. I was only 11. Not perhaps because I felt a loss, but because I was angry—angry with my father, his religion and his politics and angry with the Japanese. I thought my father and Japanese police had taken my mother away from me.

2. First Protestant Missionaries in Korea (1884-1910)

I grew up as a serious boy. I was lonely. As a preacher's kid, as they called me all the time, I had to be good and well behaved. I was always at the top of my class in Korean grammar schools, but second in my classes in Japanese middle school in Manchuria. After the loss of my mother, I became a quiet boy. I thought about religion and the Japanese and my father and my mother. Unlike my father, I didn't think the Japanese would rule Koreans forever, or that the Japanese would win the war against the Americans. I thought

Koreans could conquer the Japanese only by Christianity. God would surely deliver the Koreans from the yoke of the Japanese, like God had liberated the Israelites from the Egyptians. I attended many revival meetings. I prayed to God for the liberation of Korea from the domination of the evil powers of Japanese.

For preachers and Sunday school teachers, the story of Moses and Israel's exodus from Egypt was a favorite political story which was told and retold to raise the national and political consciousness of the hearers with regard to liberation. It was natural that they mixed this story with the story of the Korean people who were suffering under the bondage of a foreign power. Neither the preachers nor teachers would speak directly about the Korean people under the Japanese rule. They spoke only of the people of Israel under the rule of Egypt and of their hardship and servitude, but all of us who heard the story knew what was meant by it.

A missionary interpreted it as follows:

> Egypt is the shadow of the power of sin just as Japan represented a symbol of evil in their situation. Just as the people of Israel got acquainted with the power of evil and sin, the Korean people are learning about the nature of evil; just as the people of Israel became aware of God, Korean people are getting to know God. . .
>
> Just as the people of Israel prospered due to God's help, Korean people can prosper even under the Japanese rule, if God helps. This was the subject of ardent prayer of the Korean people.[2]

This was the testimony of a missionary teacher on the Book of Exodus, and on the way Korean Christians used the story of the liberation of the people of Israel. The book of Exodus was translated into Korean and published in 1909. However, even before the book was translated into Korean, the story itself was widely told in the Korean churches of the time. Not surprisingly the Old Testament, and more particularly the book of Exodus and the book of Daniel, were most disliked by the Japanese authorities, and later banned from the Korean church. The story of Moses and the Exodus were too vividly related to the national destiny of the Korean people. The story exerted its spiritual power when it was told in the light of the political fate of the Korean people. The spiritual character of the story would have been meaningless, had it not been told and heard in the light of the historical situation of the Korean people.

My father was a religious fundamentalist, and morally a Korean-style puritan. But he understood the Christian Gospel in political terms. To him Christianity was a political religion. He firmly believed that God practices politics in the world. God practices liberation politics in Korea. Liberation from the domination of the Japanese—that was to him the Gospel of Jesus. I followed his interpretation, though I did not understand him fully. Later I found in reading the history of the Korean church that Korean Christians took the Gospel as a liberating message. To the Korean people, spiritual salvation was directly translated into political liberation. When Jurgen Moltmann visited Korea in early 1975, I showed him around the streets of Seoul where many Korean Christians had been shot on March first 1919 for their declaration of independence. Moltmann exclaimed that Korean Christians had been political theologians before him! Korean Christians heard the Gospel as the message of liberation—not just as an abstract kind of spiritual salvation, but as a concrete message of liberation.

Protestant Christianity was first introduced by American missionaries in the 1880's when the old "hermit kingdom" of Korea was forced to open her doors to the West. In 1882, Korea made a treaty with the US through the mediation of China. The first American missionary was a medical doctor, Dr. Horace Newton Allen, who came to Seoul *via* China.[3] Toleration of religious propagation is not included in the Korean-American Treaty of 1882. To the Korean government, this meant no missionary activities in Korea. But sooner than Americans expected, missionaries became favorites at the royal court.

1884, the year Dr. Allen landed at Inchon, was remembered for the tragic December (4th) mutiny conspired in by the then pro-Japanese and progressive young leaders against the pro-Chinese and conservative government. The coup was bloody but not successful. One of the targets of the assassins, at a banquet celebrating opening of the first post office in Seoul, was Min Yong-ik, nephew of Queen Min. Min Yong-ik had just returned from the US where he had gone for the exchange of ratifications of the Korean-American Treaty. Min was severely wounded by the assassins' swords. Dr. Allen was called in to examine the prince at the residence of P.G. von Mollendorff, a German advisor to the king.[4] The doctor found the prince lying at the point of death with arteries severed and seven sword-cuts on his head and body.

Dr. Allen wrote in his diary dated December 5, 1884: "Last night was a most eventful one to foreigners in Seoul."[5] But Korean church historians would remember the night as a most eventful one in the history of Protestantism in Korea as well. In spite of the Korean court doctors' objections to the application of the Western medicine to the prince, and in spite of the dangers of staying in the troubled city of Seoul, Dr. Allen, his wife and small child committed themselves to the care of the prince, and succeeded in bringing him back to health. By January 27, 1885, Min's condition had improved enough that he sent one hundred thousand copper coins to Allen as a token of his personal regard. But Allen's reward was more than simply money, though this was no mean amount. Western medical skill had been spectacularly exhibited, and the first American missionary had won the personal confidence of the court. Soon afterward, Dr. Allen began to make frequent trips to the royal court as an official court physician. With his medical knowledge, he paved the way for overt missionary endeavors.

From then on, Protestant missionaries were very much in evidence among the Korean people, in the royal court and in the newly-introduced modern schools and hospitals. They were also very much involved in Korean politics. It was a time when both the Japanese and Chinese were claiming colonial rights on the peninsula and moving their soldiers onto the shores of Korea. American missionaries were in the middle of the brutal assassination of Queen Min by Japanese soldiers who invaded the already defenseless royal court in 1895. In the course of ten years of Protestant mission work in Korea, from 1895 to 1905, the missionaries witnessed the social and political turmoil, confusion and bloodshed which finally led to the fateful imposition of Japanese colonial rule. In 1905, Korea was declared a protectorate of Japan.

In this milieu of national political crisis, the people of Korea responded to the Christian message. The reason for such a response was their hope for reform of the social and political structure of the country. Arthur Brown of the Federal Council of Foreign Mission Boards in the USA wrote about the situation as follows:

> Poverty, oppression and distress, resulting from excessive taxation and the corrupt administration of justice, had begotten in many minds a longing for relief, and a hope that the missionary could secure it for them. A Methodist missionary told me that most of those who came to the missionary for the first time were influenced by this motive. Beyond any other people that I saw in Asia, the Koreans impressed me as pathetically stretching out their hands for help and guidance out of bitter bondage.[6]

It was not that the people of Korea looked to the missionaries personally for relief from social and political misery. They looked to the Christian religion and its Gospel for their salvation as a people and as a nation. Some people even saw in Christianity a training ground and the resources for national rejuvenation, reform and national independence from the domination of foreign powers such as Japan. Such was the social and political impact of Christianity on Koreans, through the opening of modern schools for young men and women and the opening of new types of hospitals for the sick and the poor. This was not the conscious purpose of the Christian mission in Korea. But people in Korea responded to the Christian message as embodying a social and political hope for liberation.

The intensity of the Korean Christian sense of national crisis and national humiliation, and the anti-Japanese sentiment aroused by Japan's protectorate of Korea, caused alarm among the missionaries about the state of their mission work. They realized the hopelessness of any political action, either by Koreans in general or by Christians in particular. And more importantly, they foresaw the danger of making the young Christian church a political agency. This was the general sentiment of the missionaries as Korean Christians faced the national crisis: "We (the missionaries) felt that the Korean Church needed not only to repent for hating the Japanese, but to have a clear vision of all sin against God. . . We felt. . . that embittered souls needed to have their personal relation with the Master." [7] Ever since, the missionaries have sought to "depoliticize" both the Christian message itself and Korean Christian activities. Such an effort was made in the following years in the Great Revival movement in Korea, and it was successful. [8]

The revival meetings were designed to be a search for religious experiences. The main features of the mass meetings were public confession of sin after stirring sermons, loud prayers and various forms of volatile emotional expression. Missionaries viewed the Great Revival of 1907 as an outpouring of the Holy Spirit, and emphasized the spiritual and religious dimension of the mass experience. Reports written by missionaries at the time of the mass revival meetings reveal their positive impressions of the "spirituality" of such a revival movement. Public confession of sin was ostensibly limited to immoral acts which concerned only the individuals involved. There was no mention of how people in the revival meetings felt about their national tragedy of the collective sin of the people as a nation.

The revival meetings of 1907 and following years were a great success, yielding a great increase in church membership. Missionaries were quoted as saying that "this work has been genuine. There has been no false fire. "[9] Bishop M.C. Harris was frequently quoted when he said in 1908:

> The effects following this movement are wholly good, the church raised to a higher spiritual level, almost entire absence of fanaticism because of careful previous instruction in the Bible, not one case of insanity, but thousands clothed in their right minds; scores of men called to the holy ministry; greater congregations searching the Word, as many as 2000 meeting in one place to study the Bible; and thousands learning to read and

making inquiries; drunkards, gamblers, thieves, adulterers, murderers, self-righteous Confucianists, dead Buddhists and thousands of devil-worshippers have been made new men in Christ, the old things gone forever.[10]

This kind of revival meeting was needed by the despondent people of Korea. As the Korean church historian George Paik saw, this revival was due to (1) a sense of failure as a nation, (2) the new message from the outside world, and (3) the determination of the missionaries to bring about such a revival. The definite intent of the missionaries was to spiritualize the Christian message and thus to depoliticize and even de-nationalize Korean Christianity. Apparently, the missionaries were quite successful in leading the majority of Korean Christians away from political involvement. These revival meetings set the subsequent tone of Christianity in Korea as emotional, conservative, individualistic and other-worldly. Even today, most people follow the "good old religion" form of Christianity that the missionary fathers gave them for salvation. To them Christianity is a religion to give material success in this world *and* spiritual success in the world after death. This view stems not merely from the success of the missionary effort, but also from the extremely harsh political and religious suppression of Japanese colonial rule. It also has its roots in Korean Shamanism (which will be discussed in the next chapter).

However, in the face of the Korean people's loss of their nation and the Japanese suppression of the people, including the non-violent Christian patriotic movement, the missionary attempt to depoliticize Korean Christians was not wholly successful. Although they were successful in depoliticizing Christians, they were not wholly successful in de-nationalizing them. In later years, Christians' nationalistic feelings were aroused in revival meetings, and their sense of national identity was intensified by such emotional meetings. One could say that eventually the great gatherings at revival meetings served to bring about a greater sense of nationalism and a sense of political *koinonia* in Korean Christians. The numerical growth of the Korean church made it possible for this sense of political *koinonia* to penetrate many areas of Korean life. The March First Independence Movement of 1919 was the culmination of the political awakening of Korean Christians which exploded in their active participation in the national liberation and independence movement of the time. With the outbreak of the March First Movement, and the active participation and leadership of Korean Christians, Protestantism became a political center of Korean nationalism. Korean Christians had interpreted the Gospel politically. Although their message was simple and emotional, their political hermeneutics of the Gospel was about liberation. The Korean church had become an exodus church.

Any indigenous theology that develops in the Korean church must take this tradition very seriously. Korean theology has to find its roots deep in the political consciousness of Korean Christianity. It is rooted in the experience of political oppression. It has grown out of the struggle to liberate itself from foreign domination. This is why Korean Christians join in easily with the Black Christians in singing:

> When Israel was in Egypt's land ,
> Let my people go;
> Oppressed so hard they could not stand,
> Let my people go;
> Go down Moses, way down in Egypt's land.
> Tell ole Pharaoh
> Let my people go.[11]

If there is any indigenous Korean theology, it has grown out of people's experience of oppression and liberation, the liberation of the people of God from bondage—political bondage. "Minjung theology" is a Korean theology of liberation. Minjung theology is deeply rooted in the people's struggles for liberation, and in the Korean Christians' political hermeneutics of the Gospel.

"Minjung" is a new term even to Korean Christians, but it is a Korean word. It is a combination of two Chinese characters "min" and "jung." "Min" may be translated as "people" and "jung" as "the mass." Thus "minjung" means "the mass of the people," or "mass," or just "the people." But when we try to translate it into English, "mass" is not adequate for our theological purpose; and "the people" is politically dangerous in anti-Communist Korea, because it has become a Communist word. Nonetheless, "the people" is close to what "minjung" seeks to convey, sociologically and theologically as well. Although "the people of God" may seem to be safest, and (perhaps) a theological expression in both Korean and English, the phrase is now almost a cliche and does not say exactly what is meant theologically and politically.[12]

Minjung theology is a Korean theology, again rooted in the historical experience of the oppressed people of Korea. The term "minjung" is a recent coinage among Korean theologians. It is a term that has emerged from the Christian experience in the political struggle for justice over the last ten or more years. The theology of the minjung or minjung theology is an accumulation and articulation of theological reflections of the political experiences of Christian students, laborers, journalists, professors, farmers, writers and intellectuals, as well as theologians in Korea in the 1970's. It is theologically and historically rooted in the theological awareness of the oppressed in the Korean political situation, a theological response to the oppressors, and it is the response of the oppressed to the Korean Church and its mission. The theology of the Minjung is a creation of those Korean Christians who have been forced to reflect upon their Christian discipleship in exile in foreign countries, in the basement interrogation rooms, in trials, facing court-martial tribunals, hearing the allegations of prosecutors, making their own final defense, and in prison cells. They have reflected on their Christian commitment in prison cells, in their letters from prison to families and friends, in their reading of books sent in by friends from all over the world, in their unemployment, in their stay at home under house arrest, while subject to a twenty-four hour watch over their activities, and even over their visits with their friends.

The theology of Minjung is a socio-political biography of myself and my father and my mother under the Japanese occupation. At the same time it is a theological story about Korean Christians in the political struggle for freedom in the 1970's of Korea. It is the way in which we have lived and acted under the Japanese occupation, under the Communist government of the North and dictatorial regimes in south Korea. This is the way in which Korean Christians have lived and acted, prayed together and participated in the Lord's Supper for liberation and salvation.

3.   Christian Gospel for the Liberation of the Minjung

I was taken into the martial law command's interrogation center to tell them the story of Korean minjung—my socio-political and theological biography. On the same floor of the interrogation center, later, I met other Christian professor friends. One was in the labor movement, one in a Christian professors organization, one in the student movement. Another was dean of the faculty of the Christian university which had had the most intensive student demonstrations for the democratization of the country following the fateful death of President Park Chung Hee, who had ruled South Korea from 1961 to 1979. We were all there to tell the story of the oppressed minjung of Korea. None of us had been taken in for any *shameful* crimes. One way or another, actively, or passively, we had each committed ourselves to working with the minjung. We had the unspoken common understanding that the minjung is present where there is socio-cultural alienation, economic exploitation and political repression. That is the place, we thought, where we should be and where we should work. Therefore, a woman is a minjung when she is dominated by a man, by the family or by socio-cultural structures and factors. An ethnic group is a minjung group when it is politically and economically discriminated against by another ethnic group. A race is minjung when it is dominated by another powerful ruling race, as in a colonial situation. When intellectuals are suppressed for using their creative and critical abilities against rulers and the powerful on behalf of the oppressed, then they too belong to the minjung. Workers and farmers are minjung when they are exploited, whether they are aware of it or not . They are minjung when their needs, demands and basic human rights are ignored, and crushed down by ruling powers.

"Why do you professors and Christians get mixed up with these people, or minjung as you call them? It should be the Christian attitude and Christian faith to be good to the authorities and to think about heaven and to worry about your soul." Pointing at other rooms, the interrogator told me that the people in there were all in trouble because they had gotten involved in social problems. He was lamenting what had happened to that good old religion. Christians are always in trouble.

The interrogator was not too interested in my formal education in the United States, after my completion of military service in the Korean Navy . He was not too impressed by my record in the Navy and honorable discharge. Nor was he very impressed by my education in the United States with a Ph.D. But he was practically shouting when he asked me why a scholar like me had to meddle with poor people, laborers, and stupid, troublemaking students. What do I know about farmers and female workers in the textile factories? What does Christianity have to do with them? He produced a document and almost hit me in the face with it, ordering me to write about its background and content. The document was the 1974 Theological Statement of Korean Christians signed by 66 leading theologians and church leaders in Korea, when workers, students, and writers were fighting for their freedom and human decency. I had signed the statement. I saw that the document was covered with red pencil marks marked by the inspection reader (or readers).

> Jesus the Messiah, our Lord, lived and dwelt among the oppressed, poverty-stricken, and sick in Judea. He boldly confronted Pontius Pilate, a representative of the Roman Empire, and he was crucified while witnessing to the truth. He has risen from the dead, releasing the power to transform and set the people free.
>
> We resolve that we will follow the footsteps of our Lord, living among our oppressed and poor people, standing against political oppression, and participation in the transformation of history, for this is the only way to the

Messianic Kingdom.[13]

What can I add to this? Looking back at the document from my present viewpoint in prison, I decided that it wasn't bad at all. We had said what had to be said. Christianity is for the poor and oppressed, and the history of Korean Christianity attests to that fact. American missionaries took the "mass-line" in their mission policies. As the number of converts increased with the untiring efforts of itinerant missionaries all over the country, the missionaries came to recognize the importance and necessity of setting up some working principles in their missionary work. The Presbyterian Mission Council, whose membership was all American, adopted a written mission policy as early as 1893.[14] This was the first statement of mission policy of the American missionaries in Korea, and a remarkable one. The most remarkable feature of the stated policy was its "mass line". The first four articles of the policy outline, adopted by the Council of Missions at its first meeting in Seoul in January of 1893, are most important and to our point.

? ⊕ (simply different aim)

1. It is better to aim at the conversion of the working classes than that of the higher classes.
2. The conversion of women and the training of Christian girls should be a special aim since mothers exercise so important an influence over future generations.
3. The Word of God converts where man is without resources; therefore, it is most important that we make every effort to place a clear translation of the Bible before the people as soon as possible.
4. The mass of Koreans must be led to Christ by their own fellow countrymen; therefore, we shall thoroughly train a few as evangelists rather than preach to a multitude ourselves.[15]

The missionaries consciously identified the lower-class population and women and children as their sociological targets for evangelization. Furthermore, in order to reach these people, the missionaries stated their policy that "in all literary work, a pure Korean free from Sinicism, should be our aim," (Article 6), and so they translated the Bible into that pure Korean, free from Sinicism. The "mass-line" which missionaries took was not something new. Their mission policy statement of 1893 was a verbal articulation and re-affirmation of the things they had been doing since 1884.

Ewha Womans University, the most prestigious women's university in Korea with a student enrollment in 1980 of more than 10,000, was founded by the frail mother of an American missionary doctor; with an alienated concubine, a poverty stricken girl and a waif. This is what Mrs. Mary F. Scranton said about her first modern school for Korean women:

> I began with one scholar. She was the concubine of an official who was desirous his wife should learn English, with the hope that she might sometime become interpreter for the Queen. She remained with us only about three months.

> The first permanent pupil came in June, 1886, one month later than Mrs. Kim. Poverty unquestionably brought the girl to us, but not many days had passed before the mother felt it better to brave poverty rather than trust her child to a foreigner. . .

> The second pupil was a little waif whose sick mother was picked up out of the city wall by Dr. Scranton (her medical missionary son) and taken first to his hospital for treatment. Koreans watched these girls very closely. As they did not find them unhappy or ill-treated, other mothers gradually gained a little confidence, and at the time of removal to the Home on the hill, the school numbered four, and the following January we counted seven.[16]

Girls were brought in from the streets and outside of the city wall by the missionary doctor, and they were treated, fed, clothed and educated. The stated purpose of education for Korean girls was to make "Koreans better Koreans only." Mrs. Scranton says:

> They, the girls, are not being made over again after our foreign way of living, dress, and surroundings, because it occasionally appears from home and even in the field that we thought to make a change in all ways. We take pleasure in making Koreans better Koreans only. We want Korea to be proud of Korean things, and more, that it is a perfect Korea through Christ and his teachings.[17]

Dr. Helen Kim, the first Korean woman to become principal of Ewha Womans College in 1938, invited me to join the faculty at Ewha in 1964. I had believed in the spirit of Mrs. Mary F. Scranton ever since I joined the international internship program at Union Theological Seminary in New York and read the writings of the first American missionaries to Korea. That was where I first met Dr. Helen Kim in 1962. Ewha is not a school for the rich and powerful; it is not a place to train those who would suppress and alienate the poor and the oppressed; and, it is not the institution of higher learning whose students become rich and powerful to exploit the poor and powerless. The school trains those who would liberate themselves and those who would liberate others.

This was also the vision of Helen Kim when she was an Ewha girl. This vision came to her as a religious experience during her first year of college.

> I struggled and prayed. . .all night long. Suddenly the illumination came to me that my sins were pride, self-will, and hatred for the Japanese. I fell upon the floor and asked God to forgive all my sins committed against Him. I immediately felt His forgiveness.
>
> This was followed by a remarkable vision. I seemed to see Him take the three bags of sins away, showing me what to do the rest of my life.
>
> He pointed out to me a big dug-out moat where a mass of Korean women were crying out for help with their hands out-stretched from the haze and confusion that covered them. The whole vision was very real to me. This must have been what is usually called a spiritual awakening.
>
> From that time on, my life has been directed by God's hand toward the one course of humble service to the womanhood of my country and the emancipation of the women of the world. I could ask of my religion no other reality than His presence with me throughout life. [18]

This remarkable lady of inspiration to many young women of Korea dedicated all of her life, in various capacities, to the higher education of Korean women and to her country. Never did she lose her vision of a big dug-out moat filled with a mass of Korean women stretching their hands out for help and for liberation.

Dr. Kim and other Christian leaders of the country were all influenced by the conscious missionary policy, from the very beginning of their mission work in Korea, to reach the poor and the deprived. These missionaries had opened dispensaries for the poor and the uncared-for sick. They had opened schools for abandoned children and orphans. The sons of the yangban, the aristocratic class, were not attracted to these schools. Perhaps this was because the founders of the Christian schools stated their purpose as not "to make 'interpreters' and 'operators' but liberally educated men."[19] This was the statement of Dr. Appenzeller, the founder in 1885 of the first modern boy's school, Pai Chai Haktang. The first Presbyterian school founded by Dr. H.G. Underwood was a boarding school for boys. As students could not afford the tuition and fees to come to school, it was natural for Underwood to call his boarding school an orphanage.[20]

In the spring of 1887, some country people in the village of Sorai in western Hwanghae Province were secretly baptized by Underwood while Hulbert, another missionary, guarded the door against possible intrusions. This insignificant but dangerous beginning of Protestant evangelism soon expanded to teach the mass of the people. The increase in Protestant membership in the cities and the countryside may be attributed to a number of causes: political, social and religious. But the missionary outreach toward the mass of common people was certainly the major reason for the increase in church membership. Those who had been oppressed and deprived for so long in a Confucian class-oriented and authoritarian society grabbed on to the liberating message of the Christian religion. The people accepted the Christian message not only for its spiritual and religious salvation, but also for its this-worldly and social liberation. The missionary emphasis on the gathering of large numbers also created a sense of community among the new believers. Such a sense of community for the socially-deprived was almost a necessity in a society that had been going through tremendous changes and confusion and chaos.

For example, while the social reform of Kabo Kyongjang of 1895 had abolished the social caste system on paper, Christianity actually worked for the lower class people and women and children, the most deprived sectors of Korean society. One good example of the liberating effort of the American missionaries was a brave contact made with the outcast class of butchers. Mr. S. F. Moore did evangelistic work among a group of butchers in the capital area, making "a large number" of converts. These butchers did not take the Christian message lightly. They organized themselves, and made a petition to the government for equal treatment. In the old Korean caste system, butchers were outcasts and "untouchables." The petition was granted, and it triggered the spread of the Christian message not only for its religious content but also for its social implications for minjung and their liberation.[21]

One of the most remarkable policies set by the first missionaries was their choice of the language of mission. They chose the language of the minjung, the Korean vernacular script, as the "official" language of Protestant Christianity in Korea. When missionaries came to Korea, they discovered that Hangul, the vernacular and vulgar script of the Korean language, was despised and neglected as the language of women, children, and the unlearned. They studied it, learned it, and then decided to use it to communicate with the people of Korea. The first Scottish missionaries, John Ross and John MacIntyre, came as far as the Manchurian part of China looking for a chance to cross the border into Korea. In Manchuria, they saved the lives and spirits of some sick and despairing Korean peddlers, the So brothers, learned Korean from them and then translated the Gospel of Luke into Korean. In making that translation they used the vulgar script. As early as 1882, this first Gospel was printed on a printing press set up in Mukden,

Manchuria. Copies of the book were sent to Korea through peddlers of quack medicines. The younger So (Sang-yun) was the first of such Bible peddlers. The British and Foreign Bible Society later published all four Gospels and the Book of Acts in the Ross version, and authorized the publication[22] of an edition of five thousand copies of the entire New Testament.

We have already mentioned the clearly stated mission policy of 1893, that "in all literary work," especially in the translation of the Bible, "a pure Korean, free from Sinicism, should be our aim." Thus the medium of the Christian message was indeed the language of the lower class people. They did not choose the official Chinese characters which were the language of Korean officialdom and the Yangban class, the educated aristocratic sectors of old Korean society.

This policy was in sharp contrast to the introduction of the Catholic message through Chinese books on Christianity. Therefore, the early Catholic missionaries did not translate the Bible into Korean script, though Catholicism was introduced to Korea exactly a century earlier than Protestantism. Christian books in Chinese had a certain advantage in that they could be read by the educated Yangban Koreans.

This "rehabilitation" of the Korean script occurred in the field of education as well. The first missionaries who opened the schools faced the problem of language, the medium of instruction. The Koreans' understanding of respectable education was to learn Chinese and Chinese classics. But the American missionaries chose the Korean alphabet for the language of instruction—the language to be taught as well as the medium of instruction itself. This was a remarkable thing to happen to Koreans, and the Korean minjung. Clearly, Christian education was designed and carried out for the minjung. The missionaries did not want to establish English schools, so they learned the Korean language to be able to teach classes. Because the missionaries used Korean script in their schools, their modern western education was looked down upon by Koreans who wanted to learn English. Therefore, at the early stage of modern education by missionaries student enrollment was low, and there was the problem of attracting more students from the upper class and learned sector of the society. Nonetheless, mission schools pressed on with the use of the Korean script for their language of instruction even during the time when the Japanese forced all schools to teach and use Japanese.

Other books and tracts were also published, and the circulation of these and the Bible became the most effective strategy for the missionaries' spreading Christianity. In 1889, the Korean Religious Tract Society was organized to publish and circulate Christian tracts and periodicals through-out Korea. In this way missionary endeavors in education were not limited to formal education in schools. The Korean Bible and Christian tracts written in the common people's script were a very important medium of education for those who could not go to schools. Religious campaigns conducted by means of Bible studies and revival meetings had become, in addition, powerful literacy campaigns. Missionaries not only propagated the Christian Gospel to the common people and the general populace of Korea, they also encouraged Koreans to discover their own language and to use it for the de-velopment of themselves as individuals and that of the country as a whole.

Eventually, literacy campaigns on the part of Korean Christians in the rural areas became, in addition, campaigns for nationalism and national self-identity in the face of the Japanese policy of total annihilation of Korean political and cultural identity. Through the reading of the Bible in the Korean script, Koreans not only learned the religious message of the book, but also discovered the power of their own language to liberate the poor and the ignorant. The reading of the Bible itself was not a dangerous thing, but reading it in the Korean vulgar script became a dangerous thing for the Japanese, because it aroused in Korean hearts a deep national consciousness. Thus, it was a common practice during the Japanese occupation for high school and college student organizations to go out to the farm villages and teach Bible reading during the day and preach in the evening services. This was the best thing the students could do to join the literacy campaign. It was a nationalistic and a religious campaign at the same time.

Therefore, in addition to the general significance of the rediscovery of the Korean script, the main significance of the translation of the Bible was the fact that it created a major "language event." It was an event because it was a revolution in the field of education. It was an event because it was able to draw the mass of people into contact with the Christian message. The message of liberation of the poor and oppressed was conveyed to the people by the language of the oppressed and the poor. This was an event because with this learning of the language, Koreans were nurtured and brought up with a sense of national consciousness and national identity. It became a political language in Korea. Also with the Christian Bible translated into the common Korean script, the Christian message itself became part of the political language. The translation of the Bible into the Korean people's vernacular language became one of the most significant revolutionary events in modern history, with implications far beyond its religious significance for the Christian church in Korea.

4. Christian Suffering with the Korean Minjung

Levites

August 29, 1910, was a day of national humiliation for the Korean people. This was the day when Korea was formally annexed to Japan. The Korean people lost their country. Now Koreans became enslaved as subjects of Japanese military rule. The Yi Dynasty of old Korea ended and the right of government was transferred to the Japanese Emperor. The Japanese government appointed Terauchi as the Resident-General in Seoul. After the signature of the annexation document on August 22, 1910, all social and political organizations were dissolved, and all mass media were either forced to close down or came under the tight control of the Governor-General.

The Korean people never accepted the legitimacy of the Japanese annexation of Korea. For Korean Christians, political neutrality was impossible. To accept Japanese rule as legitimate was neither Korean nor Christian. Whether they were Christians or not, Koreans were politically against Japanese rule. It was almost fatal for the powerless people of Korea to endure Japanese oppressive rule, but that oppression was never accepted. It remained as the "han" of the Korean people. [23]

Anti-Japanese feeling in Korea had deep historical roots. In 1592, Hideyoshi had sent generals Kato and Konishi and two hundred and fifty thousand soldiers to invade Korea and rampage through the whole land. In 1876 Japan was the first nation to approach Korea and force the country to open its doors for trade. The Japanese-instigated coup d'etat of 1884 failed, but they came back in 1894 to suppress the Donghak revolutionary movement and "rescue" Korea from Chinese domination. They forced the reform of Kabo (1895) and murdered Queen Min. This series of Japanese imperialistic moves led to the Treaty of Protectorate of 1905, following the victory of Japan against Russia in 1904. The Japanese forced the abdication of Emperor Kwangmu, the ill-fated and retarded last king of Korea. Finally, came the annexation of Korea in 1910. This is the litany of historical events that humiliated and oppressed the powerless people of Korea. Christians as well as all the people of Korea now singularly perceived that the main contradiction in Korean society and its history was Japan's rule over Korea. And more particularly, the Japanese rule aggravated societal strains, for the powerless minjung were more exploited than the rich and powerful. Therefore, the minjung of Korea had to unite with the Christians to oppose Japanese oppression in Korea.

Typical Korean Yangbans, following the Confucian virtue of loyalty to the king and to the nation, committed suicide rather than slavishly follow a life of humiliation. In 1907, the Righteous Army Movement opposed not only the disbanding of the Korean army, but also the step-by-step invasion of the Japanese into Korean affairs. In September and October of 1909, the Japanese launched a systematic anti-guerrilla campaign against Righteous Army Movement. During this two-month campaign, the main forces of the Righteous Army were crushed, and after annexation, Righteous Army actions were mostly scattered in the northern regions near the Manchurian border.

Under such circumstances, the Christian community and the people around it represented the single most powerful force confronting Japanese rule. In spite of the fact that missionary friends persuaded Christian leaders to concentrate on the education of the Korean people and not to directly confront the Japanese with arms, and perhaps because of this, leaders in the Christian community formed organizations which carried out progressive educational programs for the mass of people. One of the most influential of these organizations which emerged as a progressive force in Korea at the end of the 19th century was started and led by So Chae-pil (Phillip Jaisohn). The name of the organization was the Independence Club. The Club published the first Korean language newspaper in 1896 and advocated a constitutional monarchy. In 1909 progressive forces around the Christian community led by such men as Lee Sang-jai and Yun Chi-ho formed the semi-underground organization "The New People's Association" (*Sinmin-hoe*). This was a nation-wide organization. Its aim was to train future leaders armed with Western knowledge, to develop national consciousness through a cultural movement with the publication of monthly magazines, and to develop modern industry for national economic growth. The stated goals of the New People's Association were:

1. to increase the people's awareness of the national cause, and to encourage thinking independent of Japanese control;
2. to organize comrades to build a national people's power;
3. to establish educational institutions to promote education of youth; and
4. to promote the wealth of the people and finance commercial and industrial activities.

Associated with this New People's Association were the youth and Student Association Taesong School, Taeguk Book Store, and a pottery factory. But the most important spiritual and personal support came from the Christian churches and Christian educational institutions. At that time, the Christian community was carrying out the "One Million Movement," which was a church membership expansion campaign inspired by the Great Revival Meetings of 1907. By that time, according to the Northern Presbyterian Report, there were 962 mission schools, 500 congregations, and 25,000 Christians. Church property was worth over one million dollars; and the total annual expenditures of the Christian community exceeded 25 million dollars. The number of Americans and other foreign missionaries under extraterritorial protection was about 330.[24]

Furthermore, the language of the Korean Christian pulpit every Sunday morning was aggressively nationalistic. Our historian George Paik describes the church's language situation as follows:

> That is not all! When one looks at the language and deeds of Christians, they profess that the people of Israel under the oppression of Egypt succeeded in their exodus for national independence and liberation under God's help and under the leadership of Moses. They teach the biblical story that during war with another nation the people of Israel were vindicated by David, the Apostle of Justice who destroyed the giant Goliath. And whenever they congregate together, they sing hymns, "Believers are like soldiers of the Army!" and "The Army of the Cross." This language was easily construed to be rebellion oriented, as Christian leaders now saw."[25]

Obviously the existence of the Christian community was a formidable problem for the Japanese military government in Korea. In spite of, or perhaps because of, the Japanese effort to Japanize the Korean Christian movement, they were not able to get leading Christians to identify themselves with the new regime or to cooperate with their Japanization effort. The missionaries also took a stand against the Japanization of the Korean Christian movement. This complicated the matter, because foreign missionaries were not subject to the rule of Japan.

In response to the development of a "political theology" of the Korean church, the Japanese cracked down on the Christian community for political reasons. Under the circumstances, it was an absolute necessity for the Japanese to do so. It was a political necessity, and the Japanese were rather desperate. As early as October, 1911, one year after the Annexation, the Japanese had to create the so-called 105 persons incident. About forty of the teachers and students of the Presbyterian Academy of Sinch'on were arrested and brought to Seoul for imprisonment. Subsequently, 157 persons were arrested, and 123 of them were prosecuted. One hundred fifty of those prosecuted were Christians, including prominent leaders such as Yun Chi-ho and Lee Sung-hun.[26]

The charge was that those arrested had plotted to assassinate Terauchi, the Governor-General, on his way to the opening ceremony of the Amrok-kang (Yalu River) Bridge. The accused had allegedly organized the Sinmin-hoe (The New People's Association)—a secret society—and had established a military school in Manchuria to carry out systematic terrorist activities. Later, it was learned that the case was built on confessions extracted under extreme torture.[27]

Though passively, the Korean Christian communuty was identified as a political community standing with the people of Korea suffering under foreign domination. The "Conspiracy" case of 1911 had an important and symbolic significance. The incident clearly characterized the Korean Christianity as the nationalistic church suffering with the people of Korea. The Japanese fabrication of the case using severe torture went far beyond the legal question of human rights. The act of the regime was first of all an act of political oppression, but Korean Christians took it as religious oppression. They suffered not just because they were resisting as Koreans but also because they were Christians taking on themselves the cross of the suffering people of Korea. The Christian language of suffering was being related to the suffering of the people. This was indeed a beginning of the "historicalization" of the Gospel of Jesus' suffering on the Cross. The Korean Christian community came to find a new identity in this experience of suffering. The suffering had not only a political meaning; it came to have a theological meaning as well. The Christian message came to life in the actual Korean experience of suffering for the cause of freedom and national independence. Perhaps for the first time, Christians were able to identify themselves with their national destiny and with the suffering of the people of Korea under the Japanese rule. In the experience of Korean Christians the analogies between the suffering of the Korean people and the Biblical stories of the suffering of the people of Israel were vivid and telling. The story of the Exodus became the story of the suffering experience of the Korean people and the hope of their liberation from the yoke of Japanese enslavement. The humiliation and torture of Jesus under Pontius Pilate was considered as the cost of discipleship which Korean Christians had to bear. With the stories of the Bible, Korean Christians were able to interpret their religion politically, and they put their faith into action as they fearlessly suffered with all the suffering people of Korea.

The so-called conspiracy case of 105 Christians was fabricated by the Japanese police, and Korean Christian leaders were thus forced to bear the political cross of Jesus. But the March First Movement of 1919 was indeed initiated by Christians and through it Korean Christian leaders took an active part in bearing, with the Korean minjung, the political cross of Jesus for the independence of the nation. The March First Movement of 1919 was the pivotal experience for Korean Christians and the Korean minjung. The minjung of Korea made their decision to rise up against foreign domination and to liberate themselves from Japanese enslavement. Korean Christians committed themselves with the minjung of Korea to the liberation of the nation. The old age of medieval darkness had past, the old age of foreign domination was over, and the new era of enlightenment and liberation had come to the minjung of Korea. It was not just a movement by Korean Christians to gain religious freedom: it was not a religious movement. It was the independence and liberation movement of the Korean minjung: It was a political movement. Korean Christians took a major, leading part along with the minjung of Korea. For the first time, Korean Christians joined with the minjung, united with them, worked and suffered with them. Thus, the historical character of Korean Christianity was set as the political religion of the minjung.

Frederick Arthur McKenzie (1869-1931), a Canadian reporter for London's *Daily Mail,* wrote an on-the-spot report of the March First Movement of 1919 as follows: "On Saturday, March 1st (1919), at two in the afternoon, in a large number of centres of population throughout the country, the Declaration of Korean Independence was solemnly read, usually to large assemblies, by representative citizens."[28] McKenzie first of all characterized this Korean independence movement as a united people's movement, and a pan-religious one. He reported: "In some places, the leaders of the Christians and the leaders of the non-Christian bodies acted in common. In other places, by mutual agreement, two gatherings were held at the same time, the one for Christians and the other for non-Christians."[29] But the leaders came from the religious bodies, such as Buddhism, Chun-do-kyo, "Heavenly-Way-Teachings," (an indigenous religion that had come out of the Donghak movement) and Christianity, all of which had been accepted as the religions of the minjung of Korea.

McKenzie cast a perceptive eye on the sociological make-up of the Movement: "It was soon seen that every class of the community was united. Men who had been ennobled by the Japanese stood with the coolies, shop-keepers closed their stores, policemen who had worked under the Japanese took off their uniforms and joined the crowds, porters and labourers, scholars and preachers, men and women all came together."[30] And for the first time, Korean demonstrations became people's movements in which everyone participated. It was an egalitarian and democratic movement of the people for their national independence.

There has been some debate among historians as to the violent character of the movement. Some would deny that the movement was non-violent. Others would attribute the movement's failure to its non-violent character. However, our reporter claims: "The movement was a demonstration, not a riot. On the opening day and afterwards—until the Japanese drove some of the people to fury—there was no violence."[31] For one thing, no Japanese was hurt; no Japanese shops were looted. Against the vicious attacks of the Japanese, there was no retaliation on the part of Korean demonstrators. The instructions given to the demonstrators, according to McKenzie, were extraordinary under the circumstances:

> "Whatever you do
> DO NOT INSULT THE JAPANESE
> DO NOT THROW STONES
> DO NOT HIT WITH YOUR FISTS.
> For these are the acts of barbarians." [32]

The March First Movement for Independence was triggered by two outside incidents: One was the end of the First World War, and the other one was the symbolic end of the old Korean kingdom by the death of King Kojong, the last king of the Yi Dynasty. The self-determination of the people of Korea as an independent and free people had chosen the republic form of independence. The March First Independence Movement did not shout for the restoration of the old kingdom, and it did not petition for the improvement of the harsh Japanese colonial policies. Rather, it demanded the nation's total independence from Japan based on the ideals and institutions of democracy. The movement was triggered by US President Woodrow Wilson's famous but ineffective declaration of the rights of weaker nations. The most important sentence of Wilson's speech, which excited the Korean people here and abroad, was: "What is the task that this League of Nations is to do ? It is to provide for the Freedom of small nations, to prevent the domination of small nations by big ones."[33] What more was needed to agitate the aspirations of the people of Korea for freedom and independence? The time had come for the small nation to put an end to domination by the big nation. McKenzie put it more boldly, "If any outsider was responsible for the uprising of the Korean people, that outsider was Woodrow Wilson, President of the United States of America."[34]

A Day of National Mourning was set for the fourth of March, Tuesday. It was the day set for the funeral of King Kojong, and that was the signal day for the independence demonstrations. March 4 was not chosen for demonstrations; rather the Saturday before that week of mourning, the first of March, was chosen for the uprising. This was because the leaders expected that there would be many country people coming to the capital for mourning, and national independence would be declared to the largest possible crowd in the city.

The Declaration of Independence was prepared by the non-Christian Chun-do-kyo leader, Son Byong-hee, and a historian scholar, Choi Nam-sun. The document was signed by thirty three leaders who chose martyrdom. At first, Christians and non-Christians organized separately, but later, during the month of February, the two leading religious sectors agreed on united action. On the Christian side, the most crucial leadership came from the mission medical school, Severance Medical School and Korean YMCA student groups. Thus among the thirty three original signers of the Declaration, Christians numbered 16, Chun-do-kyo, 15, and 2 were Buddhists.

The "proceedings" of the Declaration was reported by our correspondent as follows:

> On the morning of March 1st the group of thirty-two met at the Pagoda Restaurant at Seoul. Pastor Kil was the only absentee; he had been temporarily delayed on his journey from Pyong-yang.

> Some prominent Japanese had been invited to eat with the Koreans. After the meal, the Declaration was produced before their guests and read. It was despatched to the Governor- General. Then the signers rang up the Central Police Station and informed the shocked officials of what they have done, and added that they would wait in the restaurant until the police van came to arrest them.

> The automobile prison van, with them inside, had to make its way to the police station through dense crowds, cheering and shouting, "Mansei! Mansei! Mansei!" It was old national battle cry, "May Korea live ten thousand years." Old flags had been brought out, old Korean flags, with the red and blue germ on the white ground, and were being widely waved. "Mansei!" Not only Seoul but the whole country had in a few minutes broken out in open demonstration. A new kind of revolt had begun. [35]

Because of the people's shout, "Mansei," sometimes Koreans called the movement "the First of March Mansei Incident." McKenzie was later corrected by Korean historians that not only was Pastor Kil absent from the lunch meeting on March first, but also three others were away from Seoul that day.

This was a movement of rhetoric and passive non-resistance. There was no report of any plan of action to follow the declaration of independence.

There was no plan to take over government offices or newspapers. There was no group of people organized to draw up a democratic constitution or prepare for a new government. The rhetoric of the movement was idealistic. One wonders whether the leaders really thought that the declaration would move the world to make the Japanese leave the country alone and independent, or that the Japanese would kindly leave the country. Still the language of the declaration was revolutionary, and it had power to move the people of Korea and to conscientize the minjung as both the subject and master of the nation.

The Declaration is certainly a proclamation of the emerging nationalism of the time. According to the translation of McKenzie: the first sentence of the Declaration read: "We herewith proclaim the independence of Korea and the liberty of the Korean people. We tell it to the world in witness of the equality of all nations and we pass it on to our posterity as their inherent right. "[56] But more particularly, the oppressed condition of the people under the ambitious imperial power was dramatically enumerated:

> Victims of an older age, when brute force and the spirit of plunder ruled, we have come after these long thousands of years to experience the agony of the years of foreign oppression, with every loss to the right to live, every restriction of the freedom of thought, every damage done to the dignity of life, every opportunity lost for a share in the intelligent advance of the age in which we live.

But according to the Declaration, "we have no desire to accuse Japan of breaking many solemn treaties since 1636..." and " we have no wish to find special fault with Japan's lack of fairness or her contempt for our civilization... " Later, the declaration said its purpose was to influence the Japanese government, "so that it will change, act honestly and in accord with the principles of right and truth." The Japanese government was requested to treat Koreans as an independent and free people, and such was the demand of the Declaration.

The Declaration articulated the new era of freedom of the people and their national independence. Poetically, it stated that

> A new era dawns before our eyes,
> the old world of force is gone,
> and the new world of righteousness
> and truth is here.

> Out of the experience and travail of the old world
> arises this light on life's affairs.

The insects stifled by the foe
and snow of winter awake at this same time
with the breezes of spring
and the soft light of the sun upon them. [37]

The objective of national independence and the vision of a new era was "a full measure of satisfaction in the way of liberty and the pursuit of happiness, and an opportunity to develop what is in us for the glory of our people." [38] This was a democratic declaration, full of democratic ideas and ideals emerging from the free nations of the West. It is comparable with the French "liberty, equality and fraternity," and the American "life, liberty and pursuit of happiness." The Korean language of independence was to ensure the people's liberty and pursuit of happiness through a life which would "develop what is in us for the glory of the people." This was the revolutionary vision of the Korean minjung.

The important motif of the Declaration was theological. The claim of independence and claim of the people of the right to liberty and the pursuit of happiness and life was ordained by God. The Declaration stated that "this is the clear leading of God, the moving principle of the present age, the whole human race's just claim." Therefore, "it is something that cannot be stamped out, or stifled,or gagged, or suppressed by any means." [39] The Independence Movement was appropriately claimed as a Christian movement, that is, Korean Christians played a major role in the subsequent movement for national independence. According to the Japanese police report on the religious classification of those who were arrested in March and April of 1919, 3,373 were Christians 2,283 Chun-do-kyo, 14 Si Chun Kyo, 229 Buddhists, and 346 Confucians. Persons with no religious affiliation totaled 9,394, and those whose religion was unknown totaled 3,909. [40] With these numbers one could argue that the majority of those arrested had no religious affiliation, and thus, that the movement was really non-religious and non-sectarian. But one must also take into consideration that people might have hidden their religious affiliation to protect themselves from more severe punishment by the Japanese authorities, who particularly hated the Christians in the movement.

Just to show the violent response of the Japanese and the extent of Christian suffering in the movement, let us quote the report of the General Assembly of the Presbyterian Church of September, 1919,

Total number of arrested: 3,804
Arrested pastors and elders:134
Arrested mission school teachers and youth leaders: 202

Imprisoned male members of the church: 2,125
Imprisoned female members of the church: 531
Those who were beaten (lashes as punishment): 2,162
Those who were shot to death: 41
The total number imprisoned (as present): 1,642
Those who were beaten to death: 6
Churches destroyed: 12
Schools destroyed: 8 [41]

The Japanese response was typical and as expected: Self–determination of races was utterly irrelevant to Japan, and the Japanese met the movement with relentless punishment and inhumane atrocities. Nonetheless, during the months of March and April, 1,214 demonstrations were held throughout the country, and by the end of May, there had been 1,542 such demonstrations. In all more than two million people took part in the Mansei movement, and it became a nation-wide movement.[42] This became the pivotal experience of Korean Christians in working with the minjung of Korea, and now the church had become the church of the Korean minjung. For the first time the Korean Protestant church became conscious of itself, and of its deep and unshakable roots in the vision and aspiration of the Korean people as the free master of their own national destiny and the liberated subjects of their own history. Through the March First Independence Movement of 1919, Korean Protestantism established itself more concretely as a religion with a historical consciousness deeply rooted in the minjung movement for liberation. With the minjung of Korea and the unspeakable violent sufferings of the people, Korean Protestantism found itself to be a religion of the liberating Gospel of Jesus in more concrete terms.

The independence movement was not a success. Christians and the leaders of the movement deeply felt their powerlessness. Christians had experienced the powerlessness of the minjung, in the same way Jesus' suffering on the cross only showed his powerlessness. But paradoxically Christians found power in their deep sense of powerlessness. Korean Christians found their powerlessness with the minjung, with whom they had suffered profoundly. But they had not lost hope, because they were a "Mongol nation, roughly awakened from its long sleep, under condition of tragic terror, that has seized hold of and is clinging fast to, things vital to civilization as we see it, freedom and free faith, the honour of their women, the development of their own souls." This was Frederick McKenzie's last sentence in the preface to his 1920 book reporting on the March First Independence Movement of Korea. [43]

Drum Opening the Dawn, Lee Chul-Su

2 THE MINJUNG MOVEMENT

1. Japanese and the Christians

One of Korea's leading church historians, Choo Chai-yong, marks the following periods in the development of Korean Protestantism beginning with the coming of American missionaries to Korea in 1884.

1. The period of acceptance (1876-1896)
2. The formative period of the Church of the Minjung (1896-1919)
3. The depoliticization period (1919-1932)
4. The period of the Babylonian Captivity (1932-1960)
5. The period of awakening (1960 to the present)[1]

But it is interesting to see another reading from a secular historian's perspective. He skips the first period of Choo, and identifies the period 1884-1919, as the formative period of the church of the Korean minjung. It is also the period of the Protestant contribution to the cultural enlightenment of late 19th century Korea and to the minjung's fight for freedom and national independence.[2] These two historians are not so far apart, however, in terms of characterizing the formative period of Korean Protestantism as a politically active religion for the liberation of the Korean minjung from ignorance and feudalism, and more ultimately for the independence of Korea as a nation.

Choo marks 1932 as the beginning of the Korean Babylonian Captivity after the period of depoliticization of the Korean church, while Song chooses the year 1938 as the end of the depoliticization period, and the beginning of the Korean church's submission to the Japanese authorities' demand for Shinto shrine worship. To put the matter rather simply, we may combine the two periods under the term "the period of Babylonian Captivity of the Korean Church" (1920-1945). In this section we will be concerned with this period of 25 years following the March First Independence Movement of 1919.

The most obvious characteristic of the period was its sense of failure and despair—a national despair resulting from the failure of the independence movement. Christian churches went into a different mode of operation, because the people of Korea seemed to have turned away from the churches. They thought that Christianity, despite the supposed backing of the West, could not do anything for the political independence of Korea. In order to overcome that situation, in September 1919, the church leaders launched nation-wide revival meetings such as "The Forward Movement" of the Presbyterian churches and "The Century Advance" of the Methodist churches. These denominational revival movements came from the great revival meetings of 1907 when Korea was first annexed to Japan. An all-out membership campaign for five or six years met with considerable success. In 1919, there were 1,700 Protestant churches with 144,000 members, but in 1926 there were 2,200 churches with a membership of 195,000. In 1927 the church lost 12 churches and some 35,000 members.[3]

While the Korean churches busied themselves with the drive for church membership and revival meetings for spiritual growth, the people of Korea were suffering from economic exploitation and social disintegration. Following the First World War, Japan made an all-out effort for colonial exploitation of Korea through over-investment and through a desperate war effort toward the Chinese continent. The Korean peninsula became the most convenient logistic base for the imperial advance into all of Asia.

The statistics below show that in less than ten years' time the number of factories increased 2.5 times, the number of laborers by 2 times, and capital investment over 3 times. As the number of wage earning laborers increased drastically, Korean farmers were losing their land and becoming wage earning tenant farmers. In 1920 there were 1,082,800 tenant farmers, but in 1925, the number increased to 1,184,400, and in 1930, 1,334,000. The tenant farming population was 39.8% the total farming population in 1920, and 46.5% by 1930. Farm plots became smaller while the number of tenant farmers increased.[4]

Increase in the Number of Factory Workers				
Year	No. of Factories	Capital-Investment	Total No.of Workers	Korean Workers
1920	2,087	¥ 160,744,378	55,276	46,200
1923	3,499	177,985,802	69,412	59,678
1925	4,238	265,853,369	80,375	70,281
1928	5,342	549,122,364	99,547	87,864
Korean Almanac of Economy, 1939				

Korean factory workers suffered incredibly low wages and atrocious treatment because of racial discrimination by Japanese employers. While the Japanese daily wage was ¥2,97, Koreans got ¥1,76. According to a 1931 report, the percentage of those who worked for 12 hours a day was 46.9%, 10-12 hours a day only 11.9%, 8-10 hours 28.7%, and fewer than 8 hours 0.8%. 82.2 percent of female textile workers worked more than 12 hours a day. There was no such thing as labor laws, nor any safety measures for the dangerous working conditions. Living conditions were austere, and more than 70% of the workers had heavy debts. By 1930 the number of factory workers increased to 100,000. If 36,000 mine workers and 82,000 construction and transportation workers were included, the number of Korean laborers was more than 220,000.[5]

According to a Japanese report, in the five years between 1926 and 1931, the number of beggars increased 16 times, from 10,000 to 163,000. Farmers who had insufficient food numbered 296,000 in 1926 and 1,048,000 in 1931. The number of people defined as poverty stricken rose from 1,860,000 in 1926 to 4,200,000 in 1931.[6]

We recall that this was the period following the March First Independence Movement, when Korean Protestant churches were launching spiritual revival meetings and membership drives. Propaganda also had it that the Japanese loosened their tight military control over the Korean people during this period. This was to be called a "cultural enlightenment period," with the expansion of press freedom, mass education, etc. Since the church was busy spiritualizing and thereby depoliticizing the Gospel, it drew farther

away from the minjung of Korea.[7] By contrast, the Korean minjung began to fight for their own life and destiny. Because of the tight control of the press, the majority of the Korean people and the church leaders were ignorant about them, but the number of labor disputes increased during the decade.

Labor Disputes in the 20's		
Year	No. of Incidents	No. of Participants
1920	81	4,599
1922	46	1,799
1924	45	6,751
1926	81	5,987
1928	119	7,759
1930	160	18,972
Japanese Government Report on the Security of Korea, 1933		

160 disputes in 1930 means that a labor dispute occurred on the average of every other day. There was also an increase in farm disputes in the same period. In 1920 there were only 15 incidents of tenant farmers' fights, participated in by 4,140 people. But in 1925 the number increased to 204 incidents with 4,002 participating. 1928 marked the highest number of incidents, 1,590, with 4,863 people participating. In 1930, the number of incidents decreased to 726, while the number of participants increased to 13,012.[8] Moreover, the laborers and farmers had organized themselves for their disputes. The number of organizations is shown in the table below:

Number of Farmers and Labor Organizations						
	1920	1921	1922	1923	1924	1925
Farmers	-	3	23	107	112	126
Laborers	33	90	81	111	91	128
Japanese Government Report on the Security of Korea, 1933.						

Under the tight control and severe suppression of the Japanese colonial government, it was almost inevitable for Christians to stay within the churches and focus on their inside activities, and they decided to stay safely away from the minjung. The churches of Korea were losing their roots and foothold in the real society where the minjung of Korea had to suffer. Herein can be found the roots of Korean Christian Mysticism of various kinds.

We see in the table below the statistics of labor and farm disputes in the 30's.

Labor Disputes in the 30's		
Year	No. of Incidents	No. of Participants
1930	160	18,972
1931	201	17,114
1933	176	13,835
1935	170	12,187
1937	99	9,146
1938	90	6,929
Japanese Government Report on the Security of Korea, 1939.		

We notice a sudden drop in the number of labor incidents in 1937 and 1938. This was not due to changed labor conditions in those years, and the people had not given up. With the Japanese invasion of China in 1937, the Japanese commandeered all Korean factories for the production of military supplies, thereby making the whole country their logistic base for the invasion of the rest of Asia. Under military control over the factories, labor disputes were severely suppressed.

Tenant farmers had not given up their struggles against Japanese landowners, as shown in the table below:

Farm Disputes in the 30's		
Year	No. of Incidents	No. of Participants
1931	667	10,282
1932	300	4,687

Farm Disputes in the 30's		
Year	No. of Incidents	No. of Participants
1933	1,975	10,337
1934	7,544	22,454
1935	25,834	58,019
1936	29,975	72,453
1937	31,799	77,515
1938	22,596	51,535
1939	16,452	37,017
Korean Farm Almanac		

It is interesting to note that the number of incidents increased, while the number of participants remained quite steady in the years following 1935. This means that the number of participants per farm dispute became smaller in the last half of the 30's. Under the strict control of the Japanese police it was extremely difficult for anyone to raise a voice against Japanese rural landowners. The statistics illustrate the unceasing struggle on the part of Korean farmers. The lives of the farmers had to become unbearable before they raised disputes against the allmighty Japanese landowners. When we consider the fact that more than 80% of the Korean population in 1929 were farmers, we can imagine the miserable life of the Korean people. Also, quite naturally, some 75% of Korean Christians were farmers.[9]

The Presbyterian Church recognized this statistical fact and the pressing needs of Christian farmers in the poverty stricken rural life of Korea. In 1928, the General Assembly of the Presbyterian Church organized a bureau of Farmers Affairs and began the establishment of model farm communities and agricultural technical schools, and the publication of the monthly magazine, "Farm Life." The bureau emphasized the opening and propagation of "Farmers Credit Unions," and the education of farmers in modern farm techniques. This sort of concern for Korean farmers and farming communities was an all-out effort by Korean Christians of the period. But the movement was educational mostly in terms of teaching women and children of the farm communities how to read Korean script. There was very little that Christians could teach the farmers about improving their farming techniques, or even how to organize themselves to fight against the Japanese landowners.

People were conscientized about the problems of rural areas through novels and newspapers. One of the most celebrated contemporary novelists in the 30's was Yi Kwang-Su, who wrote a masterpiece on the farm village movement by young Korean intellectuals of the time. The name of the novel was *The Earth,* and it was a best seller in 1933. Perhaps it was the spirit of the time in Korea, especially among younger intellectuals to have a deep concern for the development of rural farm communities. Dr. Helen Kim, the first Korean woman to do Ph.D. work at Columbia University, wrote her dissertation on "Rural Education for the Regeneration of Korea." She had a deep concern for Korean rural farm villages: "How to make the program for higher education relevant to our new village movement; how to bridge the great chasm between the life of the urban and rural populations; how the educated few could help the underdeveloped people to lift themselves into this new day and age." [10]

However, the basic problem of the Korean farmers would not be solved by piecemeal activities here and there to educate the unlearned in the villages and open farm credit unions or consumer unions, etc. The basic problem was the relentless exploitation of the Japanese military government. The frustration was almost unbearable on the part of Christians who moved into the countryside to work piecemeal on the improvement of farm conditions. They knew only too well that their work was closely watched by the authorities, and that the basic problem of the farm villages could not be solved until the Japanese were driven out of Korea.

Perhaps out of this kind of frustration, Protestantism in Korea became more and more an other-worldly directed, mystical and emotional religion. More revival meetings were planned by the churches, to lead the people to other-worldly concerns, and to give them spiritual or mental comfort, soothing their suffering and exhausted souls. There arose a variety of fanatical Christians and pseudo-Christian sects.

One of the most typical phenomena of this "fanatic, mystery" Christian syndrome was represented by a young pastor named Lee Yong Do (1900-1933). A graduate of the Methodist Theological Seminary in Seoul, he began preaching around the country at revival meetings, and soon became famous. He preached on the central theme of the "Suffering Jesus Christ." He was famous for his fiery sermons on the suffering of Jesus on the Cross and the suffering of the Korean people. He usually wept as he talked about the life and suffering of Jesus on the Cross, and about the suffering of the Korean people. And he made the whole congregation weep with him. He made his meetings gatherings of tears, and identified the suffering of the Korean people with the suffering Jesus on the cross. [11] Actually, there was nothing else to do but weep. The people's tears were tears of frustration, and of hopelessness. This was and is the "han" of the Korean minjung.

"Han" is a Korean word, and like "minjung" it is difficult or even undesirable to translate into another language. It is a term that denotes a person's feeling of suffering which has been repressed either by himself or through the oppression of others. This word may be translated as "a feeling of unresolved resentment against unjustifiable suffering." Usually, the word is uttered when there is actual suffering and a helpless feeling of frustration. It conveys a deep awareness of the contradictions in a situation and of the unjust treatment meted out by the powerful. This feeling of han is not just a one-time psychological response to a situation, but is an accumulation of such feelings and experiences over a long period.

Some psychoanalysts regard this feeling of han as the psychosomatic sickness of most Korean minjung. According to them, schizophrenia and other personal sicknesses stem from this feeling of han. This han could also be a socially-caused situation or disease. Under Confucianism's strict imposition of discrimination against women, for example, the very existence of a woman was nothing but han itself. Han speaks of the kind of feeling a woman has when she cannot produce a male child for the family and thus has to agree, against her will, to her husband's bringing in another woman for childbearing, or when she has to obey her mother-in-law's orders even when they are absolutely impossible and unreasonable. The feeling of han on the part of women, in this case, is due to an awareness of the structural injustice which a Confucian society imposes on women. "Han" is a psycho-social term which appears inevitably in the biography of Korean women and in their stories, novels, poems and plays.

The feeling of han, however, is not just an individual feeling of repression. It is not just a sickness that can be cured by drugs or by psychotherapy. It is a collective feeling of the oppressed. This sickness of han can be cured only when the total structure of the oppressed society and culture is changed. At a certain point in history, about half of the population were registered as hereditary slaves and were treated as property rather than as citizens of the nation. They thought of their lives as han.

For Koreans under the repressive colonization of the Japanese, all Koreans were slaves of the foreigners, so the collective life of the Korean people could not be anything but a life of han. This sense of han was experienced not only by individual Koreans, but by the Korean society as a whole. Han was a collective feeling of the Korean people. Whenever people realize that they have been oppressed by foreign power, and their sense of national independence has been repressed, the feeling of han rises up to the level of psycho-political anger, frustration and indignation, combined with a feeling of extreme helplessness. This feeling of *han* is once again an awareness at both an individual psychological level as well as at a social and political level.

In the thirties, while the Korean people's *han* was expressed in social and political terms with labor disputes and tenant farmers' collective action against exploiting landowners, Christian revivalism was more often expressed in the form of mystical union with the suffering Jesus on the Cross. Korean Christians expressed their individual and collective *han* in the form of an other-worldly and mystical but confused fetishism. Identifying the Korean people's suffering with that of Christ expressed the deep sense of *han* as a mystical union with Jesus himself. One preacher of the time said:

> I am swallowed by the love of Christ, and Christ was swallowed by my faith. Oh, what a wonderful principle of unity! Oh, mine eyes, look only toward Christ with single mind. Only look at him, the Lord. He will be caught in mine eyes, and He will stay only in me.[12]

The people's *han* may be resolved only by mystical union with Christ, and not by social or political struggles against the oppressive powers. Lee Yong Do's preaching was intended to take the people away from the world and away from their everyday social struggles. Only mystical union with Christ could solve the problem of han.

Preacher Lee went as far as to advocate a "blood connection with the Lord," with a love relationship with Christ Himself, of course mystically. And this "love relationship" with Christ was more explicitly talked about by Lee. He says:

> You must seek the love of Christ by thinking about Him and meditating on Him day and night. And go into the most intimate inner room of love. That place is the most holy ground of love. There you should embrace the true body of the Lord. . . There. . .in the shining glory of Solomon, sing out loud the song of love. [13]

Preacher Lee expressed the feeling of *han* and the experience of union with Christ in the language of sexual love. Perhaps this was the only way to connect the suffering of the people with the pain of Christ—two suffering lovers. So he would shout:

> Cry you Saints, the holy men and women, and cry. Where lies Gethsemane waiting for my blood and tears? You are sewing the red gowns, and you are

weaving the thorny crowns for me. [14]   *but you are the Rose of Sharon*

He left these words as he was dying of tuberculosis. He was condemned by the Presbyterian Church in 1933 and was stoned by the people as a heretic. The people did not seem to know how to connect their religion with their suffering under the Japanese repression. Their *han* was unresolved and perhaps unresolvable, so they turned to mystical revival meetings and became emotional, turning away from the concrete world of suffering and struggles.

This period can also be characterized as a time when Korean Christianity became fundamentally conservative both theologically and politically. One could say that Korean Christians did not know how to deal with the situation intellectually; that is, perhaps Korean Christians were not intellectually prepared for the national crisis. Thus, as in the case of Preacher Lee who used revival meetings for an all-out emotional outburst in a direction completely opposite from the world, church leaders closed their doors to the secular and intellectual world and chose Biblical fundamentalism as an alternative. Missionaries might have thought that under the political circumstances, the best they could do was to solidify ties within the church through Fundamentalist doctrine. Perhaps this was the only way for Korean Christians who were not ready to open themselves up to the world intellectually and politically. Fundamentalism was an opportune response on the part of the Korean Christian leadership to deal with the troublesome and problem-ridden world of Korea under the Japanese occupation.

First, the missionaries declared that they would remain conservative Christians, following the fundamentalism of the times in the United States. They attacked the modernists as traitors and as evil elements in Korean Christianity. This was the time when Harry Emerson Fosdick of Riverside Church of New York City was going through a heresy trial urged by George Machen of Princeton Theological Seminary. American missionaries were afraid of such modernist influence creeping into Korean churches, and more particularly into Korean theological circles. On the whole, missionaries in Korea took a stand against the onslaught of liberal Christian theological movement from the West. Instead of nurturing and developing an intellectual power among Korean Christians to cope with the on-rush of the modernizing trend from the West, they denied and resisted the intellectual trend of the time. Korean Christians remained ignorant and intellectually powerless. They were left in the world, but with only an emotional and other-worldly religion—a revival type, fundamentalist Christianity.

The course of fundamentalism was decisively set in the years 1932 and

Read George Machen

1935. The stage was the general assembly of the Presbyterian Church in 1934.[15] Two pastors were accused of being heretical. Pastor Kim Yung Joo of Seoul was reported officially to the Assembly as saying that the Book of Genesis was not authored by Moses himself, and Pastor Kim Chun Bae of Hamkyung Buk Do wrote an editorial in the *Presbyterian Weekly* advocating better status for women in the church. The latter even recommended the ordination of women as early as the 1930's in Korea! But the basic issue had nothing to do with the status of women. The problem was serious because the two Presbyterian pastors publicly questioned the literal interpretation of the Bible. While the first one questioned the authorship of the Book of Genesis, the second one questioned the authority of Paul's letter. Paul said that the women in the church should remain silent, so even today women should be silent in the church. Pastor Kim Chun Bae questioned this. That was the problem.

So, at the General Assembly a recent graduate of Princeton Seminary and professor of systematic theology at Pyongyang Theological Seminary was commissioned to examine the two pastors' writings. Professor Park Hyung Ryong not only condemned the two pastors as persons "unfit for their ministry in the Presbyterian Church of Korea," but also came out very strongly against the feminist attitude. According to him, women were not fit for responsible public work, for according to the Bible, women are more sinful than men. So, women cannot hold any responsible position, nor do they merit education and intellectual development. From the fundamentalist's point of view, women were created after men, that is Eve came after Adam, so it is only fitting for women to take a submissive role with regard to men. This has remained the official position of the Korean church until today; a proposal to the General assembly of the Presbyterian Church for a constitutional amendment to allow the ordination of women was voted down within the last five years.

The so-called "higher criticism" debate was a major issue in the division of the Korean Presbyterian Church into two factions after 1950. This is the major anathema within the theological seminaries of the conservative Presbyterian Church in Korea even today. Korean churches are on the whole characterized by a strong fundamentalist stance with regard to Biblical interpretation and the historical critical method of reading the Bible. For the minjung of Korea, this may have been a strength. The Gospel message was kept simple and strong for them to hold on to in the time of trouble and in their powerlessness. But in the long run, fundamentalism weakened their sense of reality, and facilitated the manipulation of the powerless minjung.

The decade of the 1930's was a tragic period not just for Koreans, but all over the world. The economic situation was at its worst, including the depresssion in the United States. Rumors of world war soon became a reality. In Italy, the Fascist Mussolini had been in power for years, and in Germany, Hitler and his Nazis were firmly in control. In 1935, Mussolini's Fascist army conquered Ethiopia, and the next year, Ethiopia was "annexed" by Italy. Japan's Imperial Army gobbled up Manchuria in 1934 and invaded China proper in 1937. The same year, Japan, Germany and Italy formed the so-called Axis powers—and prepared to carve up the world. In 1938 the year I was moving to my second grammar school because of my father's change of parish, Germany annexed Austria. In July of the same year Japanese and Soviet troops were fighting along the Manchurian-Siberian border. In September, the Munich Pact was signed by England, France, Germany and Italy. But in 1939, Germany swallowed up Czechoslovakia, Hungary and Rumania. In spite of the German non-aggressive pact signed with Poland and Russia in August, Hitler invaded Poland in September and ignited the Second World War.

The Japanese demanded that Koreans speak only Japanese at home, at school and even in church. We lost our Korean names, and we were forced to take new names in Japanese. (Our family name was Oomoto, and my given name during the Japanese occupation until 1945 was Eiichi.) The Japanese authorities forced Korean people, including church goers and church leaders, to bow down to Japanese Shinto Shrines.

First the Japanese authorities put pressure upon the mission schools. The missionaries refused to pay respect to Shinto shrines, because they thought it was an act of worship of another god. "The worship of deified spirit at the shrines is contrary to God's commandments," was their understanding of the situation.[16] Principals of mission schools such as George S. McCune of Union Christian College and Miss V.L. Snook of the Soong-eui Girls' High School, both in Pyongyang, were barred from running their schools. Because they refused to pay respect to Shinto shrines, in 1936 they were deported to the United States. By 1938 all the mission schools in the Pyongyang area were closed down by their American mission boards.[17] But the Japanese forced the mission schools to re-open under different names with a Korean board or with Japanese authorities. In October 1940, the American Minister Marsh ordered all the missionaries to leave Korea. However, some missionaries insisted staying on until June 1942, when the Underwoods and a few other missionaries left by way of Pusan harbor.[18]

In the General Assembly of the Korean Presbyterian Church of 1938, Korean delegates to the Assembly voted, in front of police observers, for the Shinto worship. They passed a resolution that the "Shinto Shrine is not a religion and it is not against the Christian dogmas; the worship of Shinto Shrines is a patriotic national ritual," and therefore "the delegates will not only actively participate in Shinto Shrine worship but also they will promote the same to the other members of the Church in Korea."[19] Many church leaders resisted, but they were imprisoned. In the five years of the Pacific War, more than 200 churches were closed down. More than 2,000 Christians were imprisoned and some 50 church workers died in prison.[20]

2. The Minjung and the Christians in Divided Korea

My father was taken in by the local police over the question of the Shinto Shrine worship. He refused to pay obeisance as demanded, and he resigned from the church. In 1939, when I was in the fourth grade and immediately after the General Assembly's decision, we moved to Man Po, a border town facing Manchuria where my father started a small grocery and drug store. Business went well, I think, and I recall we were much better off than we had been in the parish. But he could not continue to do such business. Within a year he sold the business, and we moved again to inland Manchuria` where my father was pastor of a Korean church. In later years I heard him say that he was disgusted with the church leaders' decision on the Shinto Shrine business. That had led him to quit the ministry for a while, but he could not quit everything, and he went to Manchuria into the Korean community of believers.

I was not mature enough to ask him about the nature of his refusal to worship at Shinto Shrines. But if I could ask him now why he refused to pay respect to Japanese Shinto Shrines, he would probably retort with anger at me that I did not know the answer. The basic and apparent reason for such refusal on the part of Christians in Korea was that it was a basic violation of the first and second commandments: "Thou shalt have no other gods before me and thou shalt not make unto thee any graven image." They refused to worship Japanese Shinto Shrines on religious grounds. Their refusal was the strongest expression of their religious fundamentalism Out of their faith, they were able to say no. This came out of their fundamentalist religious training.

Moreover. my father would have given another reason for his refusal, a political reason. By refusing Shinto Shrine worship, he was resisting Japanese imperialism and he was fighting against the political religion of the Japanese. In a sense, though he was not able to articulate it theologically, he was refusing the Shinto Shrine on the basis of his political theology. I suppose that other Christians at the time, who refused to worship at Shinto Shrines and chose the course of death, had the same spirit of resistance against the Japanese. It was the Korean Christians' anti-Japanese action which the Japanese could not tolerate. The Japanese did not really care about the Korean Christians' becoming Shinto worshippers. They did not like the Korean Christians' religious basis for political resistance against them.

However, Korean Christians had neither the power nor the resources to make their political resistance more apparent than it was. Consequently, they became more and more religious and other-worldly in their care of the remnant of believers. They took care of the poor and sick and weak souls of the minjung, directing their attention to heaven and other worldly realms. But they gave the minjung hope for the future—on the historical horizon— liberation from Egypt and the final victory of God over against the evil powers of Japan and Germany—although they could not talk about Japan and Germany. With this hope, the minjung was barely able to continue breathing for survival.

When, at last, Korea was liberated from the Japanese, Korean Christians believed that truly God's kingdom was at hand. Japan was defeated by the allied Forces, and the Second World War ended on August 15, 1945. Thirty-six years of Japanese rule had been terminated. Now Koreans were free, free at last. There was no deep thinking. We were only elated. Everything would now go well. We were free and free at last. We took out our Korean flags hidden so deeply in our chests and closets. People came out in the street to shout "Mansei" (Long Live Korea). We wept and wept, and we cried until we lost our voices. My father decided to return from Manchuria to the northern province where I was born, although there was nothing actually for him to do. There was only my mother's grave yard and her younger brother, a school teacher. My father had no plans, but he took us all back to his home area. The reason for his homecoming was that Korea was liberated. That was all.

We came home. But we were starving. We came home, but Korea was divided into two. We were locked into North Korean territory. So we were locked up once more by the repressive Communist regime of North Korea. Liberation had gone and the era of Communist captivity had set in.

Again North Korean church leaders, as under the Japanese occupation, found themselves resisting the Communist regime in North Korea. Instinctively, Christians in North Korea sensed the anti-religious stance of the Communists and felt the forthcoming persecution of Christians. Korean Christians in the north wanted the unification of Korea under the leadership of America, with an American-type democratic form of government. The

Russian-inspired North Korean regime wanted one Korea under Communist domination. For Christians in the North, liberation meant the establishment of a democratic system of government, and nothing less than that. Naturally, to Communist leaders in the North the Christians became an unwanted element in the society, not only on religious grounds but even more on political grounds.

North Korean Christians were able to stand up against the Communist repression on a religious basis. To their fundamentalistic faith communism was based upon an unchangeable atheistic stance. Christians in the North took Communism, rather correctly, as another religion with which they could never compromise. There was no "dialogue" between the Christian leaders and the Communists. It was as though no communication was possible by the very nature of the two opposing "religions." One side had to be extinguished, and that was Christianity. The Communist authorites in North Korea decided to hold an election for the establishment of a Communist government in the North on November 3, 1946. The important implication for Christians was that the election was set for a Sunday. The North Korean Presbytery issued a statement against the choice of Sunday as election day. To vote on Sunday was, for Korean Christians, another violation of the Commandments. Thus Korean Christians found a religious basis for their political resistance to the communist regime. And North Korean Communists found political reasons for further oppression of the North Korean Christians. While North Korean Christians took a strong anti-communist stance, they demanded separation of religion and politics, and independence and freedom for the Christian church. But the North Korean authorities organized a puppet "League of Christian Churches" through which they forced Christians to cooperate with the Communist regime. Many Christian pastors, including my father, refused to join the League. When the principals and professors of theological seminaries in Pyongyang refused to join the League, the seminaries were closed for a while. Later they were re-opened for a short time, under new leadership appointed by the League, until the Korean War broke out in June 1950.

As the nation was divided into two, and people of the North and the South could not visit each other, the Christian church itself suffered internal divisions right after liberation. The first schism had to do with the lapse of Christians under the Japanese occupation—the worship of Shinto Shrines. Those who came back from prison alive and those Christian leaders who had remained faithful to the Commandments demanded that the whole Korean Church show full repentance. In practical terms, the "pure" element of the church demanded that lapsarian churchmen take "repentance leave" for at least two months. However, Korean church leaders in both the North and the South ignored the suggestion, for no apparent reason. The "pure" group left the church, and started their own.

During the Korean War, while Christians were experiencing the massive on-slaught of North Korean communist forces deep into south Korean territory, and seeing the massive number of dead on both sides, right in the middle of the national tragedy, schism erupted. In the May 1951 Pusan General Assembly, the "pure" group declared themselves to be "separate" from the old Presbyterian church and named themselves the "Legal, Traditional Korea Presbyterian Church." Even more tragic, immediately after the separation the "pure" sect issued a statement denouncing the main body of Presbyterians as Communist. The Korean church was accused of receiving relief goods from the World Council of Churches, and therefore of cooperating with a pro-communist organization. Thus the Korean Presbyterian Church was indicted as a politically dangerous group of pro-communists, right in the middle of the South Korean war against the communist north.

Because of the anti-communist stance of the South Korean political leader Syngman Rhee, the bloody fight resulting from the North Korean invasion deep into the South, and the North Korean persecution of Christians in the north, there had been no way of establishing any dialogue between Christians and communists in Korea. Moreover, Communists were barred from South Korea, and it was not even permitted to study the works of Communist theoreticians. Being a South Korean was synonymous with being anti-communist. Nevertheless, there have been Christians in the South who see their mission as work with factory workers and others who are poor and oppressed in their society. And invariably they have been accused of being communist as a result. To be sympathetic to or understanding of communism in South Korea would be more dangerous than worshipping a Japanese Shinto Shrine. It is both politically and religiously dangerous. For anti-communism in the South has become almost another religion—a strong political religion.

In both the North and South, but perhaps more so in the North, a Christian stance against communism was taken on a religious basis. As we said before, the communists' atheistic stance and anti-religious posture itself was the most important reason for Korean Christians to oppose communism. Furthermore, the south Korean government's anti-communism and the cold war politics of the world hardened the Christians' anti-communistic stance. As the world was divided into North and South in Korea and East and West elsewhere, and the two camps of red and white confronted each other with arms and hostility in words and actions, already right-wing Christians could not help but harden their right-wing stance on the matter of communism. In the middle of the cold war ideological struggle, in the middle of the Korean war, and more so in the middle of North Korean communist persecution of Christians, the minjung of Korea was almost forgotten. Korean Christians had no power or intellectual resources to think and act in light of minjung—the poor and oppressed—in the rapid social changes that had taken place immediately after liberation. The official anti-communist stance of the church and the government in the South barred the church from becoming conscious of the poor and oppressed. For to think about the minjung sometimes was labeled as communist and dangerous.

This does not mean that only the communists would be conscious of the minjung, the poor and oppressed. On the contrary, North Korean Christians realized that the communists were only exploiting and manipulating the minjung in the name of minjung. That is, although they were talking about minjung as the subject of history, they were making the minjung objects of exploitation and manipulation for their own political ends. This is one of the strong reasons why Christians and communists in the North cannot come to recognize each other as possible partners for the benefit of the minjung .

In the South there has been a consistent effort on the part of Christians to work with the minjung—with the poor, with labor unions, with factory workers and with the politically oppressed—for human rights and democracy. The work with the minjung and for the minjung by Christians has been labeled as communist or communist-inspired, thus giving more credit to the communists than they deserve. In response to this kind of labeling—labeling Christians who were working for the minjung as communists—Korean Christianity became more and more religiously and politically fundamentalistic and conservative. This is the background against which Christians in the 60's and 70's became conscious of social problems and the problem of the minjung in Korea.

While Korean churches became religiously and politically more right-wing, and while they were divided during the Korean war on the basis of ideological differences, they were also divided on the basis of theological differences. The first division created the ultra right-wing church, namely, the Korean (or Koryo) Presbyterian Church; the second division created a theologically liberal church, namely, the Presbyterian Church of the Republic of Korea, otherwise known as the *Christ* Presbyterian Church; this left the "main line" *Jesus* Presbyterian Church.

Although this division of the largest denomination in Korea was not finalized until 1954, it began as early as 1938, when the missionary teachers of the Presbyterian Theological Seminary in Pyongyang were ordered to leave the country and the Seminary was closed down. Some Korean theologians known as "liberal" established a "Chosun" theological school with an announced purpose of "liberal" theological education. With indigenous funding, the "Chosun Theological seminary" was opened in April 1940 in Seoul. One of the founders of the school made it clear that this was the first time in 60 years of Korean mission history that Korean theologians were able to take the lead in theological education. Professor Kim Jae Joon criticised the missionaries' theological education policy—their fundamentalism and their negative attitude toward high quality theological education for Korean church leaders. Professor Kim declared that the new Korean theological school's purpose was to make theological education more liberal than ever.

(1) The level of the Korean Church has to be upgraded, not only in terms of mission work, but also in terms of scholarship and theological thought.

(2) In order to achieve this goal the new seminary will promote free inquiry with piety to enable students to gain and strengthen their faith independently.

(3) There shall be no suppression of free thinking by the students. Professors will introduce theological scholarship with full sympathy and understanding so that the students come to realize the validity of Calvin's theology independently.

(4) Current critical Biblical studies will be introduced. But this is for preliminary examination of the Bible, and has nothing to do with the establishment of a theological stance.

(5) Our theological endeavors shall be in the context of practical development of the Korean Church. Our endeavors have no concern for theological debate *per se*, or for unnecessary struggle among church authorities.[21]

The founders of the Chosun Theological School in fact wanted to teach their students as they had been taught theology, in the United States, Germany and Japan. It was their ambition to upgrade the almost backward and missionary-centered theological education in Korea. Their ambition was expressed as (1) free inquiry and (2) introduction of critical studies of the Bible. Their ambition was to correct thereby the anti-intellectual atmosphere of both Korean theological seminaries and the churches as well. They were not advocates of the 19th Century German Liberal school of theology, but were "liberal" because of their desire for academic freedom and free and open theological inquiry. This move was revolutionary. It was revolutionary intellectually. "Open and free inquiry" on any subject is culturally foreign to the Korean intellectual atmosphere in general let alone to church communities.

This move was also significant as reformation. It represented a break from the monolithic and authoritarian theological education of the missionaries. As early as 1896, American missionaries outlined the direction of theological education in Korea. It was not to provide the student with free and open intellectual inquiry on "the cardinal facts and truths of Christianity," but rather to "ground him thoroughly in the Word," and "let him strive above all else to be a Holy Ghost Man." This was the so-called Nevius method of theological education in a mission land such as Korea. The idea was not to educate the Korean minister too much: above the average church goer but not as high as the missionaries. The principle was expressed by the missionaries as "seek to keep his education sufficiently in advance of the average education of his people to secure respect and prestige but not enough ahead to excite envy or a feeling of separation." [22] The Nevius mission objective is in a nutshell self-supporting, self-governing and self-propagating. But the Nevius method of theological education did not allow Korean leaders to establish their own self-supporting theological education. At the time the Presbyterian Theological Seminary in Pyongyang was closed, only one Korean professor of theology was on the theological faculty. The founders of the Chosun Theological Seminary in Seoul in 1940 wanted to break away from missionary-dominated theological education.

During the Japanese war period, that is until 1945, the new theological school did not do much for Korea's own theological development, as they had ambitiously set out to do at the beginning. But when Korea was liberated from the Japanese, and Christians in the North took refuge in the south, and American missionaries came back to claim their "field," the new theological school became a problem. Conservative north Korean refugees wanted to go back to the "good-old" theological education which the missionary "fathers" had established. "Restoration" of theological education meant opposition to the new theological stance of the only existing theological school. The intellectual climate of the time was not favorable for the founders of the new theological school to maintain their power and continue as the "official" training center for Korean ministry.

Students at the seminary reported the liberal and thus "heretical" teachings of their teachers to the General Assembly of the Presbyterian Church. These students were reportedly disturbed by their teachers' use of the "historical-critical method" in Biblical studies. The General Assembly commissioned a committee to examine Professor Kim Jae Joon. Professor Kim was examined by a "special examination committee" on the question of the "inerrancy" of the Bible . It was a clear violation of academic freedom, but no one saw the problem from that perspective. This was a one-sided exercise of ecclesiastical power which was based on another theological (or non-theological) way of thinking. The church authorities took the position that fundamentalism was the "official" doctrine of the Korean` Presbyterian Church.

From 1947 until the end of 1954, all through the harsh and difficult years of the Korean War, the founders of the new theological school went through "heresy trials" over their desire for academic freedom in theological education. In 1953, at the 38th General Assembly of the Korean Presbyterian Church, Professor Kim was expelled from his pastorship in the "name of Jesus Christ," on the grounds that he taught "errancy" of the Bible without regard to the previous warning of the Assembly not to use the historical and critical method of Biblical studies. This was excommunication from a Protestant church, on a matter of doctrine, an unheard-of event in the history of the Korean Church! In June of 1954, the followers of the new theological school gathered in Pusan to establish a new Presbyterian Church. It's official name was the Presbyterian Church in the Republic of Korea, otherwise known as the "Christ" Presbyterian Church. [23]

The minjung of Korea were suffering from a most cruel war— a war with no purpose, no ending. They were suffering death, wounds, poverty, abandonment, and betrayal; but the Christian leaders had nothing to do with them or their suffering. An ecclesiastical power struggle seemed to be the only thing that would be recorded in the history of the Korean Church of those years. But perhaps this fight had to be fought, if not during the war then at another time. Korean intellectuals came to realize that the church could be the most oppresive power for suppressing intellectual development. And although it led to division of the church, it was a good fight on the part of those Christians who wanted some new and fresh air for the church in a liberated and independent Korea. The new church and the intellectual force around her soon became the firmest ground for the theological maturity of Korean Christians in the 1960's and 1970's

It was the newly-divided "liberal" church and the new theological seminary that assumed leadership in the development of Korean theology. Because of their fight for liberalization, and for free inquiry into theological problems, the young scholars in theology and the pastors and lay people of the Korean church were able to open themselves up to western theological ideas. For the first time in Korean theological development, Korean Christians were introduced to the names and ideas of neo-orthodox or dialectical theologians such as Karl Barth, Emil Brunner (who came to visit Korean Christians in 1949), Rudolf Bultmann and Paul Tillich. Only through the new "theologians" in the new Presbyterian church did Korean Christians learn about theological issues and developments in the Western world. The leaders of the new church and the new seminary opened up new and wide horizons: the exciting and breath-taking theological world of Dietrich Bonhoeffer, Harvey Cox, Thomas J.J. Altizer and other Death of God theologians, and later Jurgen Moltmann, theology of hope, secular theology, political theology, liberation theology, black theology and women's theology.

The new horizons were opened not only in the area of theological scholarship, but in the area of the mission of the church. Liberation of the new church made it possible for theological students and lay people to become concerned about the world and to go into the world. They were able to participate in the _missio Dei_, the mission of God, not particularly in the Church but in the world—in rapidly growing industries, on farms, on university campuses, in new housing developments and in squatters' villages. The new theology opened the gate to the church people for their entry into the world. Had we not had their fight for a new freedom in theological inquiry, we could not have found freedom to become involved in the world. In this sense, the new church division was an historically necessary process, for this was the radical break with the fundamentalist theological and political outlook of the past, and more importantly the radical restoration of Korean church to its original perspective. With a fundamentalist outlook, Korean Christians never would have become aware of the problems of the contemporary world and its modernization process in all of its intellectual and technological aspects, let alone the true nature of the Gospel—God's total presence in the world as a human being for the liberation of the world.

With this new thrust of the church movement and theological development, leading theologians in Korea were exposed to the basic issues of Christian mission—how to translate the Christian Gospel from a Western language into relevance for a rapidly industrializing society which had long and rich religious and cultural traditions. The new development gave courage to Christians to look into new and current theological developments in the Western world and introduce them in popular monthly journals and weekly church papers in Korea. Younger theologians and theological students were sent to American and German theological schools for academic and mission training in light of theological developments in Korea. When they returned they became deeply committed to the development of theological education and theological scholarship in their respective institutions. In the 1960's the Korean Association of Accredited Theological

Schools (KAATS) was organized with the help of the Theological Education Fund (TEF), which became a center for theological leadership training and the development of theological scholarship in Korea.

The Korean theological leadership which had been involved in the development of a new theological climate in Korea became deeply involved in two major issues in the 1960's. One was the issue of indigenization of Christian theology, and the other was the issue of secularization. In other words, Korean theologians began to grapple with the problem of traditional culture and religion in Korea in and through which the Gospel was translated and spoken, namely, the problem of two stories—the stories of the people of Korea and the stories of Jesus Christ in the Gospel. For the first time, with a perspective different from that of the missionaries, Korean Christians took a careful look at Korean cultural and religious traditions. This made it possible to create new interest among Korean Christians in looking seriously at the traditional Korean religions—Shamanism, Buddhism, Taoism, and Confucianism—as well as the cultural and political history of Korea, her literature and folk drama. (We shall go into this development in the next chapter, as we examine the roots of minjung theology in the Korean cultural and religious soil.) But without the struggle of the "new theologians" in the 1950's, there would have been no awakening of theological concern for the "hermeneutics of the two stories" or the issue of the *missio Dei*.[24]

I was fortunate enough to be admitted to a small church-related liberal arts college in Montana in 1956. That was the condition on which I was able to terminate my service in the Korean Navy. Rocky Mountain College in Billings, Montana was where I learned the significant meaning of "a small church-related college" in the American educational tradition. After five years' of military service I was an old student in terms of age, but at heart I was as young as any other student there. I enjoyed almost limitless intellectual freedom in almost any field of study. My hunger for learning was almost fully satisfied. I majored in philosophy and religion. I read Plato and Paul Tillich, and I was excited about reading the major English novels of Melville and Hemingway, Lawrence and Joyce.

I aspired to the teaching profession and went to the graduate department of philosphy at the University of Illinois. I was confused. Although I had some undergraduate backgroud in the history of philosophy, I was ill-prepared for the technical philosophy of linguistic analysis. While teaching world religions as a teaching assistant, I had a difficult time mastering contemporary philosophical development in positivism, conceptual analysis, and the philosophy of language. In two years' time, I was becoming a pretty good imitator of linguistic analysis, echoing their lingo and jargon, examples and jokes. In an inconsistent way, I was able to produce a few analytical papers and to introduce some of the prominent names in the British school of linguistic analysis. Theological language—language of God, or God-talk—these came to my mind. If man is a language user, and if that is one basic way of defining man as man, ultimately man is the user of the God language. He speaks of God; he speaks the language of God; and he acts on the language of God. What would be the grammar of the language of God, if there were such a thing as the grammar of the language of science? What would be the correct use of the language of God? What would be the misuse of God language?

Carrying these questions and frustrations, I went to Union Theological Seminary in New York in 1962. It was the time when most of the theological giants—Tillich and Niehbuhr—were gone. But Union, I thought, was re-aligning itself intellectually and politically with new developments in a new era of American society. It was a never-settled place, and therefore, an ever-changing and dynamic place. And to me, New York was an entirely new world in every possible way. I was quite comfortable in philosophy and theology, or philosophical theology and the history of theology, because I was fascinated to review and survey the entire western development of dialogue and the conflict between philosophical ideas and theological thinking.

I was to become a philosophical theologian, *a la* Tillich's correlation method. I wanted to combine my own philosophical training with a theological response to it. Western philosophy is the hard core and the essence of Western culture, and I was fascinated by the whole of Western theological development as a response to its cultural tradition. The more one is to take theology seriously, the more one must take philosophy seriously also. But I was led beyond the confines of certain philosophical schools to the entire question of the cultural traditions of the west, arts and technology and the way of life of western man. This was something I could not deal with all at once. But in later years, after returning to Korea, I continued my interest in the western way of life and in the traditional Korean culture and religion in connection with the formation and development of Korean theology. I did graduate study in the area of philosophical theology at Vanderbilt University and wrote a dissertation on the question of the language of God in connection with James Austin's analysis of performative languages.[25]

Interestingly, my experience at Union seemed to coincide with theological developments in Korea during the early 50's. As the Korean church was struggling with a new way of reading the Bible, I was going through a series of shocks in learning how to read the Bible. I hung on to it. I had many sleepless nights, not just keeping up with heavy reading assignments, but also sorting out some of my old fundamentalist hang-ups against the so-called historical-critical studies of the Bible. A country church boy from a mission wonderland of Korea had a very hard time getting rid of the idea that God wrote the Bible word for word. And then he had a hard time combining the idea that the Bible was not written by God himself with the idea that it still is the Word of God. In the end my notion of the Bible was somewhat, if not entirely, demythologized. I found myself, however, bravely trying to find the new modes into which the Gospel was to be retold or remythologized.

I think this represents, in a way, the Korean theological struggle to find a new mode of language in which the demythologized Gospel may be proclaimed again. That mode may be the traditional language of Korean culture and religion. That mode may be the rapidly changing and securalizing language of the contemporary world. Biblical studies in the first semester of my Union experience were daring and radical for me. Because of this shocking experience, I gained courage to make a daring and radical attempt at understanding the message of the Gospel. Courage to turn around, to take a look at things from a different perspective, to be critical about my own prejudices—this was what I needed in understanding the Gospel. And this I learned in the Bible classes at Union.

The year I went to New York for my theological education, the civil rights movement was at its height. Students there were most concerned about the movement, some of them joined the movement, and some of them came from that movement. Professors like Stringfellow and Clark were respected by the students who were deeply involved in inner-city field activities. Most of the students want to go into the inner city as their field work. The whole seminary seemed excited about tearing down the wall between the seminary, the city of New York and the world at large.

My field work was in Jamaica, an integrating suburban Methodist church. For the first time, I worked with black youth, I visited black homes, and I was invited to black homes for their "southern hospitality" to young seminary students. I ate many, many chicken drumsticks and enjoyed the warmest hospitality. I had to confront the hostility of black young peoples as well, and experience their anger and frustration. For the first time I was able to meet with black people as people—the suffering people of God. Later, I changed my field work to the Columbia University Protestant Center to serve as one of its assistant counselors. I worked with students at a nearby Korean Church, while I was taking university chaplaincy training with the Columbia University Protestant chaplains.

My field work experience was not just to go through tough experiences with the congregation. That was important, but what was more important was to reflect upon the experience—how to look at it, how to interpret it. We were fortunate to have extraordinarily good field work tutors at Union who could lead students to think about their own experience and to reflect on their failures and successes in the field. We were also challenged to make an effort to combine experience in the field with the theologies we learned. We were asked to question the validity and relevance of theologies we learned in the classrooms. We were challenged to learn to practice theology from the perspective of our own field work experience. In order to do that, we realized that we needed more training in how to look at a situation, at its social, political and economic make-up. Out of that learned experience, we would take a look at theology and the Gospel—its meaning, its relevance, and its action. Here we learned the secular meaning of the Gospel. We tried to answer Bonhoeffer's question about how to speak the language of the Gospel in a secular way. We tried and learned, or at least sensed, that we should speak the language of God politically, in concrete, socio-economic language. At least that was the feeling and atmosphere at the time at Union.

In my first year at Union, I was fortunate enough to become friends with the Rev. Park Hyung-Kyu, who was a pastor from the "Christ" Presbyterian Church, the new church. He had come to do his master's work with John Macquarrie. He gave me a sense of Korean reality, and he gave me the warmest pastoral care in my first year of theological training. I owe him a great deal in terms of my personal development at Union in a most difficult period of formulating my own theological thinking and reflecting upon my experiences in Korea and in the United States. He was my theological therapist for a whole year. I talked about myself—my upbringing, my education, my theology, my frustration and my successes and achievements—with him, and we reflected together and shaped my own thinking direction. I began to direct my attention to Korea and to pay more attention to Korea and the Korean theological scene.

I was also fortunate to meet Dr. Helen Kim who had come to Union as a visiting scholar at the invitation of Henry Pitt Van Dusen, then president of Union. Helen Kim had just been forced by the military government to retire from her presidency at Ewha Womans University. The military government ordered every university president over the age of 60 to retire. She asked me to come to Ewha to teach in the future, and she was kind enough to invite me to take up an internship at Ewha. In 1964 and 1965, I took an international internship at Ewha and was married on the Ewha campus to an Ewha graduate on its faculty. That was the beginning of my association with Ewha Womans University, and I have since committed myself to this institution of higher learning.

3. Rediscovery of the Minjung

It was 1964 when I came to Ewha Womans University on my theological internship from Union. I was placed in the University Chaplain's office and appointed a full-time instructor in the Department of Christian Studies in the College of Liberal Arts and Sciences. As a younger theologian, I was actively involved in the student Christian movement in Korea, and I committed myself to university student Christian activities in Korea. I was well accepted by the university faculty and by the students, and I decided to return to Ewha to teach after I finished my Ph.D.

When I came back in 1969 with my degree from Vanderbilt University, I was appointed Chairman of the Department of Christian Studies. Full power was given to me to steer the direction of theological education for women, and of the whole religious climate of the campus. I was the youngest on the faculty, but the whole faculty accepted me warmly with full support. I had accepted the important call to the religion faculty of the most prestigious women's university in Korea. Significantly, Ewha has traditionally been a Christian university; it was founded by a Methodist missionary in 1886 for the education of Korean women, the first school of its kind in Korea. Ewha is regarded by the public as the best among the women's universities and colleges. The University administration is deeply committed to Christian higher education, that is, the Christian character of higher education in Korea. Students of Ewha are the brightest among their peers coming from the middle and upper class sectors of Korean society. They are also the most keenly aware of the social and political problems of Korean society, and they are often among the first university students to move and speak out for the cause of democratic development of their country. The whole university faculty itself is one of the greatest resources for the development of campus ministry, in their intellectual, educational and artistic resourcefulness.

I reorganized the department's student activities to promote more studies and social action. I also tried to mobilize the whole university for a more secular understanding or a more academic translation of the Christian message in the rapidly secularizing university and the society at large. In the week-long, university-wide religious emphasis week, I spoke on the new religious way of living. I selected my speech titles from the titles of popular songs of the time. I tried to speak about the Christian Gospel from and through the language of the students—the secular language. I tried to make religious language meaningful to them, while speaking it from the center of their everyday experience and everyday life.

I asked a professor of modern dance to translate *Jesus Christ Superstar* into a form of modern dance, and students from the Modern Dance Department performed the dance version of *Jesus Christ Superstar.* The dance play was given on Easter Sunday morning of 1971, and ever since this has been the "passion play" of the year performed by Ewha's Dance Department.

The early 1970's may well be characterized as an era of counter-culture in Korea. Besides long hair and mini skirts, young students in Korea were in search of their own style of life, their own language, and their own arts. I translated the entire play *Godspell* into Korean and had Ewha students perform it in 1974. It was a great hit, and immediately became the song and the language of our young students. *Godspell* was a language of liberation for our students, and it became a political gesture for the liberation of Korean students. More importantly, it was looked on as an important possibility for a creative youth counter-culture in Korea. I did not have to interpret this as my application of Paul Tillich's theology of culture. I simply wanted to let the young people speak their own language to understand and live the life of liberation. They spoke freely their own language of liberation as they participated in the musical.

But after two public performances of *Godspell* the authorities banned the songs and the performances on the ground that the musical was subversive, agitating the students to political action. They took, quite correctly, the whole language of youth expressed in the musical as the political language of liberation. The authorities had in effect, politicized the whole musical play, *Godspell.* From the Christian point of view, these two musical plays are artistic expressions of the life and teachings of Jesus. These plays make Jesus a human being, a friendly human being, with passion and anger and laughter and jokes, just like any other young person with joys and frustrations. He becomes a friend of the sick and the poor, girls and boys, prostitutes and tax collectors. Our students could easily identify with Jesus in the musical plays, when he was taken in by the Jewish and Roman authorities, beaten, and tried and imprisoned and put to death on the cross.

From the students' point of view, these plays were speaking of the experiences of the students and the people of Korea in struggling to make their country more democratic and humanized. The plays coincided and correlated with the stories of the students and the stories of Jesus in the Gospel. The actors of social action for justice in Korean society were the performers of the musical plays. The stage was a microcosm of their larger world where they acted in behalf of the suffering people, and suffered but rejoiced for the future of resurrection. They wept as Jesus was beaten, they laughed with the stories of Jesus, and they shouted when Jesus was victorious.

This was also the time when Korean university students rose up against the more and more repressive government of Park Chung Hee, and when Korean students became more and more politically conscientized. When I returned home for good to teach at Ewha in 1969 President Park was in his second presidential term. He was successful in taking over the weak and ineffective civilian government which followed the downfall of the autocratic Syngman Rhee regime in the student revolution of 1960. Mr. Park forced the people to agree with his normalization policy with Japan in 1964, and he sent Korean troops to the jungles of the Vietnam War in 1965. President Park was reelected in 1967 for his second and last term of office. In 1969 he forced the people to pass a proposal to change the constitution so he could run for a third term; Christians and students strongly opposed the idea. The Korean National Council of Churches issued a statement against the constitutional amendment, and the students demonstrated against the national referendum.

There were widespread arrests of student leaders and closure of university campuses. But as soon as the universities were opened for the second semester of 1969, Park's ruling Democratic Republican Party unilaterally passed his third-term proposal in the National Assembly, and it was confirmed by a 65% majority in a national referendum that October. Again President Park had broken his promise to make the Korean political system more democratic. He used the possible military threat from the North as his excuse for prolonging his power and military rule. Ideologically, he advocated an ever stronger anti-communist stance and fabricated the so-called "Korean style" democracy. "The Korean style democracy" meant that his government was legitimate, ideologically stemming from the traditional Confucian style of authoritarian government. Korean style democracy was necessary. Koreans are used to the authoritarian traditions of Confucianism, and these traditions were more necessary than ever under the threat of the North Korean communist regime.

After his narrow victory over opposition Presidential candidate Kim Dae Jung in the third term presidential election in 1971, Park and his party moved very swiftly to organize the government into a dictatorial system for his lifetime. Only a year had passed after his inauguration when all the universities were seized by soldiers, and in October 17, 1972, martial law was declared with suspension of the Constitution and dissolution of the National Assembly. Park and his followers formulated the new Yushin Constitution, and under martial law the new Constitution was passed in another national referendum. The new Constitution received a 91% affirmative vote, and in December the new president was elected by the newly-formed 2,500 member electoral body called the "National Conference for Unification." President

Park was the only candidate for the first of an unlimited number of six-year terms as president. His permanent control of dictatorial power now seemed tight and complete.

The people of Korea had been forced into a modern Babylonian Captivity. With the Yushin System, President Park had seized almost absolute political power over the nation. The name democracy was a mockery; in the name of Korean-style democracy all the democratic rights of the voters, the masters of the nation, were robbed and denied to them. There was no freedom of the press, no academic freedom to discuss and criticize the Constitution, no religious freedom to pray for democratic development of the country or for basic God-given human rights. The power of the National Assembly was drastically reduced; the President had the power to dissolve it at any time, as well as the power to hand-pick up to one-third of its membership. The Supreme Court was also to be picked by the President, and it was not given authority to deal with constitutional matters. The President had virtually all the powers of the three supposedly and formally separate branches of the government.

President Park had seized the people of Korea for a Babylonian Captivity through his absolute rule by emergency decree. Until he was shot to death by his own CIA chief in 1979, he ruled the country with emergency decrees Number 1 through Number 9. The Constitution gave him the power to take "necessary emergency measures" in "the whole range of state affairs, financial and judicial affairs" in times of "national calamity or a grave financial or economic crisis and in case the national security or the public safety and order is seriously threatened or such a threat is anticipated." There had been no such threat, except that his own power was threatened by public discontent. "Popular discontent—escalating sense of crisis among the ruling group—intensified repression—escalation of opposition movements"–this was the sequence of the vicious circle for more than ten years of "emergency decree" rule until the president's death in 1979.[26]

The President's emergency decrees were carried out by his own centralized police system, itself a Japanese colonial legacy. Besides the regular police force, the Korean Central Intelligence Agency was his most trusted strong arm for controlling the press, universities, students, faculty, Christian ministers, Catholic priests and labor unions. It was supposed to fight against communist infiltrators from outside, but it was used against internal critics of the government. Universities were manned by KCIA agents. They had control over the hiring and firing of university professors. They checked the professors' lecture notes. They were to know any and all student movements against the Yushin government of President Park. In spite of, or perhaps because of their tight and harsh control over student activities, student protest movements on the major university campuses continued.

In April 1974, commemorating the student revolution of April 1960, students organized the "National Federation of Democratic Youth and Students" (NFDYS). The students' statement demanded that the nation "punish at once the ringleader of the corrupt power group and guarantee a minimum standard of living for the laboring people and their freedom of labor movements, and to release all the patriotic leaders who had been imprisoned." [27] Ultimately the students wanted the Yushin system and the KCIA to be dissolved.

Emergency Decree Number 4 was declared on April 3, 1974, in order to crush the massive April student demonstrations organized by the National Federation of Democratic Youth and Students. It imposed heavy penalties of from five years in prison to death on all persons guilty of involvement in the NFDYS. Article No. 5 of Emergency Decree Number 4 stated quite clearly the repressive measures against the university campuses. "It shall be prohibited for any student to absent himself from school or refuse to attend classes or to take examinations without legitimate cause; to hold an assembly, demonstration, rally, or any individual or collective sit-in, outside or inside the campus, except normal classes or research activities conducted under the guidance and supervision of the school authorities . . ." [28]

The National Federation was used by the authorities as a good excuse to arrest a large number of students and professors, charging them with plotting "the largest communist-led rebellion to overthrow the state." More than 1,000 persons were detained and interrogated, and over 700 were jailed, and of these 253 were tried before a special military court-martial. Among them were Christian students and Christian leaders of the country, including well-respected Christian professors. Former ROK President Yun Po Sun, Bishop Tji of the Roman Catholic diocese of Wonju, Rev. Park Hyung-Kyu, pastor of Seoul's First Presbyterian Church and close friend of mine since my time at Union, Dr. Kim Donggill, a Lincoln scholar teaching American history at Christian Yonsei University and the only brother of President Kim Okgill of Ewha Womans University, and Professor Kim Chan Kuk, Dean of the School of Theology at Yonsei University, were among those tried and convicted on August 9 by a military tribunal for supporting the student uprising in April. In the same trial the most popular poet and social critic Korea has ever produced, Kim Chi Ha, was sentenced to death. Other men were to serve in prison 15-20 years with their civil rights suspended thereafter.

Catholic and Protestant church leaders rose up to oppose the emergency measure and demanded the immediate release of the political prisoners on human rights grounds. Purely by coincidence, on August 15 (anniversary of Korea's liberation from Japan in 1945) which was the date requested for their release, instead of an announcement by the government, fateful and tragic news came with the bang of pistol shots. An assassination attempt on President Park by a Korean resident in Japan had failed, but the assassin's bullets had killed his wife. On August 23, President Park suddenly cancelled Emergency Decrees 4 and 1, explaining that the assassination attempt had sufficiently aroused the people's awareness of the "danger of provocation and invasion" by the North.

On several occasions I went to a country prison about 25 miles south of Seoul to visit Dr. Kim Donggill, though his sister, President of Ewha, was not allowed to see him. President Kim Okgill could take money and clothes to the prison, and she managed to get some news from the cell from the prison guards. An English major in college, Dr. Kim opened a "free university" in his cell according to the news from prison, and out of sheer memory he recited the Bible and English poetry to the 15 student prisoners in his cell. It was a severe Korean winter that he and his students had to endure in an unheated Korean prison cell. But no one died because of the cold; everyone was cheerful as "secular saints" because of their belief in democracy and faith in Christ. On February 15, 1975, three days after another national referendum on Park's Yushin Constitution, the government announced the temporary suspension of sentences and the immediate release of the political prisoners.

The imprisoned students and professors were never taken back by their universities. Poet Kim Chi Ha was taken back to prison again, after a few months of freedom. However, university campuses did not remain silent, for students were determined not to be silent until the Yushin system yielded. Campus surveillance on the part of the government was tightened. Students were the single most powerful group which opposed the Korean style democracy and Yushin system of the government. Instead of responding to student demands and criticism, the authorities criticized the students for being too politicized, and instituted an all-out suppression of any creative and critical student activities and movements.

Historically speaking, Korean students have provided the most forceful ideological leadership in their society. They became the first enlightened element in Korean society when Korea was opened to the West and to modern education. They were the ones who led demonstrations for the independence of Korea when Japan and the Western powers were threatening the selfhood of the nation. Students here and abroad in 1919 were the leading elite in the March First Independence Movement. In 1929 teen-age high school students in Kwangju, a southern provincial city, rose up against the Japanese. Students went to farm villages to work for the improvement of Korean rural life, giving up their success and gains in the cities and in the ruling sectors of society. Along with the Christian church students became the hope of the Korean people for national independence and liberation. In Korean history, nationalistic and liberation movements have been led by students. So, Korean students and the national liberation movement have been inseparable.

This was witnessed in the April 19 student revolution of 1960, an uprising for viable democracy against the dictatorial Syngman Rhee regime. Korean students are the element of society most sensitive to political changes and to false political consciousness, and in Korean political history students have been the most volatile and progressive force. Even in traditional court politics, students of the royal college got a full hearing at the court when they criticized royal policies. The people of Korea from time immemorial have respected students; Confucian tradition gives highest respect to learning and therefore to the learned as well, especially when they are with the people and for the people. By contrast, the ruling sector of society has adopted a supreme authoritarian Confucian attitude and has tended to suppress the opinions of youthful students as immature and too idealistic.

When I returned home to Korea in 1969, students were not only a critical political force. They were also deeply involved in rural villages and newly developing industries as well as in helpless slums and squatter areas. Christian student activities were especially remarkable. The Korean Student Christian Federation had already started a social action program called the Social Development Service Corps. This program was ecumenical, not limited to Christian students but open to non-Christian secular students as well. Its purpose was to go into the slums, factories and apartment buildings to learn about the social and political realities of modernizing Korean society, and to find ways to work with the people. Students mobilized their learned resources to prepare sociological studies on the areas they had chosen, to set up strategy meetings and to go out to help organize the people for action. Students discovered the minjung of Korea, the suffering of the minjung. They learned of the total social injustice imposed on factory workers and slum dwellers, and their situation of total powerlessness. As the students became keenly aware of the minjung of Korea in their powerlessness, they formed a community of the minjung which was born out of a keen sense of the historical contradictions of power. The students were conscientized as the minjung became conscious of their situation, and they helped the minjung mobilize themselves to change the situation, to become the masters of their own destiny and the subjects of history itself.

As student consciousness of the minjung's suffering in the process of industrialization, "modernization" and development increased, the faculty of Ewha's Christian Studies Department began an industrial internship program. Our intent was to sensitize our students to the factory situation and that of the teen-age girl workers in the factories, in order to help the students seek new directions for Christian mission in the world. Heretofore, the Christian Industrial Mission's objective was to evangelize factory workers so that they would be obedient to the managers. But the newly arising Industrial Mission work in Korea was taking on a different posture. It was to work with the workers and conscientize them about the basic value of the individual, human rights, and their own resources and potentialities for transformation.

Our department program was set up in conjunction with a Christian Ethics course to give the students time to reflect on social problems and Christian social ethics. The faculty selected two students from those enrolled in the course to go work in a factory during the summer vacation months. As they went into the factory, they hid their student identity. Our students were hired as regular workers in a textile factory where most of the employees were young girls. Our students lived with the factory girls. They worked together, suffered together, and learned together about the structure of economic exploitation, the structure of low wages, and the structure of poverty. Our students also learned the precious wisdom of organizing laborers and the problems of labor unions completely controlled by the government. As expected, the students came back to school having gained more than they gave to the girls in the factory. Our students showed courage and maturity and a sense of wisdom. They shared much with the faculty, as they reported back to the students and faculty what they had learned about the meaning of participation in suffering and about the meaning of the Gospel of liberation in the contemporary economic world.

The program was continued, with wide-spread impact on the campus among Christian and non-Christian students. Working with the audio-visual education students, I created an audio-visual aid which showed the problems of the city, factories, slums and the poor farm areas. The program was named "One People in Two Worlds," to show the two worlds existing in one country and in one city–two divided worlds, north and south, haves and have-nots, the poor and the rich. The whole campus seemed to have been disturbed by the program, shown in the university chapel during religious emphasis week. Challenging the students who came from well-to-do families, we spoke of the tradition of missionary founder teachers who had built Ewha for the liberation of Korean women from poverty, ignorance and social and cultural oppression.

Secret
Octed

Finally, one of our students who was in the factory was discovered by the factory girls and eventually by the factory managers to be a university student. The whole program was publicized by a daily newspaper. It became an embarrassment to the factory, and a challenge to the so-called development policy of the government. The President of the University asked me as chairman of the Department to go with her to visit the President of the company which owned the factory where our student had worked as a student intern. We met the company president, expressed our regret and explained the purpose of our program. The matter was ironed out in a very oriental way with exchanges of bows and smiles, but I had the impression that the factory president was deeply challenged and disturbed by the presence in his factory of not only our students, but of the president of the university herself. It was the event of 1973. As the Yushin system set in with the imposition of harsh emergency decrees, student involvement in slum areas and factories had to be withdrawn, and students had to mobilize themselves otherwise for the struggle for freedom and democracy.

The Christian Urban Industrial Mission (UIM) in its present form had been active since 1965, although individual denominational industrial mission work existed since 1958. The UIM activity has the tradition of acting as a counter or critical force against the government-controlled labor unions in Korea. UIM workers were the organizers of labor-centered labor unions in the factories, and they were the only ones in the factories to speak up for the basic human rights of the factory workers. The Protestant UIM and the Catholic JOC (Young Catholic Workers) have made very significant contributions to the Korean labor movement, in contrast to the government-controlled labor unions.

An American missionary labor worker, Dr. George Ogle, was forced by the Korean government to leave the country in December 1974 because of his open doubts about the execution of eight People's Revolutionary Party members and his active involvement in the labor movement in Korea. Ogle reflected on the Korean Christian labor workers' contributions as follows:

> Their contributions are primarily two: first, the support that comes from standing alongside the workers in their struggle for justice; and secondly, the help given the workers in formulating a rationale for their demands and a philosophy upon which their goals and values can be expressed.[29]

One of the foremost Christian labor leaders in the movement states the theology of the Christian labor movement in one word: "presence." It was good enough to be with the workers—work together, think together, suffer together and win together.[30]

Mr. Cho quotes an interesting dialectical sentence which well depicts his theological posture: "The Christian presence is a Christian absence; and the Christian absence is Christian presence." [31] In the early 1970's a young garment factory worker burned himself to death to express his agony over the contradictions existing in the world of labor with its inhuman exploitation. He was not a Christian, but in him young Christian students encountered the Christian presence. And the young Christian students went into the labor world with their identity. Christians, students, and laborers–these have come together in the struggle for justice, equality and humane life in contemporary Korea. In this togetherness with the people, in this presence and participation in their suffering and struggles for a more humane life and just society, Christians have identified themselves as true disciples of Jesus Christ and have found themselves in the tradition of the Korean church that worked for the liberation of the Korean minjung.

It is an historical irony, and perhaps the grace of God, that Korean Christians discovered their own identity clearly in the historical traditions of Korea. The Yushin government emphasized a "Korean type of democracy" as its rationale for going against the development of Western democratic ideas and ideals. Government ideologues spoke of "rejuvenation" of Korean history and traditional consciousness, in order to justify their Confucian style authoritarianism in all walks of life. Their emphasis on national consciousness in the history of Korea made a significant contribution to the development of historical research on things Korean. While the scholars were doing research on the history of the rulers, kings and ruling classes, students and writers were doing more serious research on the history of the people: downtrodden, oppressed, socially and economically alienated people of the minjung. While the government was commercializing the traditional folklore and folk arts, the students re-created them in the present political consciousness, making folk plays the living arts and life of the oppressed people.

Students at Ewha Womans University, for instance, organized a study group to learn the traditional performing arts of the common people. They learned from the old performers of Korean traditional mask dances. The Korean mask dance is genuine people's art. It is a uniquely Korean art form, so that it can be easily exploited by the government as good propaganda material for the traditional arts of Korea. But Korean mask dances were born in the consciousness of the Korean minjung. They speak of the minjung's suffering and their agony and their transcendence. Korean mask dances have the minjung's body movement and their own music—straight and strong with a natural beauty and dynamic balance. The stories of the Korean mask dances are about the lives of the minjung. And they are critical of the ruling class— to show how unfit are the ruling aristocrats to rule the people, and to show that the religious leaders are too deeply corrupt to give salvation to the people. They laugh at the rulers, they laugh at their jokes, and they laugh at themselves. This is the "feast of fools." The minjung are laughing at themselves, at their own suffering, and at their own powerlessness. But they transcend themselves and overcome their foolishness and their powerlessness. They sense the power of laughter and the feast of togetherness. They sense the power of the solidarity of a community. Their language is vulgar and unrefined and spontaneous. Korean mask dances speak the language of the body and the language of the minjung.

Our students learned the spirit of mask dances and performed them in public on campus, which heightened the consciousness for the minjung, the people, and the present political situations. Our students adopted the mask dance form for the creation of their own contemporary plays. These were more powerful than the performance of *Jesus Christ Superstar* or *Godspell*, because, in spite of their power, they are still Western plays coming out of a Western consciousness. In a word, they were still foreign to our students. But the Korean mask dances were Korean expressions, and they were the language of the suffering people with whom Christians were to identify themselves. Korean Christians became more and more conscious of their own historical roots in their active participation in the people's struggle for socio-economic justice. They started over again in looking into the traditional religious consciousness of the Korean people, in identifying themselves with the culture and language of the common people of the minjung, and in studying the history of the development of Korean Christianity.

All the theological questions of the 1960's : indigenization of Christianity, the problem of text and context, and the issue of demythologization and interpretation of the Biblical language—all turned around to discover the language of the Gospel of liberation in the Korean consciousness, in its art forms, in its literature and music, and its dances and plays. Korean Christians found their own stories to tell alongside the stories of the Bible, the stories of a liberating Jesus and the Christian Gospel. The theology of the minjung was therefore born out of active participation in the struggle of the Korean people for a more humane and just society.

But it is more than a political theology. It is rooted deeply in the consciousness of Korean history, its religion and its culture. It is a cultural response to the minjung of Korea. It is a cultural theology. It is a cultural theology not in the style of Tillich. It is not a kind of theology which would respond to the western and aristocratic forms of culture which Tillich knows well and loves so dearly. It is a Korean Christian response to Korean culture, and the Korean minjung's way of life. And it is not like Paul Tillich's correlation method which presupposes a Christian stance over against a given culture. Korean cultural theology is a Christian response within the culture, right in the middle of and at the center of the culture of minjung. (In this sense, Harvey Cox's criticism of Tillich is quite close to our present concern in the development of minjung theology).[32]

With the development of student consciousness and concern, as well as the re-creation of the Korean traditional culture of the minjung, coincidentally, and out of this consciousness of the students, the world of poet Kim Chi Ha was born. He used the traditional rhythm of Korean folk tales in song form (Pan sori). He told traditional stories of the common people with their suffering and "han." He created the stories of the minjung in his long poems. He was critical of the ruling class, as were the mask dances. Actually he was creating mask dance poems in the contemporary Korean situation. Extremely funny and extremely sad at the same time. Extremely joyous and at the same time extremely angry. He showed his passion for the final victory of the minjung and his vision of utopia, the time and place where the minjung become the subject of history.

Kim Chi Ha spoke of the "han" of the Korean minjung in his now banned poem, "The Story of the Sound" published in 1972. The story is about "very strange bumping sounds" which "if heard by people with money and power would cause them to tremble like aspen leaves and break out in a cold sweat." The whole story is about the origin of a bumping noise. A bumping sound is heard coming from a deep prison cell. A poor prisoner named Ando is expressing his deepest "han" over his unjust and cruel treatment in prison. His head and legs were chopped off; and the trunk of his body keeps rolling and bumping against the prison walls. This is the noise. The "han" of the oppressed people and the "han-cry" of the unjustly-treated people are heard as strange bumping sounds day and night, posing an incredible threat to their oppressors. This noise is not just the cry of the minjung in the prison cell and in the prison-like conditions of the society. It will accumulate to make the noise of revolution. Revolution is the explosion and culmination of the oppressed people's cries and shouts of "han." According to poet Kim, the work of a poet is to transmit the "han" of the people in his/her poetry as an expression of political imagination. "This little peninsula is filled with the clamor of aggrieved ghosts. It is filled with the mourning noise of the 'han' of those who died from foreign invasions, wars, tyranny, rebellion, malignant diseases and starvation. I want my poems to be the womb or bearer of these sounds, to be the transmitter of the 'han' and to communicate a sharp awareness of our historical tragedy." [33]

This was not a solo play of poet Kim Chi Ha. There were other novelists and poets who wrote about the historical suffering of the Korean people in the late 60's and early 70's. Their materials are not limited to traditional stories. They boldly used the contemporary materials of labor problems, the rapidly changing urban situation and life in the slums and factories to raise the consciousness of Korean readers. Some of their works were banned by the authorities, and some of the writers were even investigated and convicted on charges of pro-communism. But their works are a search for humane society and humanity itself in a historical situation which is in a process of rapid dehumanization.

As the dehumanization of politics, a total alienation of the minjung from the political process, and total exploitation of the workers were in progress, Korean intellectuals and Christians were drawn more and more to one issue—mobilization of the minjung. Korean church historians looked at the 100 years of Korean Protestantism from the perspective of the liberation of the nation and the *han* of the oppressed people. Korean secular historians read the history of Korea from the perspective of the development of the minjung's self-consciousness. Some Korean Buddhist writers began to interpret the Maitreya Buddha as the messianic Buddha of the Korean minjung (Ko Eun, to whose thesis we shall come back in the following chapter). Student demonstrations were not limited to demands for more democracy; they were more and more related to the economically exploited workers and minjung of Korea. The whole movement for democratization in Korea of the 1970's was not just power politics or party politics to support one party over another. It was a populist movement for the rights of the minjung, their livelihood and their humanization.

On October 24, 1975, as the struggle against the Yushin Constitution and for human rights escalated among religious leaders and students, the heretofore silent press community came alive and joined in the struggle with its powerful resources. On that day about 200 workers at the nation's major daily newspaper, the *Don-A-Ilbo* issued a "Declaration of Freedom of the Press." As soon as this move to protect press freedom was made, other major dailies such as the *Chosun Ilbo*, the *Chung-ang Ilbo*, and the *Hankuk Ilbo* joined the struggle. It spread nationwide; in a few days twenty-two other newspapers followed the declaration of the freedom of the press. In spite of the government's stern warnings to the religious and press communities, solidarity between the religious sector, the students and the press became stronger than ever. Out of this solidarity on November 5 a Christian Council to Protect Democracy was formed, and soon a more broadly based National Council for the Restoration of Democracy was formed.

As expected, the formation of a united democratic front posed a serious threat to the Park regime. Instead of a head-on collision against the united front, the authorities used an indirect method of attacking the members of the front. A university professor who had joined the National Council for the Restoration of Democracy, a Harvard trained English Literature professor and editor-in-chief of the nation's leading liberal quarterly, *Creation and Criticism*, was dismissed from his teaching post. I drafted a statement against his dismissal and organized some 44 university professors to sign the statement demanding the immediate reinstatement of the dismissed professor on the grounds of academic freedom. No result. And no response from the Ministry of Education except that I was investigated for my intentions and the process of organizing professors to sign the statement. The *Dong-A Ilbo* published our statement as a "Declaration of Academic Freedom." [34]

In the military interrogation center in the summer of 1980, long after the death of President Park, I was asked again to write about the "Declaration of Academic Freedom" of 1975. I protested the inquisition, but the reply was that I had a dangerously wrong sense of history. According to the interrogator, the Yushin system was not over yet, and Park was not totally dead. This was legally correct, perhaps, because at that time no new constitution had been written.

In response to the Declaration of Freedom of the Press issued by the leading newspapers in Korea, some 300 reporters, editors and printers were fired. The Korean Christian Faculty Fellowship, a Christian university professors' group which had been actively involved in the students' and religious leadership in the struggle, joined in the protest movement. In the spring of 1976, the Ministry of Education fired some 160 university professors and junior college teachers on the grounds of incompetence and lack of qualifications. Among them, the government included against the will of the respective university presidents, some 15 Christian professors from prestigious universities. These dismissed professors were well qualified and well respected professors, most of them Ph.D. holders from respected American and European universities. They were in no sense incompetent. They did not have "political ambition" like their fellow professors who worked for the repressive government as technocrats and ideologues. But the dismissed professors were accused of being "politically active" or "meddling in politics" by the same government which was mobilizing all available intellectual resources for its own power and political survival.

I was listed as one of those to be dismissed in 1976, according to rumor–a rumor which no one cared to clarify as factual. But according to another rumor, (in a time of extreme press censorship, rumors are the only reliable source of information), the President of Ewha Womans University, Kim Okgill, a woman, was the only university president who refused to fire members of her faculty, including me.

At the interrogation center, I was asked to write about my activities in the Christian Faculty Fellowship in support of Christian professors dismissed from their respective universities. The last paper I had to write was about the Theological Declaration of 1974 which I had signed along with 65 other Korean church leaders and theologians. The interrogator concentrated on the following passage and demanded that I translate it into plain language, giving the background and intention of such a statement:

> All powers that be come from God (Romans 13). This passage of the Bible expresses the limits of political power before it speaks of obedience to it. The political ruler is commissioned to preserve life, property, and freedom, which are fundamental human rights, and the exercise of political power should be within this limit. Political power that violates the life and the freedom of man, his fundamental human rights, is in rebellion against God. Christianity understands that if the relative thing is absolutized it is called an idol. Traditionally Christianity fights against such an idol. Therefore, when absolutized power violates human rights, the church has no choice but to struggle against it. [35]

This is a strong and clear expression of the political theology of Korean Christians from the beginning, more particularly under the Japanese domination of Korea. Korean Christians have interpreted the first and second commandments more politically than any other contemporary Christians in the world. Moltmann's political theology, [36] and his political hermeneutics of the Gospel were put into practice with blood, and so have matured in the bone marrow of Korean Christians. This has been the call of God to struggle against the demonic political forces in the world that make themselves all powerful political idols—that is why Korean Christians had to bear the cross of suffering as they fought against the Japanese, against the North Korean communists, and now against the Yushin regime. The decision on the part of the interrogator was quite clear: he told me that I was "impossible and could not be saved," but should be sent to the military tribunal to be tried for my agitation of students to bloody demonstrations.

What was more troubling to the interrogator was the passage in the theological declaration of 1974 immediately following the one quoted above.

Common survival and mutual help are necessary for people to create meaningful and fruitful lives. Christians are fighters against the power of evil which prevents the possibility of such common survival. Thus, the church is commanded to fight suppression, on the side of the poor and the oppressed, to liberate them and to restore their human rights. [37]

This was a clear statement of the Korean Christians' commitment to the Gospel of liberation—the Gospel that is committed to and proclaimed for the liberation of the poor and oppressed and alienated. This is the root of the theology of the minjung in the history of the development of Korean Protestantism.

When I finished writing my confession of Christian faith in my cell room, interpreting the declaration of fellow Christian theologians and our community of faith in Jesus Christ in this particular history of crisis, it was already my second Sunday in the cell. Someone in the next room started singing hymns, and the military policemen who were guarding us in the corridor joined in. Almost all of the Christian professors who were writing their biography of struggle for the minjung were eventually dismissed from their teaching posts. (Some 87 professors were dismissed in the summer purge of universities by the new military government of 1980.) We heard the voice of the minjung as we were silently humming the hymns of liberation.

Paul in prison.

The Cross, Lee Chul-Su

Mother, Lee Chul-Su

Dream of a Female Worker, Lee Chul-Su

PART 2

RELIGION AND CULTURE
OF KOREAN MINJUNG

3 SHAMANISM: THE RELIGION OF HAN[1]

1. Korean Shamanism

Sounds of music. The whole town is already excited by the clang of cymbals and the thump of drums. Neighborhood children are dancing toward the house where the music comes from. But there is no circus in town. There is trouble, perhaps sickness or death. It is the *mudang's* music for a *kut.* The troubled house must be exorcised of evil spirits. Neighborhood women are so curious about what is happening to that house that they have to go to see the *mudang* and the *kut.*

I too want to go and see what is happening. I like that kind of music. I like to see the evil spirits being exorcised. I want to see the *mudang* dance. But I cannot go. My father is a Christian minister, and I am a Christian. My mother wouldn't let me go to see the *mudang,* because Christians are not supposed to be mixed up with other religions such as Shamanism. For me, it is a sin to see the *mudang* and participate in the *kut.* Besides I am afraid that I may be

Mudbugs page LOL

contaminated by the evil spirit—just by watching the *kut.*

Korean Christians have been isolated from the other religious cultures of Korea. The missionaries taught us that to accept Christianity means to cut ourselves off from the old way of life—the old way of religion. To become a Christian means that we must get rid of the household spirit shrines and forget about them. This is conversion, and an act of conversion. *Mudang* and *kut* have nothing to do with Christianity. Christ is *against* our culture, no matter how old and how strong it may be. Christianity is different from other native religions, and it is better than the rest. This we must accept and believe.

Despite the missionaries' teaching, shaman music and dances are still attracting women and children and sometimes men. And shaman faith or custom is the most pervasive form of religious culture in Korea. There are many shamans around an urban neighborhood, with green or white flags on the roof alongside the tall television antennas. Korean Christianity, although so western in its liturgy and appearances, is obviously quite shamanistic in its belief and behavior. In the final analysis, we may be all shamanistic, and Korean Christianity may be characterized as shamanistic Christianity. The shaman ritual, the *kut,* gives expression to the very soul and essence of the Korean people and their culture.

Shamanism is the pervasive religious custom and culture of the Korean *minjung.* But shamanism has no hierarchy, no church, no building, and no doctrine. It is practiced inside and in the courtyards of ordinary houses. A *mudang,* a Korean female shaman, comes to a house to perform a *kut.* She brings a drummer girl with her for the music and dancing. But for a special occasion, you could arrange a big *kut* in a shaman shrine on the top of nearby hill in Seoul. There are two shaman shrines in Seoul. But the one that I visit regularly has a seating capacity of less than 30, in contrast to a big church we have in Seoul that seats more than 10,000. Basically, shamanism builds no temples. It is practised at home, or even in front of an elm tree on the road leading to a village.

Mudangs may be called the priests of Korean shamanism. A *mudang* is usually a woman. Some are very young and some quite old; most are middle aged. Most of the *mudangs* I have seen and met have husky voices, rather refined body movements, are beautiful, and stand out from the other women attending shaman rituals. Korean shamanism has no known founder, or prophet, or leading priest(s). Korean shamanism is a religious practice centered around the *mudang.* A *mudang's* dance and her music are the liturgy of Korean shamanism. In her ritualistic trance she utters the "word of spirits" or "words of god." There are no scriptures, no written rubrics of religious practice. Therefore, the *mudang* is the single-most important figure in

Korean shamanism.

The group of women who perform *kut*, the shaman ritual, are known by different names.[1] *Mudang* is a common name for women who dance in trance to mediate between gods and people. But the name varies according to geographical area. For example, in the northern half of the Korean peninsula a polite name for *mudang* is *Mansin*. The latter, as it is written in Chinese characters, means "ten-thousand gods." The shaman is a recognized professional who manifests the gods in her own person at will and interprets the words and visions they send her.

Sometimes shamans are called a Buddhistic name such as *Bosal*; it is quite natural for the Buddhist Koreans to use this more Buddha-like name. Sometimes *mudangs* are called *shinsun* or *Sunkwan* out of respect. (The Chinese character "sun" refers to a Taoist visionary. This name comes naturally to Koreans with a long and deep influence of Chinese Taoism. But these are rather rare cases. *Mudangs* are usually called *mudang*, or *Jumja-nagi*, meaning diviner or fortune teller. This is a functional name for *mudangs*, because they practice divining and fortune telling when they are not dancing and making music for a big *mudang kut*.

One does not become a *mudang* through a process of education, examination and ordination, or through initiation rites. *Mudangs* simply learn the *mudang* "skill." They usually inherit the tradition from their families, learning an orthodox ritual preserved in the family for five or six generations. In the southwestern region of Korea, those who inherit their mudang knowledge are called *danggol*, meaning "regular customers". But in Cheju Island, they are called *Shimbang*, meaning "the room of gods." In spite of their family tradition and the learning process for the job, there are no reports of young *mudangs* becoming "professional" *mudangs* through ordination or initiation rites.

Most revered and respected are the "real" *mudangs* who have become *mudangs* through divine inspiration or "spirit illness" (*shinbyung*). In literal translation they are described as women who "entered into the gods" and "upon whom gods have descended". When spirits and gods enter into a girl, she becomes sick. This "spirit illness" or *shinbyung* syndrome seems to be a form of mental illness, hysteria or psychosomatic disorder. The symptoms of one destined to be a shaman include a persistent illness without apparent cause, appetite loss, unwillingness to eat meat and fish, craving for cold water, weakness or pain in the limbs, dreams, hallucinations, and crazed wandering.[3]

During and after the spirit illness the mudang-to-be sees hallucinations and dreams about mountain spirits or soldier spirits on horseback. Then she goes to a *mudang* for consultation or for exorcism. There and then she may begin to dance in the *kut*, or just start fortune telling for others. Thus, a new *mudang* begins her apprenticeship for the professional job of practicing *kut*. An anthropologist who observed Korean *mudang* extensively writes that "A *Mansin* (*mudang*) engages in a tug-of-war with the gods from the very beginning of her career." [4] Those who refuse the will of the gods and resist becoming *mudang* die raving lunatics. The following words of a *mudang* interpreted by an American anthropologist describe well such tugs-of-war between gods and men.

> They don't know what they're doing. They yell, 'Let's go!' and go running out somewhere. They snatch food from the kitchen and run out in the road with it. God-descended people snatch things and run away. They strike at people and shout insults.

> If I were a god-descended person and my husband were hitting me and calling me 'crazy woman!', I'd shout back at him, 'You bastard. Don't you know who I am, you bastard?' That's what the Clear Spring Mansin did. Then she sat beside the road talking to the chickens, so funny!

> It's very difficult for them. They're sick and they stay sick, even though they take medicine. And there are people who get better even without taking medicine. There are some who can't eat the least bit of food; they just go hungry. There are some who sleep with their eyes open, and some who can't sleep at all. They're very weak but they get well as soon as the gods descend in the initiation *kut*. For some people, the gods descend gently, but for others, the gods don't descend gently at all. So they run around like crazy women.[5]

A distinction can be made between a god-descended person and someone struck temporarily insane. According to the *mudang*, "Insane people look like they're in pain, but god-descended people wander here and there, singing out, "I'm this god, I'm that god!"[6] For the god-descended person, an initiation *kut* is performed in which the initiating *mudang* invites the gods to complete their descent and allow their chosen one to dance and sing as a *mudang*. Thus ushered into *mudang*-hood, as it were, the initiate is called upon to bring blessing to the living by appeasing spirits and gods in the invisible world, and curing illness by exorcism.

According to shamanistic tradition, in early Korean history there were male shamans, and shaman practice was dominated by men. During the Yi dynasty (1392-1910), when Confucianism was the state religious ideology, male shamans gradually disappeared. Male shamans, called *Paksoo*, comprise about 30% of the present Korean shaman population. According to the 1960 census, there were some 21,932 shamans in South Korea. However, this figure does not include *Paksoos*. A *Paksoo* is a teacher of dance, and a musician skilled in the double reed flute, single reed flute, two-string violin and drums, as well as being a shaman. The word *Paksoo* is a derivative of *Paksa*, meaning a person who knows many things by learning, someone with a Ph.D. A *Paksoo* knows by heart three hundred or so texts, songs and chants, and he interprets the ancient Korean and Chinese texts. Because of their learning, *Paksoos* do business in cities as "name makers," for newborn children and for new businesses. They are professional fortune tellers.

A 1972 survey estimated that there is one *mudang* of some sort or other for every 314 people in Korea. This is high density. By comparison, 1982 government statistics indicate that there are some 35,000 Protestant ministers in Korea, or one for every 1,000 people. According to the same statistics, there were even fewer Buddhist monks, 20,755, than Protestant preachers. It is interesting that the 1982 government statistics do not include the number of *mudangs*, or the number of people who go to a *mudang* for *kut* and on various occasions of religious need.

The Ministry of Culture and Information, which compiles and issues such statistics, does not classify shamanism as a religion. This is understandable, since *mudangs* have no church where they practise their religion. There is no *mudang* organization which produces statistics for the Ministry which oversees the religious affairs of the nation. And *mudangs* would be the last to acknowledge, on their "citizen's identification card" or on their tax return, that their profession is *mudang*.

Scholars of Korean shamanism carefully avoid the term "religion" in defining the *mudang* phenomenon. In Korean, they call it "customs of *mudang*," [7] not "kyo" (敎) or religious teaching, but "sok" (俗) or custom. And *Musod*, or the customs of *mudang*, may be defined as "a form of people' s faith in traditional religious phenomenon centered around the *mu-dang*." [8] When scholars call this religious phenomenon "customs of *mudang*," they contrast it with religion, which has teachings and doctrines. They want to call it "people' s faith," or "folk beliefs."

Despite its lack of teachings or doctrines, Korean shamanism still deserves to be called a religion. The Latin *religio* is derived from *religare*, which means "to bind" or "to attach" and "to relate." The original meaning of the term religion, "a contractual obligation with a divine being," is fulfilled in the "customs of *mudang*," Korean folk religion or the faith of Korean people. This religion is "folk," "popular" or "people", and now "*minjung*," not only because it is shared by the majority of the Korean people but also because it has been officially ignored, if not openly persecuted, first by the literati of the Yi dynasty, and then by the new and modernized governments, Japanese and then Korean.

This is a properly Korean religion because it predated Buddhism, Taoism, Confucianism or Christianity. According to the *Sam-Kuk Ji*, written by a Chinese historian of the third century, the peoples of the Three Han (ca. 1000 B.C.) believed in "spirits," and had "parts of villages set aside" where a large tree was hung with small bells and drums as a form of worshipping the gods. The place was called "Sodo" or "Sottae." [9] And according to the Chinese historian, an ancient people of Korea had an October festival wherein they worshipped the gods of the heavens and drank, sang and danced day and night. The festival was called "Heavenly Dances."

Today in Korea it is rare for a whole village to participate in a shaman ritual for the well being of the community. It is a religion of households, of women, and of the common people. Although Korean scholars call the phenomenon "customs of the people," this expression is unknown among the believers and among the *mudangs*. It is a religion which is pervasive in Korean minds, and which is alive in the Korean way of life. It may not properly be called shamanism, and we have no popular Korean term for it. It cannot strictly be called an "ism" because it has neither explicit doctrine nor sacred texts. It is no ideology, nor does it have systematic teachings. It may be called the religion of *mudang*, but it is not practised by *mudangs* alone. It is the basic religious mind-set of the Korean people high and low, the basic religious mentality of the Korean people. It is an old, indigenous, informal and nearly unconscious kind of popular religion, the religion of the Korean minjung.

Although Korean shamanism is not organized, with an established hierarchy and political representation, it is pervasive in Korean political life. And although it has no permanent shrines or sheltered places of assembly, no institutions for the training of workers, no press or any other audio-visual means of propagation, it is everywhere in Korean life—in all the formal religions, in the education system, and in the media. It is a religion completely secularized in the everyday life of the Korean people; and it is more than any other religion, for it incorporates the traditions and the spirit of the Korean people.

Because customs of the minjung, the common folk, do not involve a dogmatic belief system, they can exist side-by-side with other religions. Yes, it is a nameless entity, a nameless religious phenomenon without a belief system. But it is a religion, and the religion of the Korean minjung has sustained them through the crises and perils of this world and other-world.

2. "Theology" of Korean Shamanism

There is no theology of shamanism as such, although the practice of *mudang* "presupposes" some kind of theology. There are "gods" that are addressed. And there are many gods around Korean households and Korean villages and factories. *Mudangs* dance in front of a pantheon of Korean household gods. But Koreans do not "worship" their gods, in the way that Western Christians go to church and "worship" God. No Korean *mudang* would define their gods as "that which nothing greater can be conceived," or "the unmoved mover." The gods of the *mudang* are everywhere, maybe great and maybe not so great. They can be objects of worship, but they are not the awesome figures that the Hebrew prophet Isaiah encountered in the temple. But they are all around the believer, and take care of his well-being. This may be polytheism, with some resemblance of Greek religion . But there is no hierarchy among the gods, and no coordinated activity among them. Each god is in charge of its own particular type of activity and acts independently within its area of responsibility, as it were. For this phenomenon where the gods exist and act side by side, a Korean shamanism scholar has coined the apt term "parallelotheism."[10]

A Christian missionary quite rightly observed of Korea in the 1920's, "It is a land of demons."

> The name of its pantheon is legion, for its gods are so many. . . It simply swarms with them, spirits of the earth, and spirits of the air, spirits of the waters and spirits of the hills, spirits of the living and spirits of the dead, spirits in rocks and spirits in trees, spirits which act in a rational manner, and frolicsome, capricious spirits like the "Tokkeibi" goblins, who spend all of their time playing pranks upon these stupid unresisting mortals.[11]

One American missionary could say the same thing even today, standing in the middle of a high rise apartment building in downtown Seoul.

He lists many different gods of the *mudang* religion in Korea in the 1920's. One may be misled by the list–"spirits of the earth, and spirits of the air, spirits of the waters and spirits of the hills, – spirits in rocks and spirits in trees. . ."into thinking that *mudangs* believe in "natural gods," or "nature gods" which reside and act in natural phenomena and natural objects. Certainly, *mudangs* believe that behind nature there is a movement of gods, and that "supernatural" beings control the course of nature itself. And in order to control natural phenomena, particularly in time of natural disturbances and natural disorders, a *mudang* would seek to pacify the nature gods—the gods and spirits in rocks, trees, winds, waters and in the earth.

However, *mudang* religion is not practised in terms of "natural religion." There are no "cosmological arguments" for the existence of gods. There is no magic to convert natural power for human purposes. When nature gods are invoked or worshipped, that becomes a religion of a community or a nation. It is interesting to note that the "nature" gods of Korea are closely related to community religious activities. That is, for a better harvest or better fish catch, Korean farmers and fishermen would approach the "nature" gods as a group, as members of the farming and fishing communities. The worship of "nature" gods in Korea is a community religious activity, not an act of individual religious worship.

Koreans call such community religious activities "village rites" or "village festivals". They offer music and dance and food to the "nature" gods, such as the gods of mountains or waters, in order to secure the well being of the community to which they belong. To the mountain gods, members of the community pray for divine protection from natural disasters and for a rich harvest. To the gods of waters, the whole fishing village comes to pray for a big catch and safe fishing.

There are two types of community rites: (1) the quiet or Confucian type, without music and dance by *mudangs*, which is conducted by the male village elders; and (2) a *kut* festival conducted either by *mudangs* with music and dance or by farm dancers. The two types are not always clearly separated. Sometimes they are mixed rather liberally, depending on the particular purpose, the occasion and the province. For example, in the Chulla Province area the most popular village religious activity is "Dansang-Je," a combination of a Confucian-type mountain spirit rite and a *mudang*-type farm dance festival. Interestingly, there is no involvement of female *mudangs*. Village elders and all male farm dance groups are the officials of the "Dansang-Je" rite-festival. This rite-festival has two components: religious rites to the mountain gods and a music and dance *mudang* festival. The farm dance festival is not just for recreation or for fun; it is a religious festival to exorcise evil spirits in the village and to invite good fortune to the village community. In the central act of the farm dance festival, the farm dancers dance around the whole village, visiting each house—symbolically making the house soil hard for the good fortune of the household. The ritual is called "Stepping on the ground gods."[12] In this religious festival the members of the village and the gods of the village come together to drink and dance for the good life. Therein, the whole community comes together with the nature gods who protect the community. This is a festival of music and dance for god and man.

There is a village *kut* called "Dodang-kut" in which female *mudangs* participate. This village *mudang kut* is practised in the Seoul area. In 1979, this particular *kut* was performed in a village near Seoul (in Buknan-San), Some 184 households donated nearly $600 necessary for the *kut*. This community *kut* begins with music and dance and ends with the drinking and eating of the sacrificial foods and singing and dancing by the participating villagers. The participants in this religious festival pray to the mountain gods of the northern Seoul area for the safety of the whole community. The religious activity and the great festival of songs and dances involve the whole village community. They dance with gods, they eat with gods for good fortune, and they burn white paper for each household in the village, praying for good fortune and safety.

In the port city of Kangnung in Kangwon Province, on the east coast facing the Eastern Sea (otherwise known as the Japan Sea) , a week-long May Festival is held annually beginning on May 5 on the Lunar calendar. This May Festival is a typical community *mudang* festival for the safety and blessing of the seagoing fishing villagers of the region. It begins at a nearby mountain shrine with a civil ceremony of Confucian form, presided over by the civil leaders of the community. But the whole festival is conducted by *mudangs* with songs and dances and excessive drinking and eating. This is the happiest time of the year for the farmers and fishermen around Kangnung.

In the southern port city of Pusan, Kyongsang Province, a similar fishermen's *mudang* festival is held every two or three years. The *mudang* community festival is called *Pyulshin Kut*, meaning a special *kut* for the Sun god. (In some areas, this *kut* is held once a decade.)[13] The *Pyulshin* Kut is also performed elaborately among merchants to ensure their business success; it is sometimes called "special market *kut*." In this case *mudangs* visit each store to give blessings for business success. This *kut* is not too different from the *Dodang Kut* performed in the village near Seoul. But this *kut* is performed by the learned or inherited *mudangs*, while the *Dodang kut* is usually performed by god-descended (Naerin) *mudangs*. The *Pyulshin Kut* is also a village festival with drinks and food, and with music and dancing day and night.

It is important to stress that the *mudang kut* in Korea is essentially and traditionally a community religious activity. In the earliest records, tribal communities set aside a special site for community festivals for gods in the months of May or October, before the sowing of seeds and after the harvest. These festivals involved prayers to gods and festival with drinking and eating, and dancing day and night for several days. The climax of these community *mudang* festivals is the burning of white paper by every household participating in the festival. This comes at the end of the festival, when the village representative, usually the leading elder of the community, reads aloud the intercession of the whole village written out on the paper. An example of the intercession is:

> Bless us some 80 households and thousand members
> of the village with safety and well being,
> Bless particularly with health and safety, those who
> are traveling afar and those soldiers fighting in Vietnam,
> Bring us good fortune in whatever we plan to do
> this year, and bring us a big harvest.
> Give us a reunified nation.[14]

As the prayer paper burns and the flame rises into the May night sky, the people begin the village festival with songs and dances, for fellowship and with gods. The festival is not only to petition the gods of the village for a better harvest and for an abundant catch of fish; it is also to secure the fellowship and unity of men and gods in music and dance. The *mudang kut* and the village dance are the dances of gods. Through them the unity of the community and the unity of god and men are established. Drinking and eating are the central part of the festivals, drinking and eating with the gods and drinking and eating of the blessings. This is the freest occasion of the hard working minjung of Korea—they can forget about their tough lot as tenant farmers and liberate themselves from the repressive Confucian social system and greedy landlords. This is the time for solidarity among the village minjung, and for temporary liberation from daily toil and from the secular and mundane world. This is also the time for the Korean minjung to meet the gods and drink and dance with them.

Most nature gods are associated with village community festivals. Mountain gods, enshrined in the nearby mountains, are the prime object of festival worship for farmers and fishermen. Sometimes, the dragon god or water gods are included in the *mudang* festivals of fishing villages. Tree gods, which supposedly inhabit a prominent old tree at the village entrance, are also venerated in village festivals. Thus, most nature gods are intimately connected with community religious activities and with the various *mudang* festivities.

The more popular gods in Korean shamanism are the household gods that dwell in individual houses. There are more household gods than nature gods. Everywhere you turn in a Korean house you encounter a god or spirit–at the entrance gate, in the court yard, in the main beam of the house, in the kitchen, in the inner room, and even in the bathrooms. It is safe to say that almost all of the Korean shaman gods are around the house. Korean gods are household gods.

The Korean household pantheon is numerous. To name just a few: (1) Chishin or site god, (in Korean, Tujoo Daegam). One finds them behind the house, perhaps in small jars with a few pennies in them, sometimes covered by peaked tent-like roofs of thatch. Once or twice a year, (more often if necessary), cooked rice or rice cakes and fruits are spread out before the gods and the members of the family bow and pay respect.

(2) Sungjoo, the main spirit of the house. When a new house is built, a *mudang* comes to offer a *kut* honoring the Sungjoo who resides in the central beam, which is visible in the ceiling of the main hall. According to a *mudang*, "Every house has a roof beam, so every house has a House Lord; there is a House Lord in the beggar's hovel and a House Lord in the tile-roofed house."[15] Elaborate and traditional rituals for venerating the Sungjoo (House Lord god) are rarely observed these days in the Seoul area. But according to Clark in the 1920's,

> *Mudang* makes a rude sort of paper envelope, puts some rice and money in it, soaks it in wine, and, after appropriate ceremonies, pastes it to the side of the ridge pole, where it hangs all puffy with the enclosed air. Dry rice is thrown at it, and, if much of it sticks, it is considered a favorable sign. [16]

When things go wrong in the household, the family feels the need for a *mudang kut* for the House Lord, and invites the *mudangs* to repeat the same ceremony in order to alleviate the misfortunes besetting the family. (One should not step on the threshold of the house, for that is believed to be the neck of the god, Tujoo Daegam or the House Lord.)

(3) Samshin, the birth gods or the gods of the children. (Clark translates this "Three Spirits," making it sound like a "Trinity." But "sam" here does not denote the number three, but rather "birth" or "san" in Korean.)[17] Samshin is worshipped by women who long for children, particularly boys. Samshin looks over the shoulder of little children until they are ten years old. Samshin is called friendly, the Birth Grandmother, for she is sort of guardian spirit or angel. Samshin or the Birth Grandmother is well placed in the inner room, which is where the lady of the house receives her husband. Samshin oversees conception and the successful rearing of children, particularly male children. She is placed in an earthen jar or paper bag, or sometimes in a gourd containing rice and some strips of paper with writing on them, placed there by the *mudangs*. Periodically the lady of the house spreads out rice cake and water, and sometimes bean, candy, nuts, fruit and lightly pickled vegetables. The Birth Grandmother is known to be fond of sweets and soft food.

When worshipping household gods, the lady of the house sets down the rice cake, bowing deeply, and rubs her hands in prayerful supplication, praying: "Please make us rich; please make this house peaceful and safe; please make the children turn out well." These are the only household offerings and prayers, except when a *mudang* executes at the home of a client much longer and more elaborate forms, sometimes with song and dance. The lady of the house then cuts up the rice cake and distributes it to the neighbors. (When I was a child, and my mother received a gift of rice cake from the non-believer neighbors, she inquired about the occasion for the gift. If the rice cake was from the offering tables for the household gods, she politely refused, saying that her Christian religion would not allow the eating of spirit offering rice cakes.)

What is more important to notice in the village *mudang* rites or in the household *mudang* rites is the nature of the gods or spirits which are venerated by the Korean people. What is most striking is that the gods of Korean shamanism are mostly value free and morally neutral. They are neither good nor bad. They have no character. Korean shaman gods are not anthropomorphic, although people talk about their *mudang* gods as being like human beings with feelings and wills. They are usually harmless, they are no devils unless they are offended. But they are not by nature benevolent either unless they are pleased with drinks and food and entertained with music and dance. Korean shaman gods are not good, loving, just or benevolent *by nature.* They are morally neutral; Korean shamanism does not know of any gods of love, of revenge, of beauty, of creation, of songs, of dances, etc. And none of them is the "supreme being" of heaven and earth; none is omnipotent, omnipresent, and eternal and transcendent.

But Korean people turn to these gods in times of crises: in poverty, in sickness, in pain, and in suffering from the loss of small fortune or from the failure of their children at school or in business. Instinctively they believe that their shaman gods are benevolent and good, and if they maintain a good relationship with the gods, the gods will bless them with wealth, fortune, peace and health in the household and the village community. Their gods are powerful enough, if not almighty, that they can bring happiness and peace to the family and the community. So they pray again this morning to a household god, or to a tree god back of the village: "Please make us rich; please make this house peaceful; please make the children turn out well." If they are sincere enough, if they put their minds into it (Jung-sung), and if they pray continuously and patiently, their wish will be fulfilled.

Kut (Shaman Rite), Hong Song-Dam

3. The Shaman Rituals

Korean shamanism is a religion of wish-fulfillment, and it is practised by the deprived. Since it is practised by female *mudangs* and by the women of the household, it may be called a religion of Korean women. Women and oppressed groups in Korea participate in *mudang* religion, primitive or peripheral religion, in order to redress the deprivation inherent in social peripherality. Or perhaps the Korean *mudang* religion is primitive and peripheral because women and the oppressed minjung participate in it. Shamanism in Korea is the least respected religion, even despised. Its practitioners are the most despised and oppressed. Korean shamanism is a religion of the Korean *minjung*. The Korean minjung turn to the Korean *mudang* religion out of their social deprivation, poverty, ignorance, suffering and misfortune, imposed upon them by their social fate. In this religious practice Korean *minjung* can bring their *han*, their troubles, their tears, and their frustrations. The Korean *mudang* religion is an expression of the powerlessness of the Korean minjung.

Besides the rather simple form of household *kut* for blessings or for a sick patient, there are two kinds of full-dress *mudang kut*, one for the cure of the sick and another for the dead in the family. Commonly in these elaborate *mudang kut* the *mudangs* follow twelve steps to complete the whole ceremony. The steps may be divided into the five parts: (a) prelude, (b) protection, (c) exorcism, (d) blessing, and (e) postlude. No matter what the external form, or name of the *mudang* ritual, the basic structure remains essentially the same. First, an invitation to the gods to descend. The *mudang* sings "Chungbae-Ka," the song of divine invitation, and dance:

> When you come, oh gods of eight provinces
> come with blessings
> to the sons and daughters;
> around their neck
> tie the iron necklace
> of long life . . . .
>
> We pray and we pray
>
> Please accept our small offerings
> oh, fathers and gods of the mountains and rivers.[18]

While the *mudang* sings and dances slowly to a staggered beat of the drum, she goes into a trance. Eventually the drum beat becomes faster and faster and the *mudang* jumps higher and higher. During this ecstatic jumping dance, the spirit comes down and possesses her body. The *mudang* might look like she has blurred vision, for her eyes seem to lose focus, she looks at no one around her, but gazes into the middle distance.

The second general step is to "play" with the gods through songs and dancing. In between songs and dances the *mudang* relays the message of the gods to the participants, usually the sponsoring person or family, friends and visitors. The messages of the gods are usually from the spirit of an ancestor summoned in the *mudang* trance. A dialogue ensues between the ancestor spirit and the family. The *mudang* and the family talk back and forth about the situation. Sometimes the deceased comes back through the *mudang* to describe his or her tragic death in a traffic accident. Or a deceased father may complain about the mistreatment of his son or daughter-in-law. Or sometimes the ancestors and the spirits called upon by the *mudang* will ask for more money and more food and drink. And sometimes, the members of the sponsoring family will negotiate with the summoned ancestors or the spirits for more blessings for the family, in return for more offerings and money. (This is the way the *mudang* receives generous "tips" for the *kut*.) At the end of this part of *kut*, the *mudang* concludes by singing:

> Thus says the spirit
> he will receive your small offerings
> as a big mountain, and
> he will bless you,
> put aside your worries, for
> he will take care of you . . . .

During this dialogue the summoned ancestor or the powerful spirit, speaking through the *mudang*, gives directions for the family well-being, suggests medicinal remedies for sickness, and gives good counsel to various members of the family. Sometimes, the *mudang* will cry aloud, become hysterical or angry, and smoke cigarettes and drink rice wine as the summoned relative or ancestor would have done while they were alive. At times she will joke with the members of the sponsoring family. This is a lively session, with songs, dances, costume changes, tears, shouts, jokes and laughter. This is essentially an entertainment session, bringing all the family troubles and problems into the open.

The third and final stage of the *kut* may be called a postlude in which the *mudang* sings and dances briefly. The songs of the final stage are usually pleasant ones which praise the good and big-hearted spirits of the ancestors and bid farewell to them. The *mudang* will come out of her trance or possessed state. And she will sing beautifully:

> Please stay and play,
> Play with us,
> O gods and spirits of the mountains
> and spirits of fathers . . . . [19]

The most elaborate and lavish kind of *mudang kut* is the *kut* for the dead. It is sometimes called *Chinogi kut*, a peace-giving ceremony for the dead, or the releasing of the soul of an ancestor. *Chinogi kut* is performed some three months after the death. A *kut* performed immediately after the death, for the "freeing" of the dead, is usually called *shikim kut*. The *kut* for the dead is to guide the dead soul to "heaven" in peace. When it is mixed with the Buddhist ideas, this *kut* is to free the souls of ancestors imprisoned in Buddhist hell and allow them to enter heaven. In the northern provinces of Korea, it is called a "bridge" *kut* (*dari kut*), building a symbolic bridge to enable the dead soul to cross the chasm between this world and the other world. In a sense this is a *mudang* farewell ceremony for the dead, praying for a safe and peaceful journey to the nether world. People in this world do not want to be bothered or harmed because they did not send dead parents and relatives safely and properly to the place where they belong.

When a person dies, he or she dies only physically. The soul lingers around the body "observing" what the relatives are doing. The soul is not dead yet; that is, the soul has not departed to its proper place. A farewell *kut* is needed to help the soul to go to the place for the dead. Some dead are not ready to die; some die by accident and some die too young. But the death itself is something sad and unhappy and unpleasant. There is a lot of "han" in a death. Thus, the *kut* for the dead is to release the sad feeling, or *han*, which the dead person has accumulated during his life time. Even if the dead person led a happy life without any *han* (which is most unlikely), the death itself is a great *han* for him, and the person needs release from the *han* of death itself.

At a *kut* for the dead, the dead soul is called back by and through the trance of a *mudang*. And through the mouth of then tranced *mudang* the dead person talks about and enacts his *han*-ridden life. Through such talk and enactment, the soul releases its *han*, leaves its last words in the form of a will and blessings to the family present, and sets off peacefully on its final journey. The whole *kut* also asks the heavenly officials of death (Buddhist origin) to lead the souls to the proper place. When this is done, a white cotton cloth is spread out in front of the food offerings, to symbolize the road to the gate of heaven.

At the *Chinogi kut*, the *mudang* sings the epic poem of *Parikongju*, who is the mythic ancestor of all *mudangs*. According to the epic story, Pari is the seventh and last daughter of a royal family which desperately needs a male heir. But Pari's parents, having produced a seventh girl, angrily put her in a basket and throw her into the open sea. But the compassionate Buddha happens to find the princess in a basket and makes an old mountain guard take care of her. The Pari princess grows up beautiful and intelligent, knowing the "heavenly reasons" and the "earthly geography." Eventually, her parents fall sick. According to the heavenly messenger the sickness is because of the princess Pari. So, the king sends for the princess, and she is brought back to the palace. But this does not cure the fatal illness of the king and his wife. Again, according to the heavenly messenger, Pari's parents need a heavenly herb which may be obtained only in the other world. Only a sacrifice of death can bring the heavenly herb to this world. All of Pari's sisters refuse to go to pick up the heavenly herb for their sick parents. But when the question is put to the seventh princess Pari, she sings out:

> Seven princesses were called out
> for sacrifice
> to save the lives of father and mother.
>
> Though I received no favor
> from the country and the court,
>
> I was given life for ten months
> in the womb of my mother.
> To save my mother's life
> I will go.

So Princess Pari journeys to the nether world where she meets a mountain spirit (a Taoist god figure) who asks her to marry him in return for the mountain herb for her sick parents. In order to get the needed herb, she agrees to marry him, and gives birth to seven sons. Upon her return to the royal palace, she meets the funeral procession of her parents. She flings open the casket lids and puts the mysterious mountain herb on the bodies of her parents. Her parents come back to life, and she is invited back again into the highest place in the royal court. She refuses, and asks instead to become the first ancestor of all *mudangs*. Her primary function is to lead the dead into heaven, safely and peacefully.

The epic of Pari Kongju depicts the *han*, life and death of women in Korea. And because of her sacrificial life and death, she can lead the souls of the *han*-ridden dead to the peaceful land of heavenly paradise. By reciting the epic of Pari Kongju, the first ancestor of all *mudangs*, a *mudang* can lead the soul of the deceased into the heavenly paradise. Thus at the end of *Chinogi kut*, the Pari Kongju epic is chanted as the *mudang* descends to lead the soul of the deceased out of hell. A *mudang* dressed colorfully as Pari Kongju circumambulates the altar twice, breaking open the gates of the ten stages of hell. Finally, at the end of the *kut*, the *mudang* rushes through long strips of burlap and muslim cloth, and rips the cloth. This is to lead the soul into heaven, freeing it from hell. In an elaborate *Chinogi kut* there may be a flowery gate through which the *mudang* passes with songs and dances to indicate that the spirit is moving happily through the gate of heaven. With a final thanksgiving for the safe journey of the dead, the *kut* comes to an end.

From the *mudang* ritual for the souls of the dead, we learn an interesting idea of "life after death." Korean shaman rituals do not describe heaven or hell except by borrowing from Buddhism and other religions. There is no good place or bad place to go after death. But it is good to die completely. That is one's soul should not linger around somewhere indefinitely, neither here nor there, to bother the living. This is the most unfortunate state a soul can be in. One should die "completely," and go to the proper place for the dead.

Another point in the *mudang* ritual for the dead is that the soul of the dead is not necessarily rewarded or punished by what he or she has done in this life. There is no reward and punishment system in the *mudang* "theory" of life after death. The unknown area of death is primordial chaos, from which life probably sprang. Life after death is immortal and the human soul is eternal, but death is morally neutral; it is not caused by any form of "original" human sin. And the nature of life after death is not determined by the moral life of the living. The proper death is completed by the *mudang* ritual. Dying is sad and horrible; therefore, the soul wants to linger among the living. The soul should be sent off properly by sincere performance of a *mudang* ritual. And the *han*-ridden soul of the dead has to be gotten rid of, so that the living can live in peace.

Another feature of *mudang* understanding of the dead soul is that there is no notion of rebirth of the soul, as in Buddhism or Hinduism. Once one dies and moves into the eternal primordial chaos, that is the end of it. But an interesting irony is that the living will not let the dead stay dead. The people call the souls of the dead back again and again, through the help of a *mudang's* trance, and ask for blessing. The living want the dead dead, but at the same time they want the souls of the dead to come back at their convenience to cure the sick in the family and for blessing. Dead or alive, one cannot escape a tight relationship with family and community.

A *kut* is full of symbols, gestures and objects, and only a few words are spoken. There may be some words of admonition and a few words of consolation. But a *kut* is essentially a religious ritual without words or linguistic explanation. There is no sermon to speak of. There is singing, chanting, drumming and dancing to induce the spirits to this world, and to please them. The *mudang* provides blessings in the present visible world by invoking the spirits of the invisible world. The *mudang* invokes the spirits of family ancestors—the spirits of the past which "reside" in the invisible world. The *mudang*-shaman is an intermediary between the world of men (visible) and the world of spirits (invisible). In order to make contact with the spirit world, the shaman altar is filled with a pig's head, cooked meat, sweet rice cakes and white rice wine. Cooked grains are used to exorcise, dried fish and live chickens to expel evil, balanced swords to indicate blessing. The entire *kut* is a drama between man and spirit, the spirits of the past come into the world to give blessings to the men of the present. It is a drama of cosmic fighting between spirits. There is singing and dancing. There are tears and weeping which soon turn to joyous laughter and happiness. There are jokes, and consolation and harsh words, all coming from the nether world of the past.

4. Mudangs and Minjung

The shamanism or *mudang* religion of Korea has been assessed and evaluated in various ways. When Christian missionaries came, the *mudang* religion was the first thing they attacked. To the Confucian literati of old Korea, the *mudang* practice was an embarrassment. A Western observer once said to me, however, that a Korean carries a Confucian head, a Buddhist heart, and a Shamanistic belly.[20] In other words, Confucianism is a religion for the intellect, Buddhism for the heart and feeling, and Shamanism a religion of intuition. Another way of saying this is that the basic religion of a Korean is shamanism, and in the final analysis the basic religious character of a Korean is shamanistic. An American missionary named Hulbert who first came to Korea in 1886, wrote in a 1907 book of Korean history, *The Passing of Korea*: "As a general thing, we may say that the all-around Korean will be a Confucianist when in society, a Buddhist when he philosophizes and a spirit-worshipper when he is in trouble." He concludes that "the underlying religion of the Koreans, the foundation upon which all else is mere super-structure, is his original spirit worship."[21] A contemporary observer of Korean religions, Palmer, agrees with Hulbert: "Shamanism is the primitive ethos of the Korean people. It is the basic instinct of the masses. . . ." It is the religion of the Korean minjung.

No religion in Korea has been more suppressed and persecuted than the *mudang* religion. A nationwide and systematic persecution was launched by the neo-Confucian government of the Yi Dynasty. The old Confucian king-dom prohibited all *mudang* practices inside the four gates of the capital. The *mudangs* were pushed out of the royal palace ground and into the country-side. The king's court ordered all *mudang* books to be confiscated and burned. The *mudangs* were outcasts, despised as the lowest class of people. Despite such persecution, the *mudang* religion persisted among the minjung of Korea and even among the people of the king's palace. The colonial government of Japan saw the *mudang* religion of Korea as an embarrass-ment to a modernizing nation. The Japanese despised the home *mudang* rituals, and barred community *mudang* festivals on political even more than religious grounds. The Japanese wanted to eradicate anything Korean, and they did not want village people to gather for religious festivals for fear that the group might turn into a demonstrating mob against the foreign rulers. In spite of such suppression, and the more they are persecuted, the tighter the minjung clings to this most despised, primitive *mudang* religion..

The Korean *mudang* religion is the religion of minjung's han. A *han*-ridden Korean woman comes to visit the *mudang*, or invites her to her home for a short *mudang* ceremony. The *han* of a woman is revealed to the *mudang*, and the *mudang* exorcises it for her, chasing the evil spirit out of the household. The *mudang* gives the *han*-ridden woman consolation, and prays for blessing. For the Korean *minjung*, there is no other way to cure sickness in the family which has not been cured by the modern doctors in a Western-style hospital. A modern hospital is a prohibitive place for the Korean *minjung*—too expensive, too foreign and too clean. Family misfortune and family sickness are attributed to neglect of the spirits of the dead in the family. One's fortune is directly related to the doings and feelings of one's dead ancestors. These worldly happenings are directly connected with the world of the invisible spirits. The helpless *minjung* of this world have no other place to turn, except to the invisible spirits of their ancestors. After all, parents and relatives are the only reliable support, dead or alive, in this world of political suppression and economic exploitation.

Psychological studies of the *mudang* religion of Korea have shown clearly that the *mudang kut* is a dramatic process of counseling. Projection, catharsis, transference, consolation, admonition, release or salvation, all these steps and processes are present. Projection and the power of suggestion call forth excuses or reasons for a woman's illness and misfortune. Her misfortune is projected out of herself. It is not her fault, it is because the dead ancestors' spirits are bothering her worldly affairs. Since her misfortune is the doings of the spirits of her dead ancestors, she can talk about it. That is, she can talk about her *han*-ridden, unfortunate life. This desensitizes her guilt feelings through abreaction by means of the *mudang*'s trance, talking with dead parents and explaining away her worries. And she will have a catharsis. She can cry out loud. And through her tears, laughter, rage and expressed frustration, she will relieve pent-up emotions and *han*, the unexpressed and unresolved resentment. She reveals all her *han* to the *mudang*. It is a common thing to see, during the *mudang* dance, a daughter-in-law beating her mother-in-law, or the lady sponsoring the *kut* beating the *mudang*.[22]

Evil spirits and feelings are expelled by the use of chickens, swords and other exorcistic devices. The transference technique of the *mudang* removes the cause of evil in a human body or family and "transfers" it to other objects. The most interesting thing in the whole process is its community centeredness. The *kut* is a family affair, if not an affair of the whole village. Particularly in the *mudang kut* for the spirit of the dead, the entranced *mudang* will give the whole family didactic instructions–admonishing them to mutual cooperation, filial piety, loving each other, sharing the wealth generously among the relatives and so on. Basically, the *mudangs* seem to believe that the basic cause of sickness and misfortune in the family is a lack of giving, care and concern and love among the members of the family. When such an admonition is given through the mouth of the entranced *mudang* to the whole household, it turns out to be group therapy. The *mudang kut* brings about a renewed spirit of love among the members of the family.

The *mudang* religion of Korea, in spite of and because of its pervasiveness among Korean minjung, has been criticized for its projective approach towards all human problems. All problems are attributed to spiritual causes or forces apart from individual awareness and responsibility. Sickness comes from the petty anger of the spirit heroes of the past, of an ancestor who is still suffering in purgatory. It is not because of the behavior of the living; it has nothing to do with loose living, bad food, or poverty, or an immoral life. One has no responsibility for sickness or misfortune, and thus does not have to take action to eradicate suffering. The *mudang* is asked what to do. And the entranced *mudang* will provide a message from the most feared ancestor or powerful spirit.

The *mudang* religion does not teach any sense of moral responsibility, or give a sense of independence to do whatever is necessary to eradicate pain and suffering in the family and in the society. A complete dependence on ancestral or unknown spirits of the past in the invisible world is encouraged. The minjung is completely powerless, and the minjung of Korea has been told time and time again that he is incapable of doing anything for himself. He has no other place to turn for help and salvation from the worldly suffering and pain of *han*. The *han*-ridden minjung of Korea has been taught to rely on the spirits of the family dead. Only the dead spirits of his ancestor can help him; they are much more powerful and benevolent than the living members of the family. The dead spirits of family ancestors are much more reliable than any powerful government. The government has betrayed him many, many times, but his father's spirit will not betray him. This illustrates dramatically the complete powerlessness of the Korean minjung, his *han*, and his *han*-ridden life of helplessness.

The *mudang* knows what to do. The *mudang* will not preach to him. The *mudang* understands him, his *han*-ridden life of trouble and tribulation as a powerless and oppressed person. She will listen to his *han*-ridden story of life, and she understands. For she herself has experienced the *han*-ridden life of the oppressed and despised, as a woman and as a Korean *mudang*. The *mudang* was once sick with a mental sickness (*Shinbyung*). She was once called mad and spirit-possessed. The *mudang* has the experience of overcoming and transcending her illness, spiritual illness and the suffering of mental sickness. Therefore, she understands her patient's grievances and suffering. She will resolve his *han*. She will cry with him, she will laugh with him, and she will hold his hands tightly and give him sincere and heart-warming consolation. The *mudang* is full of *Jung* (heart-warm feeling). *Han* can be resolved only through the *jung* of others. And when *han* is resolved, the feeling of *jung* is created between persons. His *han* resolved, he can live in this terrifying world with the warm feeling of *jung* in his family and among the people of his society.

Michael Saso has this to say about the "positive" or humanistic approach in understanding the *mudang* religion:

> In the best sense of the *kut's* social and cultural impact on the community, the Shaman rites definitely promote a sense of peace and smooth function-ing of society in the Korean traditional mentality. A sense of historic signi-ficance, of social importance of touching the deepest sensitivities inside the human psyche, perhaps for years behind social sublimation, are a part of the *kut* experience. One feels that the best and worst of the human con-dition is touched and appreciated in the symbolic drama of the *mudang*.[23]

The *mudang* religion may be criticized as a manipulation of the Korean minjung towards submission to his fate and to the powerful. But this *mudang* religion has enabled the Korean minjung to survive his fate and the exploitation of the powerful.

Another point to be mentioned with regard to the humanistic approach to understanding the Korean *mudang* religion is that while it projects problems to unknown and invisible spirits in the other world, it does not project life itself into the other world. The Korean *mudang* religion is thoroughly this-worldly. It affirms the importance of the living and life of this world. It is not pessimistic about this world, and it does not long for the other world. It is not cynical about this life, although it is filled with suffering, pain and *han*. One's *han*-ridden life is still precious; it should be cured and blessed with health and wealth and success. The Korean *mudang* religion does not question the importance of this world and this life. Religious salvation in the *mudang* religion is not a release from the life of this world. The *mudang* does not pray for a better life in another world, but for this life in *this* world.

Earlier, I mentiond the festiveness of the *mudang kut*. There is food, lots of food. There is a lot to drink. The whole process of *mudang kut* is singing and dancing. It is a festival religion. There is laughter and joy. It is a free religion. People come and go, take a break for coffee or for a lunch or dinner. This is a religion of dialogue between the *mudang* and "congregation"–a lot of give and take between them. Anyone can participate fully in the *mudang kut*, singing and dancing together with the *mudang* and the other participants. It is in a way a liberating religion, liberating the people from the stiff proceedings of a religious ritual. It gives a sense of liberation. People loosen up, and sing and dance together. This is a religion of songs and dances. It is a dramatic religion filled with drama. Although it has no cathedral to speak of, it is filled with color and art and symbols. It has no wealth to boast; it has been the religion of the poor and oppressed minjung for many centuries.

5. The Shamanized Christians in Korea

When Christianity came to Korea, conversion meant conversion from the *mudang* practices to Christ. The *mudang* religion was despised by Christian missionaries and Korean Christians. It was a "Christ *against* Culture" model *par excellence*. It required a radical conversion–burn all the *mudang* stuff–before one came to Christ. Early mission success stories featured the new converts burning all of the house spirits of the *mudang* religion. But now we ask whether the success stories of Christian mission did not come about because of the culture of the *mudang* religion in Korea. The growth of Korean Christianity has a lot to do with the shamanistic mind-set of the Korean people, despite the fact that Christianity in Korea opposed Shamanism and set out to destroy the *mudang* religion. Korean Christianity was able to set deep roots in the religiously fertile soil of the *mudang* religion. And the branches, the healthy leaves and the various fruits of Korean Christianity grew out of the soil of the Korean *mudang* religion.

Korean shamanism is by no means monotheistic. It is a religion of many gods and many spirits, as we have seen. There are debates and disagreements among scholars on the question of whether there is a supreme being or spirit or god which stands above all other "nature" and house spirits. Early missionaries tried to find in Korean shamanism something similar to the Christian God. Linguistically, Koreans look upon heaven as the supreme "nature." When the heaven is anthropomorphized, it is called "Mr. Heaven," or *hanunim.* A supreme being resides in heaven. One of the earliest American missionary linguists, Hulbert, translated "Mr. Heaven" or *hanunim* "Sky Master."[24]

Because of the peculiar ambiguity in pronouncing the Korean word for "sky" or "heaven," "Sky Master" may be read *hananim* or "One" or the one "Great One." This is another American missionary linguist's rendering of the Korean religious word for "heaven" or "sky." So, it is not "sky" or "heaven." It is "One" or "the One," or "the only great one in heaven." [25] With this way of rendering the Korean word for god, early missionaries wanted to say that, "In Shamanism generally, there is a supreme god over all." [26] And Clark went even further to say that,

> *Hananim* is unique. There is scarcely a question that he goes far back into the dim ages of Korean history long before any of the foreign religions came into the country. In the earliest history of Shamanism, we noted how the Ye Kook people worshipped *Hananim.* It was *Hananim* whom Tangoon worshipped on his high altar on Kanghwa.[27]

Underwood quotes a Buddhist priest in a temple who said, "*Hananim* is, of course, supreme. Buddha is one of the lesser gods."[28] Underwood reported that "the supremacy of *Hananim* is apparently acknowledged alike by Confucianists, Buddhists and Shamanists.[29]

When Roman Catholics originally named the Christian God in Korean, they used Chinese characters "Chunju," meaning "Heavenly Master," but today they use the Korean word "Hanunim," meaning "Sky Master," as Hulbert suggested about a century ago. Protestants in Korea call the Christian God "Hananim," emphasizing the "oneness" and the supreme monotheistic character of the Christian God.

What I am trying to establish is that in spite of its belief in many spirits and gods, in Korean shamanism there is the notion of a supreme being who stands out as a "heavenly being" or a monotheistic "single being." There is no shaman theology that articulates meaning of "Hananim" or "Hanunim." All one could say about "Hananim," is very well described by Clark:

> Koreans universally say that Hananim sends the harvest, that he sends the rain, that by his grace we live and breathe. The Rain Bringing Ceremonies of Confucianism are addressed to Hananim, not to Sangchei, or any other of the Chinese names. In times of mortal danger, almost the first cry of the Korean is to Hananim. Hananim seems to dominate their lives, since his name is continually on their lips, but curious to note, they seem never to really worship him, unless we except the Rain Ceremonies. They say that he sends the harvest, yet in the Fall they offer their sacrifices not to him, but to the gods of the hills, or to the house gods, or to the ancestral tablets. He seems everything to them, and then again he seems to be nothing, judging from the way in which they disregard him when all goes well.[30]

Nevertheless, the Hananim concept allows a kind of preunderstanding of the Christian God in the Korean mind. Because of this religious concept of "Hananim" as a supreme being which stands over and even against other minor spirits, the monotheistic one and only one God of Judeo-Christian God is understood and accepted by Koreans. The Judeo-Christian God of YHWH was planted in the soil of the *mudang* religion which has the fertile notion of a heavenly being that is one and great. But perhaps when the Christian notion of deity is implanted in the minds of the believers of the *mudang* religion, it does not go beyond the "theology" of *hananim*. That is to say, even though the Christian notion of God as the most supreme being of all gods and spirits is very well understood by the Korean converts. Christian theology has not transformed the shamanistic understanding of Hananim. To the shamanist the Christian or Western missionary God is much more powerful than the shaman gods. The Western missionary God will do better things for the people; this God will bring more money and success to your family; and this God is modern, enlightened and enlightening. But in shamanistic "monotheism" there is no sense of history, prophetic function, or moral understanding of a supreme being. The shaman concept of Hananim is ahistorical and amoral. To this ahistorical, amoral and even asocial notion of Hananim, the Judeo-Christian God was added, making Korean Christianity conservative, ahistorical, amoral and asocial in many ways. The ahistorical, asocial or apolitical parts of the Judeo-Christian deity were readily accepted by the religious mind-set of the Korean people. But the moral and political aspects of Judeo-Christian deity have to be understood by way of another element of the Korean religious tradition, Confucianism.

There is almost a complete lack of a framework in shamanism to understand Christology as such. There is no understanding of a personal Hananim who would "send" His only begotten son to this world. There is no concept of divine incarnation, coming to this world for the salvation of the secular world. There is no "humanity" of God or the spirits to facilitate understanding of the human Jesus. Jesus might have been a great *mudang* who performed miracles, cured the sick and cast out evil spirits. Jesus might have been the greatest counselor *mudang* for the poor and deprived. But in the shamanistic mind-set, the idea of Jesus as the son of God is beyond comprehension.

Ryu Dongshik, in his extensive study of Korean Shamanism, attempts to connect the *mudang*'s spirit illness with "the dialectic of the sacred." The *mudang*'s initiation sickness and spirit possession are interpreted as a death experience, the death of the divine itself. The *mudang* thus experiences the death of God in her possession sickness, *Shinbyung*. The mudang falls into hell. But through the *mudang* initiation *kut* she comes back to life as a new being, a *mudang*. The dialectic of *Shinbyung*, the *mudang*'s spirit sickness, is the dialectic of the Sacred, or the dialectic of the spirit itself. This drama of suffering, death and resurrection, according to Ryu, is the drama of Jesus' suffering, death and resurrection. [31]

Ryu's interpretation is interesting. But he is trying to interpret the *mudang* spirit illness from the point of view of "Hegelian" dialectic. There is actually no way in the Korean *mudang* thought pattern to interpret the Christian or Pauline understanding of Christ Jesus. Christology is entirely foreign to the *mudang* religion. And the historical Jesus is even more foreign to *mudang* theology. There is no such historical figure in the *mudang* religion. It is very difficult to connect the divine incarnation in Christian theology with the possession sickness of the *mudang*.

However, the possession sickness of a *mudang* may be very directly connected with the Christian charismatic movement. The *mudang*'s possession sickness is directly interpreted as the possession of the Holy Spirit. To receive the Holy Spirit in Christian terms and be converted to the Christian religion is to be possessed by the Christian spirit. With the power of the Christian Holy Spirit of Christianity, one can speak in tongues and cure the sick as the *mudang* used to do. To be a Christian is to be possessed by the Holy Spirit. The *mudang*'s understanding of the spirit world and spirit possession, in other words, make it possible for Koreans to understand the nature of receiving the Holy Spirit of Christianity and its great power. Christian faith is almost exclusively interpreted as receiving the Holy Spirit, as the *mudang* falls into possession sickness. The signs of receiving the Holy Spirit are similar to the signs of the possessed *mudangs* who cure the sick and exorcise evil spirits. But the Christian pentecostals in Korea who claim to cure the sick and exorcise spirits disclaim the *mudang* origin of their practice and understanding, although many of them come from shaman backgrounds.

Kim Harvey reports on a Korean *mudang* who was converted to Christianity with the help of her theological student son. In an intensive interview Deaconess Chang, the former *mudang*, revealed her "transition" experience from *mudang* to Christianity. She suffered "indescribable physical affliction" during the transition period. And that "indescribable physical affliction" was "all the old symptoms which had plagued her during her *shinbyung* episodes." [32]

> Her migraine headache returned to befuddle her mind, while her eyelids swelled up and sties recurred to make her vision hazy. She suffered from paroxysmic attacks of chills and fevers that left her exhausted. Her extremities felt as though she were being pricked by a thousand needles. She was sure at times that her palpitating heart would burst right out of her chest. Her list of symptoms is endless. She says that Christ tested the firmness of her faith for five years by visiting these afflictions upon her. [33]

Now, Deaconess Chang is the most respected and awed member of her Christian congregation because of her "spiritual power," which comes from the "spiritual experience" of her conversion to Christ, which is similar to her *mudang* possession sickness. Kim Harvey reports what the converted *mudang* does with other Christian friends in their prayer groups.

> The morning prayer meeting begins with a brief prayer by one of the deaconesses, followed quickly by hymn singing and scripture reading by the entire group. This formal phase is comparatively short. The marathon session of individual prayers which follows generally lasts for two uninterrupted hours. Each woman takes her turn at prayer, reporting in impassioned detail all the pains, injustices, and temptations she has suffered as well as giving thanks for happy events since the last meeting. Usually, suffering and pain are the dominant themes, and their exorcism the main activity of the prayer group. They moan, groan, and wail as though their entrails were being ripped open. They sob paroxysmally, sometimes pounding their chests with clenched fists as if to break loose the grief dammed up inside. Their emotions are so intense that they sometimes lurch forward under their force. [34]

This is usually the way Korean pentecostals gain the "spiritual" power to speak in tongues and cure the sick by exorcism. And one may observe this kind of thing in the pentecostal churches in Korea even during the regular worship services on Sundays. It is a matter of degree in different churches in Korea: spirit possession is transferred to faith in the Holy Ghost. The practice, theology, and structure of spirit possession is the same in the *mudang* religion and Korean Christianity. This may be the strength of Korean churches. But it is also an extreme case of the seduction of the spirit, as Harvey Cox has seen it: Korean Protestantism has almost been reduced to a Christianized *mudang* religion. That is, the form and language of the worship service are Christian, but the content and structure of what Korean Christians adhere to are basically the *mudang* religion. Although missionaries rejected shamanism and thought it had been destroyed, Korean Christianity has become almost completely shamanized.

When Christianity was accepted by the Korean people and the Korean minjung, it was accepted within the mind-set of Korean shamanism, for Korean shamanism is the religion of the Korean people and the Korean minjung. For the powerless minjung, the power of the spirit, more particularly the power of the Holy Ghost, is most respected and awed. To become a Christian is to believe in the power of the Holy Ghost which is much more powerful than their shaman spirits. Korean Christians have made the Christian worship service more casual and freer than traditional Western style worship. They sing loudly and well, like in a *mudang kut.* There is a sense of joy in their service, and even the sense of festivity they experience in the *mudang kut.* They experience a close sense of community, relatedness and togetherness with other persons in the service, as in the case of the *mudang kut.* They share their sorrows, sufferings and pains as the poor and deprived and oppressed, and they also share a sense of liberation and salvation in the act of sharing. The *mudang* pathos is embodied in Christian worship and Christian pastoral care. A young Korean Presbyterian pastor who works in a Seoul slum church once remarked that he is not ashamed of being called a "Christian *mudang.*" He does not want to seduce and manipulate religiously the spirit of the people. He acts as a Christian *mudang* to take care of the *han* of the people. He would be with the people, suffering together with them in the midst of their everyday existence, and sharing their tears and laughters. He would exorcise the evil spirits in people and the evil spirits in the politics of society, to set free the oppressed and deprived, the poor and the sick.

Korean shamanism is a religion of *han.* It expels and resolves the deep rooted *han* of the Korean minjung, Korean women, the sick and the poor. The *mudang* religion of Korea is the religion of the *han*-ridden minjung in Korea. Korean Christianity has its deepest roots in this *mudang* religion, and thereby, Christianity put down roots in the minds of the minjung. Thus, Korean Christianity has been able to grow in numbers, and become one of the most powerful and dynamic religions in Korea.

Dance, Lee Chul-Su

4 MINJUNG AND SPIRITUALITY [1]

1. Spirituality Abounds

Korean Christians are impressive in their spiritual life. A casual tourist in Seoul at night cannot miss the pink neon cross towers shining over the skyline of apartment houses, hotels, bars, and discotheques. According to the recent city census, there are more church buildings than tea houses in Seoul; this is to say that Korean people are more serious about religion than about drinking tea and coffee, and more serious about meeting God than meeting people. On Sunday mornings, the city is filled with Christians, clad in their Sunday-best and rushing to get the best seats in the crowded churches. Serious-looking people–old and young, men and women–with black, leather-covered Bibles and hymnals in their hands, throng the streets near church buildings.

Inside one church, as many as 10,000 seats are already filled with people and there is no vacant place, so you are cordially invited to sit on the floor in the aisle. It is just fifteen minutes before the 11 o'clock Sunday service which is one of the five main services of the world-famous Full Gospel Church on Seoul. For the foreign spiritual tourists, earphones are provided for simultaneous translation of the worship service. The choir of beautiful young singers and the orchestra are presently producing the sweet sounds of spirituals. The congregation sings hymns in loud and joyful voices, sometimes in harmony and sometimes off-key, but surely strong and clear with assured spirituality. There is no bodily movement, no clapping of hands, no dancing or foot-tapping. Stiff bodies, stiff necks and serious faces produce this joyous, loud music. The hymns they sing are mostly 19th-century European and American melodies, whose lyrics have been translated into Korean by American missionaries and corrected by the Korean converts over the span of a century.

After several hymns, a pastoral prayer is offered; the people shout "Amen," "Sssheee," "Chooyuuu" (Lord) at the end of every single sentence of the prayer. Enthusiasm fills the air, and some people start pounding their chests and the pews; you give up your effort to make some sense out of the pastoral prayer and give in to the enthusiasm of the people. At the end of the pastoral prayer, the people join in praying loudly, all at the same time; and the huge dome-shaped church is filled with the strange amalgamation of human voices, at times in consonance and at times like a storm at sea. If you were not praying with them, you might feel nauseated by the shouts. But when the table bell rings, the prayer stops all at once, perhaps right in the middle of your sentence, and people hush up and regain their worshipful composure. The choir is first-rate by any standard. The sermon is an inspirational "positive thinking" and "can do" message, pouring forth a sense of confidence, comfort, and assurances of amazing and abundant grace of the almighty God of Jesus Christ. People around you are desperately in need of such assurances; they look like poor people recently settled in the city, having moved from farm villages and now looking for jobs in the stores and newly opened factories.

The people in the churches do not leave quickly, but stay on the whole afternoon for various activities: men' s mission group, housewives' meeting, etc. This is not all: after a short dinner break, in the late evening, the faithful gather again for evening devotions. History has it that the missionaries named the Sunday evening devotions "Evening of Praise," so the time has been devoted to the practice of hymn-singing. These days the Sunday evening devotions are used for Bible study conducted by the pastor, or for meetings by the different church organizations. Usually one tenth of the number at the Sunday morning service attend the evening devotions.

Korean churches do not stop with Sunday gatherings. Most churches in the cities and countryside have a mid-week service on Wednesday evening. And many house churches are organized to meet for Friday evening devotions. But the spirituality of Korean Christians shows most definitely at the daybreak prayer meeting, every single day of the week from 4:00 a.m. Some pastors give a brief Bible lesson and comment, but generally, it' s the church people who come and offer daily prayers—mostly in loud voices. You will find people crying out, panting, moaning, stretching out their hands, and twisting their bodies.

Protestant Christianity in Korea is one of the fastest-growing religions in the world: the unofficial count of Protestants in South Korea in 1970 was 2 million,and now in 1985, 10 million out of a 40 million population. Students of the sociology of religion try to explain the phenomenal growth by saying that political and military insecurity, rapid social changes, and the division of the country, which necessitates the continued military confrontation, have contributed to the religious fervor among the people of Korea. Pastors in these fast-growing churches would not agree, however; the phenomenon is a loud and clear indication of the work of the Spirit, it is the clear sign of the spirituality of the Korean people.

2. Religion and Spirituality

If one says that Korean Christianity is very spiritual, you will also find plenty of spirituality all over the country. Early in the morning before daybreak, if you walk up into the nearby hills overlooking the deep sleep of downtown Seoul, you will come upon blinking candlelights which kindle the earnest faces of women, rubbing their hands together in appeal to the mountain spirits for their sons and daughters and their family business. When you follow the trail down from the hill and stop by a city Buddhist temple for a drink of water from their "mountain spirit spring well, "you will find hundreds of men and women lined up for the Buddhist monks' morning prayer, "Namiamitahbuhl," accompanied by the sound of the wooden gourd.

Even if a Korean is neither Buddhist nor Christian, he or she is occupied on certain days of the year, such as the lunar New Year, the memorial day of one' s deceased parents or in-laws, birthdays, and one day each in spring and fall, taking care of the family gravesite. On these particular days, the women of the family are supposed to prepare food and drinks for the ancestral spirits, while the men of the household must offer rituals at the ancestral service. All the members of the household are supposed to bow down in front of the wooden plate on which the ancestor' s name is written, offer incense, and pray for the well-being of each and every member of the family. The male head of the house officiates at this Confucian house assembly, held in the evening or the early morning before daybreak. The Confucian family ancestor rites are conducted in the most solemn manner, without songs, movement or noise.

If you want to meet and experience Korean spirituality, you must go to a special place, leaving your tourist hotel, your home, your regular location. Religious spirituality seems to have something to do with *space*. You climb up a hill leaving the lowly downtown Seoul behind you, find a secluded place, and kneel down in front of a sacred rock or tree or spring. If you do not climb a hill, you may go to the chapel or temple to meet God, or Buddha. If you do not go to a temple, you may set up a place in the house to pay homage to your ancestor spirits. That space is a holy space, set aside for the spirits and for spiritual practice. It is different from the secular places where everyday life is going on. That space is clearly marked to separate the sacred from the secular. Interestingly, the space is not in itself holy or sacred, it is just another space within the general space; but human spirituality sets aside a certain space as different, and names it holy and sacred. This is to say that human spirituality demands a space away from the ordinary space.

The second element in religious spirituality has something to do with *time*. The earliest time in the morning, the darkest hour before dawn, is the time for all religious ones to come before the spirits. A certain time is set aside for prayer and meditation. Eleven o' clock on Sunday morning seems to have become the sacred hour of the Christian week. Four o' clock every morning is set aside for devout Korean Christians to assemble for morning prayer at nearby chapels. Three o' clock in the morning in the Buddhist Sun (Zen) hall is the time for all the students and masters of Sun to face the great white wall for meditation. This time, this hour, is holy hour, different from any other hour in one's life. It is supposed to be a purified and sacred hour which should not be polluted or disturbed by the unclean secular history. This time, like the holy space, is eternal and transcendental. It is not measured by man-made clocks or hourglasses, but only by itself, by its own time, and by eternity.

But the third element in the religious spirituality is what one does in this space and time of the sacred. An immediate answer is worship, prayer, singing, and sometimes dancing. It may be called relating oneself to another. This *relationship* is with God, with Buddha or with one' s ancestral spirit; or perhaps it is a relationship with oneself or with nothingness, or with Brahman, or the Great Universal Will. One' s spiritual relationship is one's religion, for religion is to relate one-self to the holy other (s). This establishing of a relationship is what you do in religion and in the sacred space and time. The nature of the relationship is determined by the other to whom one relates, and by what one does with the relationship.

3. Religious Spirituality

In my observation and analysis of Korean religious spirituality, I find this element of relationship most ambiguous and frustrating. When you ask the devout what they pray about, the usual answer is for the health and wealth of the family as stated in the *Third Epistle of John*, "Behold, I wish above all things that thou mayest prosper and be in health, even as thy soul prospereth." I have quoted here from King James, because it brings out and focuses on "prosperity." Our Korean Full gospel preacher named it "Three Beat Blessings," to mean health, wealth, and spiritual prosperity. And actually, what the people basically pray for in their early morning prayers in the Christian churches or in front of the hilltop rocks and trees, is the same: health and wealth and the spirit. Our religious spirituality is being used for the incessant and desperate petition for magical power to achieve health and wealth in this world.

In this religious spirituality we meet the poor and oppressed. The poorest of the poor come to the churches before daybreak, before their sons and daughters wake up for the day, and they are the ones who cry out to the spirit to give them the power to make their family healthy and rich. It is such a poor woman who cries out to sweet Virgin Mary that she has been beaten up by her drunken husband. It is such a poor mother whose child is sick or crippled. Also in this religious spirituality, we meet those who have "made it" recently: they've made it but they need more and want to keep what they have gotten. The "Three Beat Blessings" attracts the religious spirituality of the poor and those on the way to economic development and prosperity.

4. Characteristics of Religious Spirituality

In the religious spirituality of the "Three Beat Blessings," as the people ask for the blessings of health and wealth, they relate themselves to the *deus ex machina*, the ancient, almighty problem-solver. The theology of this religious spirituality is basically materialistic, capitalistic, this-worldly, anthropomorphic and amoral, i.e., morally neutral. The gods of the religious spirituality are supposed to be powerful enough to give the people the "Three Beat Blessings." And this spirituality is a task on the part of the person who asks for such blessings. The "ethics" of such religious spirituality is consistency, sincerity, and insistence. The gods of this religious spirituality are dead ancestors, though neither saints nor heroes, and those who have shown unusual military might in the nation's history. The gods of religious spirituality are Amita Buddhas, or the unknown spirits hanging around the neighborhood elm tree. The most recent gods of religious spirituality would be the seemingly sophisticated Western version which claim to perform faith healings and strange and awesome speaking-in-tongues, accompanied by money and social prestige.

In religious spirituality, religion and ethics are separate enterprises. That is to say that the gods of religious spirituality are amoral, or morally neutral; apolitical or politically neutral. The gods of religious spirituality are power without justice, and love and mercy without righteousness. They hand out the "Three Beat Blessings" to those who ask, pray, and are religiously loyal without regard to politics, moral life and works. Thus, there is no sense of sin and guilt, and thus no forgiveness involved. There cannot be forgiveness when there is no repentance. It is only the forgetfulness of being, the forget fulness of morality, the darkness of the pre-dawn sleepy consciousness that reaches out for help in search of meaning and prosperous life.

5. Paul and the Gifts of the Spirit

A very interesting, but at the same time a very disconcerting aspect of religious spirituality is its empiricism and its empirical claim. Religious spiritualism, as we have seen, is related to a certain space and time, where you can go and place yourself, and set yourself up a religious alibi. And just as we have learned that the Puritanic religious spirituality was able to show empirically in one's socio-economic success that this person was predetermined to be saved, our religious spirituality demands empirical and even "verifiable" signs of health and wealth in this world. "Have you been saved?" "Have you been baptized by the fire of the Holy Spirit?" And if you are not quick in answering these fiery questions, there comes another question: "Can you speak in tongues? Can you heal the sick with the power of the Holy Spirit?" If you cannot answer these questions in the affirmative, your theological education is a failure; you have gotten theological education without spirituality.

Paul was infuriated when he wrote to the Corinthians and listed for them the "gifts of the Spirit." In the first Letter to the Corinthians he names these as follows: (1) the utterance of wisdom (2) the utterance of knowledge, (3) faith, (4) healing, (5) working of miracles, (6) prophecy, (7) ability to distinguish between spirits, (8) various kinds of tongues, and (9) the interpretation of tongues. (I Corinthians 12: 8-10, RSV). What more could he add to this list under the pastoral circumstances of his time? And what addition could we make to this list? Perhaps, how to speak in foreign languages, Chinese, Japanese, Greek, or Swahili, and how to organize this kind of workshop, and perhaps how to run the awesome body of the World Council of Churches. But would we change the order of the list? If we take seriously what Paul had to say about speaking in tongues, that he would rather speak five words with his mind, than ten thousand words in a tongue, we should not reverse the order of the list. Paul would have been very stubborn about keeping the order of the list, according to what he says:

> I will pray as I am inspired to pray, but I will
> also pray intelligently. I will sing hymns as I
> am inspired to sing, but I will sing intelligently
> too. . . . Thank God, I am more gifted in ecstatic
> utterance than any of you, but in the congregation.
> I would rather speak five intelligible words, for
> the benefit of others as well as myself, than
> thousands of words in the language of ecstasy.
> (I Corinthians 14: 15-19, *New English Bible*)

You did it for me

Looking closely at the list and the order of it, we might think that Paul was a rationalist after all, deeply influenced by the epistemology and metaphysics of the Greeks and Romans, to put "wisdom" and "knowledge" at the top of the list even before "faith." But this was not quite so. When we encounter the thirteenth chapter of First Corinthians, which comes right in between this list of the gifts of the spirit and the problems of speaking in tongues and in reason, we see Paul putting the spiritual gift of love at the top of the gift list.

> Love will never come to an end. Are there prophets?
> Their work will be over. Are there tongues of ecstasy?
> They will cease. Is there knowledge? It will vanish away
> (v.8-9a, *NEB.*)

added throughout

When Paul says, "I may speak in the tongues of men or of angels, but if I am without love, I am a sounding gong or a clanging cymbal," he is talking about the spirituality of love, and love as the spiritual gift.

HS. 2x

6. The Spirituality of Jesus

When we talk about the spirituality of love, and love as the spiritual gift, we must turn to the spirituality of Jesus. And as we turn to the spirituality of love in the life of Jesus, we come to notice the three most important points of his life: (1) the temptation at the early stage of his "ministerial formation," (2) the first declaration of his mission, and (3) the Cross.

(1) **The temptation.** Luke reports "Full of the Holy Spirit, Jesus returned from the Jordan, and for forty days was led by the Spirit up and down the wilderness and tempted by the devil." (Lk. 4:1,2. *NEB.*) Immediately after his baptism by John the Baptist, Jesus was taken to the wilderness for his theological education. The Holy Spirit has to do with the theological education of Jesus, and spirituality has to do with temptation, a theological reflection on faith and ideology. This is the place where a theological alternative is being sought, and the place where hermeneutical suspicions arise. And this is the place where one's theological spirituality is to be tested.

The problem of the poor was raised in the spirituality of Jesus. This was not just a materialistic and economic question, but a spiritual one. When he was hungry, and the devil urged him to tell the stone to become bread, he refused to do so. He chose hunger and poverty. He became voluntarily poor to indicate to us, throughout Christian history, that spirituality and poverty go together. And we go among the poor and hungry to find profound spirituality. The Biblical spirituality is not only to feed the poor, but to be with them and on their side, for the poor are blessed with the kingdom of God (Lk 6:20). This is precisely the spirituality of love of Jesus Christ in his being with the poor and in his feeding of the hungry crowd with five loaves and two fishes. The spirituality of love of Jesus is solidarity with the poor which feeds the poor and hungry, not by bread alone but with love, care and solidarity.

The second temptation according to Luke was a political one. This is an indication of Jesus' spirituality of theological politics. The spirituality of Jesus in his political theology is downright iconoclastic. He would not recognize the absolute political power, and would not bow down before the political idols. As Scripture says, "you shall do homage to the Lord your God amd worship him alone" (Lk. 4:8). This is Jesus' loyalty to the first two commandments as the basis of his political theology, and this is his spirituality of theological politics. He will stand against the kingdoms of power that would revolt against the kingdom of God. Jesus' spiritual politics is consistent when he says, "Pay Caesar what is due to Caeser, and pay God what is due to God" (Lk. 20:25). You should not pay Caesar what is due to God, and you should not pay God what is due to Caesar."

The political spirituality of Jesus reverses the political order and the political relationship. Jesus says, "In the world, kings lord it over their subjects; and those in authority are called their country's 'benefactors.' Not so with you: On the contrary, the highest among you must bear himself like the youngest, the chief of you like a servant" (Lk. 22:25-26). The spiritual politics of Jesus opens up an entirely new power relationship between the rulers and the ruled, the dominant power and the dominated, the first world and the third world, men and women, masters and slaves, blacks and whites. As feminist theologians have perceived in "the spirituality of feminist theological politics," we cannot separate spirituality and politics. "That spirituality is inextricable from political and social responsibility is no new notion," but what is new in the spirituality which the feminist theologians propose is "that it has to do with the liberation of women of all racial ethnic heritages." [2]

Furthermore, according to their understanding of spirituality, it is basically political and communal and not a private enterprise.

> ...the quest for God, and the concomitant desire to stand open to the power of Spirit, are not, in either the first or final place, a private enterprise. Spirituality is fundamentally a communal commitment, a bonding between and among us, a relational pilgrimage–with God precisely as God is engaged and accepted in our love of neighbor as self. [3]

The feminist theologians' resolute conclusion is that "if we are consumed by that spirituality which is of God, there is no way to get ourselves off the hook of being justice-makers." [4] This is in line with Jesus' spiritual politics for the Kingdom of God. And here we see the basic difference between the politics of religious spirituality and the spiritual politics of Jesus.

(2) Jesus' declaration of mission. I would like to insert Jesus' declaration of mission, in order to make the connection between his spirituality and mission, and between his spirituality and politics of the kingdom of God. To the question "What would be Jesus' political alternative as he refuses to pay homage to the worldly politics which the devil offered?" Jesus answered in this declaration of his messianic politics. And here in his declaration of mission, we clearly see the nature of spirituality being political, and hence Jesus' spiritual politics:

> The Spirit of the Lord is upon me
> because he has anointed me;
> He has sent me
> to announce good news to the poor,
> to proclaim release for prisoners and
> recovery of sight for the blind;

H.S.
So
many
times

to let the broken victims go free,
to proclaim the year of the Lord' s favor.
(Lk. 4:18-19).

Jesus' spiritual politics is liberation politics, i.e., political liberation and liberation of politics. Jesus' spiritual politics of love is to proclaim the year of the Lord' s favor, which is to create a just relationship between human beings and to create the kingdom of God amongst us. This is the reason why we would not separate spirituality from politics, and this is why those of us who are struggling for the politics of human rights would humbly submit that our politics is spiritual and our spirituality cannot but be political. And we humbly beseech God that our political struggle would be guided by the Holy Spirit, and be "anointed," and that our politics be spiritual and our spirituality political.

What is important to notice in the spirituality of Jesus is that he breaks down the space and time of spirituality. He does not get away from the everyday life, social space and history of the mundane world of politics. Jesus' spirituality takes place in politics, where there are the poor, where there is sickness, where there are demonstrations and tear gas, where there is oppression and bondage, where there are political prisoners, and where there is absolute power which is corrupting absolutely. Jesus' spirituality is here being demythologized, secularized and made public, and is moving historically in the world of politics. In contrast to the religious spirituality of the temples and cathedrals, the Biblical spirituality of Jesus is open to the world and struggles for the establishment of a new political relationship.

(3) **Spirituality of the Cross.** The third temptation of the devil to Jesus may very well be connected with the death of Jesus on the Cross. At the top of the temple tower, the devil says to Jesus: "Throw yourself down, if you are the Son of God, His angels will take care of you" (Lk. 4:9-10). The military officers who stood looking at Jesus on the Cross jeered at him, "He saved others; now let him save himself, if this is God' s Anointed, his Chosen" (Lk. 23:35). Spirituality does not mean acting as a "superman," but it is falling down from the top of the temple and hanging on the Cross. The spirituality of Jesus is martyrdom, a lonely death, and the cry of *Eli, Eli, Lama Sabachthani.*

It is to carry your own Cross, and it is thus a costly discipleship. The temptation of the devil is not to make you fall down from the top of the temple or to take up the cross, but to induce you to ask the guardian angels to protect you from falling down or to enable you to avoid taking up the costly discipleship. The spirituality of Jesus not only means not testing the power of God, but it means taking up the cross, to participate in suffering, and refusing the ideologies of religious spirituality. Jesus' temptation and the cross are the crucial moments where his spiritual politics confronts the ideology of religious spiritualism. Religion may test God, but the spirituality of Jesus suffers with God on the Cross.

At his religious temptation, Jesus flatly refuses religious spirituality to test the power of God. Jesus flatly rejects the empiricism involved in religious spirituality. Jesus would not fall into the temptation that, if you have received the gift of the Spirit, you should try tongue-speaking or faith-healing. Jesus' spirituality has nothing to do with such spiritual show; he is free to heal or not to heal. Jesus' spirituality is to cast out the political demons, the demons that oppress the poor. The temptation of religious spirituality is to gain individual and private comfort and security of mind in the troubled world. It is not to risk your life for others for the causes of justice and peace. It is the temptation to call down the all-weather-proof protection of guardian angels.

The religious temptation at the top of the temple is the temptation of the dominant ideology. Jesus has been challenged by the ideologies of the law, the temple and the Sabbath, that is, the ideologies of the dominant Pharisaic religion of his time. In the desert, in his spiritual formation, Jesus struggles with the question of the religious ideology of the Jewish religion. He raises hermeneutical suspicions about his religious tradition. Jesus searches for a new form of spirituality, which is not of the law and not of the Sabbath, but of grace and of love. Jesus' theological education in spirituality in the desert is a critical analysis of the tradition and the dominant theological ideology. Jesus refuses the ideology of guardian angels that would protect religion and religious spirituality with the worldly ideologies of power.

The Cross is the point at which spirituality and politics meet. Jesus has to bear the cross because of his spirituality which opposes the Pharisaic ideology of religious spirituality, and he has to be crucified because of his politics which oppose the dominant Roman political ideology. Therefore, one cannot separate the Cross of Jesus from his spirituality nor from his politics. The Cross of Jesus is the climax of his spiritual politics, that is, the power of his spirituality and the powerlessness of his politics. The Synoptic Gospels are unanimous on the reports of two trials before the Cross: the first before the religious leaders and the second before the political authorities. And Jesus was not stoned to death as a religious criminal, but put on the cross as a political criminal—a religio-political criminal.

Finally, the Cross of Jesus is the decisive point at which the bond between faith and ideology breaks down. It would be right to say that faith without ideology is dead.[5] And it would be right to say that faith without culture would be lifeless. But when faith is swallowed up in the dominant ideology and the domineering culture and religion, faith is lost. The Cross is the iconoclastic power which breaks down ideologies. The cross breaks down religious spirituality in order to gain the life of faith, and the life of spirituality of the Cross. The Cross is death to the false ideology of religious spirituality, and the life of faith in true spirituality. The spirituality of the Cross becomes transparent when the Cross is interpreted in a non-religious way, and is demythologized and de-ideologized.

7. The Spirituality of the Feast

When we talk about Christian spirituality and especially when we connect the spirituality of Jesus with the crucifixion, we cannot help becoming deadly serious. Spirituality is, of course a serious matter. The Spirituality the Cross is needless to say, a deadly serious matter. But the Biblical spirituality is the spirituality of resurrection; it is the spirituality of life and creation. Jesus wept with the sick and lonely, he prayed and baptized and tempted, fought against the devils, but also he dined with the sinners, the rich and the poor. And finally, he was utterly happy when a woman poured expensive, foreign-made perfumed oil over his head, a sight which Judas Iscariot could not stand and which moved him to leave Jesus in disappointment to betray him (Mt. 26:6-16).

In his study of Korean mask dances, Hyun Yong Hak loves to point out the humor in the drama as critical transcendence—in the dancers' laughing at the religious and the powerful and even at their own miserable lot. The spirituality of resurrection is in the feast, eating and drinking together on the journey to Emmaus (Lk. 24:24 ff.). The spirituality of resurrection is the spirit in the humor, the jokes, the storytelling, the laughter, and in the play, games and dramas. It is the free movement of the body, the liberation of the body and the spirit. The Christian spirituality of resurrection is not about death, but about life; it is not impoverishment but enrichment; it is not crying but laughter. When you can laugh even at your own spirituality, you are truly in the spirituality of resurrection.

Reading I, Lee Chul-Su

Shim Chung, Lee Chul-Su
(A girl who sacrificed herself for her
blind father.- A Buddhist legend.)

5 MINJUNG AND BUDDHISM IN KOREA

1. Korean Buddhism

When people are settling down for their evening meal, the sound of a nearby temple gong can be heard. The sound of a nearby temple gong at twilight in the middle of the tired city streets makes children rush home to their waiting mother in the kitchen. The sound of the temple gong makes them hungry, hushed and homebound. It makes people calm and quiet, hushed and settled. The sound of the gong is coming from a temple on a nearby hillside, or perhaps right in the jungle of skyscrapers. It is a low-key sound with a long tail of vibrations and resonances. Gong . . . Gong . . . Gong . . . The quiet sound enters the house, the home and the mind. There is peace in the sound, and there is a certain peace of mind in hearing it and being absorbed in it.

At Buddhist temples near the modern cities or deep in the mountains of Korea, there is a smell of burning incense and the sounds of a man's deep voice reading the Buddhist scriptures and a wooden gong. Inside the main building one or three women may be bowing in front of a huge sitting Buddha statue which looks down on them. Korean Buddhist temples are favorite tourist spots, because they are located in the most scenic mountain areas of Korea. But there are also a few Buddhist temples in the middle of

Seoul, the capital city of South Korea, and in its suburbs.

In the spring, April or May, Buddha' s birthday (also the day of enlightenment and death) is celebrated all over the country. It is now a national holiday. The temples themselves and whole mountains and whole neighborhoods become excited with festive mood. Thousands of people visit temples and pay their respects to Buddha. They come to offer incense and candles for the colorful lanterns. They come to visit a small shrine behind the main Buddha hall. The small shrine is a shaman shrine where they come to pray and to be blessed. They come to celebrate the birthday of Buddha. They come to the temple for celebration and festival. They sing aloud, dance together, and get drunk. They all have great fun. (In recent years, the authorities have tried, to no avail, to regulate the loud singing and dancing on or near the temple grounds.)

In Korea the presence of Buddha, Buddhism and Buddhist temples can be experienced everywhere—their calmness, arts, statues and sculptures, stories and myths, noise and festivities. Korea is a Buddhist country. According to South Korean government statistics, as of January 1982, 29.05% of Korea's 35 million people are Buddhist. Protestants, the next largest religious group, comprise 19.93%. There are 7,253 Buddhist temples throughout the country with 20,755 Buddhist monks, male and female. Buddhism is not only the most popular religion in Korea with the most adherents; it is the oldest imported religion in Korea as well.

Buddhism was introduced to Korea at the end of the fourth century in the Three Kingdoms period. In AD 372, an Indian priest named Sundo brought the Buddhist scriptures and Buddha images to the Kingdom of Koguryo in the northern most part of the Korean peninsula. Another Indian priest, Marananta, came to the kingdom of Paek' che by way of China in 384. The southern kingdom of Silla was about half a century behind in its acceptance of Buddhism, and the first Buddhist priest to enter that kingdom was a Koguryo priest named Mookhoja, sometime between AD 417 and AD 457, during the reign of King Noolchi. But missionaries were not active for another century, until the martyrdom of Ichadon (Pak Yumchok) in AD 528.

Buddhism flourished in the northern part of the Korean peninsula under the Koguryo kings of the fourth century AD. Ado, another Indian Buddhist missionary who came two years after Sundo, built Sungmoon and Iboolnan Temples in 375. King Kokookwun stipulated in 392 that the people must believe in Buddhism. The Great king Kwangkaeto constructed nine Buddhist temples in Pyongyang (the capital city of North Korea in 395, in order to defend the country from possible and actual aggression by the two kingdoms to the south. Movement to and from China for the exchange of

Buddhist priests and books was also allowed. Priest Uiyon went to China to study the history and doctrine of Buddhism in 576, and other priests such as Chikwang came back from China to preach and teach the Buddhist *Sutras* in Koguryo.

The Kingdom of Paek'che followed the way of Koguryo, sending Buddhist priests to India and China for the Buddhist studies. While Buddhist temples were being built, the learned priests began working on the translation of the *sutras*. Priest Kyumik who studied in India made the scriptural school predominant in Paek' che. By the middle of the sixth century, the kingdom of Paek' che seemed to have made Buddhism the national cult. A six-foot high Buddha statue came in 545, and a royal decree in 595 prohibited the killing of living creatures. The kings of Paek' che kingdom also erected great temples for the national defense. King Moo (600-640), for example, built Mireuk (Maitreya) Temple, the largest temple in the Orient at the time. A stone pagoda, which still stands on the site, is the oldest in Korea.

Buddhism gained popularity in the kingdoms of Silla and Paek' che because of royal patronage. Both kingdoms saw the apotheosis of Buddhist culture throughout the sixth century. In this golden age, international religious exchanges were frequent. Not only did the kingdoms send their priests to China for advanced studies on Chinese Buddhism; they also sent many Korean priests and artisan emigrants to Japan to plant Buddhism there. The year 552 is cited as the year when the first Buddhist missionary from Paek' che set foot in Japan. The Paek' che king Sung sent Buddhist statues and scriptures, along with a seven-man missionary group led by Priest Dosim. In 554, King Widuk sent nine missionaries to Japan and again in 577 he sent many other *sutra* and *vinaya* (rules) masters, along with Buddha statue artisans and temple architects. A high Japanese official named Sogaumako learned about ordination from the masters of rules sent by the Paek' che kingdom. Thus Paek' che' s national effort to propagate Buddhism in Japan helped Japan achieve the rich Buddhist culture of the Asuka period. Buddhist missionaries from Paek' che helped lay the foundation of the Buddhist culture of the Asuka and Nara periods in Japan.

Korean Buddhism, introduced during the three kingdoms period, flourished in the unified Silla kingdom from the fifth to the tenth century, until the fall of the Silla kingdom in 935. This period, which corresponds to that of T'ang, is called the golden age of Korean Buddhism. The Buddhism of the period was a national religion devoutly followed by kings, aristocrats and the common people. The type of Buddhism initially introduced to Korea was Chinese Mahayana Buddhism; the Sun sect was introduced during the latter part of the Unified Silla period (779-935). The *Kyo* Buddhist sect, exclusively concerned with the teaching of scriptures and doctrines, subsequently evolved, centering around the court and aristocratic classes. But the Pure Land and Tantric Buddhism, mixed indigenous beliefs, were popular among the common people.

The Buddhism introduced to the Three Kingdoms was from the beginning a miracle working religion in a most simple form which promised to bring health and wealth to an individual and prosperity and security to the nation. It became easily meshed with the native popular beliefs and shamanistic customs of the time. Buddhism was popularized among the rulers as a religion with the occult power to defend the country from all evil, under the protection of the royal court. But Korean Buddhism in the Unified Silla period produced great theologians who set forth the unique doctrines which have characterized the development of a "minjung" Buddhism in Korea.

Korea has had roughly a 1,500 year history of Buddhism. The Three Kingdoms period may be called the childhood period of Korean Buddhism, while the Unified Silla period was the time of youthful development of Korean Buddhism. During the Koryo Kingdom period which lasted until 1392, Korean Buddhism came to its full growth. But when the Yi Dynasty (1392-1910) embraced Confucianism as its state ideology, Buddhism was suppressed and banned until the end of the dynasty. Nonetheless, Buddhism is the first religion of contemporary Korea and the most popular religion among the minjung of Korea today.

2. Buddha, the Founder of a Minjung Religion

Siddhartha Gautama, the compassionate Buddha, was born in northwestern India six centuries before the Christian era. The Buddha was born in an aristocratic family of Kshatriya, a military class equal in social standing to the priestly Brahmins but less involved in sacred affairs. His father, Suddhodana, centered his own life around that of his son and heir. Legend relates that the father took every precaution to protect the son from any possible experience of distress or unhappiness. Gautama was not allowed to leave the palace compound. Nonetheless, Siddhartha, according to the story, chose not to obey these parental rules, and made several secret and forbidden ventures outside the palace grounds. Inevitably, he encountered the four signs of life on these trips. According to the Buddhist Scripture, "Gods of the Pure Abode . . . conjured up the illusion of an *old man*, so as to induce the king's son to leave his home. When the king's son saw the old man, he asked his charioteer the meaning of old age. Upon hearing the explanation of old age the prince reacted to the news like a bull when a lightning-flash crashes down near him . . . He sighed deeply, shook his head, fixed his gaze on the old man, surveyed the festive multitude, and was deeply perturbed . . . ."[1]

The scripture goes on: "On a second pleasure excursion the same gods created a man with a *diseased body*," and "on the third excursion the same displayed a *corpse*, which only the prince and his charioteer could see, being borne along the road . . ." [2] The fourth sign was seen when Siddhartha was in great distress questioning the reality of life and the ways to happiness. While wandering outside the palace gates, he saw a passing ascetic with calm eyes and an alms bowl in his hands. Siddhartha decided to leave the palace grounds forever, leaving behind him his wife and a son. He was twenty-nine years old when he left his kingdom and became an ascetic in search of a solution to the universal suffering of man.

After six years of wandering about the valley of the Ganges, meeting famous religious teachers and ascetics who gave him no satisfaction, at the age of thirty-five, Siddhartha attained Enlightenment under a Bodhi tree at Buddha-Gaya. The heart of the enlightened Buddha's teaching lies in the four Noble Truths which he expounded in his very first sermon to the five ascetic colleagues at Isipatana near Benares. The Four Noble Truths are:

1. *Dukkha,*
2. *Samudaya,* the rise or origin of *dukkha,*
3. *Nirodha,* the cessation of *dukkha,*
4. *Magga,* the way leading to the cessation of *dukkha.*

The first noble truth is translated by almost all scholars as "The Noble Truth of Suffering." It means that life is nothing but suffering and pain. Walpola Rahula analyzes the concept of *dukkha* in three aspects; (1) *dukkha* as ordinary suffering, (2) *dukkha* as produced by change and (3) *dukkha* as conditioned states.[3] Rahula lists in his first category: birth, old age, sickness, death, asssociation with unpleasant persons and conditions, separation from beloved ones and pleasant conditions, not getting what one desires, grief, lamentation, distress.[4] In addition to these ordinary forms of physical and mental suffering, Buddhism teaches that human life in the world has to be seen more realistically as "imperfection," "impermanence," "emptiness," insubstantiality," "conditional" and "contingent."

It is interesting to note here that the first noble truth comes to grips with the crude reality of life and the world. But one cannot help noticing the almost completely "philosophical" and "metaphysical" understanding of *dukkha*, devoid of any social understanding of worldly suffering. The minjung that approach the compassionate Buddha are the very ones who suffer most. They suffer lives of poverty, oppression, and social deprivation. They are born into the poverty stricken families. They are born into the sick-ridden homes. They suffer material poverty. They suffer social alienation and are deprived of social privilege. The whole life of minjung is nothing but *dukkha, dukkha,* coming from the life experience of the society itself. *Dukkha* is not only a metaphysical instability; it is also the result of social and political and economical instability. The minjung suffer the comings and goings of kingdoms and empires. They are the first to realize painfully the first Noble Truth that life is nothing but suffering and pain. The Korean minjung come to cling to Buddhism for freedom and salvation from their suffering and pain in life. The minjung*'s* painful realization that life is *dukkha*, and this same realization by the compassionate Buddha himself almost invariably draw the minjung of Korea to Buddhism.

The second Noble Truth explains the origin or the cause of *dukkha*. According to the Buddhist scripture: "It is this "thirst" (craving) which produces re-existence and re-becoming, and which is bound up with passionate greed, and which finds fresh delight now here and now there, namely, (1) thirst for sense-pleasures, (2) thirst for existence and becoming and (3) thirst for non-existence (self-annihilation)."[5] According to the second noble truth, human life itself is craving and thirst for life, and therefore, life is nothing but *dukkha*. But this is too metaphysical, or psychological an understanding of human life and the world. The minjung have no chance to cultivate their cravings for sense-pleasures. If they crave anything it is food, the basic nourishment of life itself. That cannot be the cause of their suffering. Perhaps the very fact that the minjung have to work for food is *dukkha*. Only the haves—those with enough to eat and enough to spend—have other cravings, selfish desires to rule, to dominate and to exploit. It would be a better interpretation to say that Buddha ascribed the pain and suffering in human society, especially the *dukkha* of the minjung, to social and political causes: the rulers' craving for money and power. Social oppression and exploitation are caused by the selfish desire of the powerful to manipulate and dominate.

The Third Noble Truth is the cessation of *dukkha*, more popularly known in its Sanskrit form of *Nirvana*. This is emancipation, liberation and freedom from suffering, from the continuity of *dukkha*. It has been stated in imperative form: "Kill your selfish desires, and be liberated from *dukkha*," or "eliminate your cravings and you will be saved from *dukkha*." "Nirvana" has not been interpreted in such sociological terms as a "messianic kingdom" on earth that can be realized in human history. Nor is this freedom from the selfish desires of man interpreted as freeing the minjung from their poverty and oppression and alienation.

The Fourth Noble Truth points the way to the cessation of *dukkha*. This is known as the "Middle path," or the Noble Eightfold path:

1. Right Understanding
2. Right Thought
3. Right Speech
4. Right Action
5. Right Livelihood
6. Right Effort
7. Right Mindfulness
8. Right Concentration.

Practically the whole teaching of the Buddha for forty-five years dealt in some way or other with this Path. He explained it in many different ways to different kinds of people. But the traditional understanding of the essence of the Eightfold Path is to gain wisdom and compassion. But it should be noted that the way to *Nirvana* began with right understanding, or correct seeing, and right awareness, or conscientization. Liberation begins with painful self-awareness by the minjung of their condition. Conscientization of one's social and political condition is the first step toward liberation.

3. Boddhisattva and the Minjung

Siddhartha did not stay in the state of bliss experienced in his great enlightenment. He did not monopolize the state of *nirvana*, the eternal grace, unto himself. He did not leave the society of man, the bonds of personal earthly laws and ties. Rather the Buddha remained among men to teach. According to the scripture, the "Great Buddha Heart of Infinite Compassion prevailed," and he decided to live among the people, work with them and give them enlightenment. The Buddha stayed in the world, teaching people the Path for the attainment of enlightenment.

A contemporary American poet, Allen Ginsberg, depicts Siddhartha's epochal decision as follows:

He drags his bare feet

                        out of a cave
                                under a tree
        eyebrows
                        grown long with weeping
                                and hooknosed woe,
        in ragged soft robes
                        wearing a fine beard,
                                unhappy hands
        clasped to his naked breast–
                        humility is beatness
                                humility is beatness–
        faltering
                        into the bushes by a stream,
                                all things inanimate
        but his intelligence–
                        stands upright there
                                tho trembling:
        Arhat
                        who sought Heaven
                                under a mountain of stone,
        sat thinking
                        till he realized
                                the land of blessedness exists
        in the imagination–
                        the flash come
                                empty mirror–
        how painful to be born again
                        wearing a fine beard,
                                re-entering the world
        a bitter wreck of a sage:
                        earth before him his only path.
                                we can see his soul,
        he knows nothing
                        like a god:
                                shaken
        meek wretch–
                        humility is beatness
                                before the absolute World.[6]

Siddhartha dragged his bare feet out of a cave under a tree, and came into the world, the world where the minjung live. He gave up the ideal of the *arhat*. As Arnold Toynbee saw, this is a contradiction not only of the Buddha's personal inclination but of his basic doctrines as well. This is a contradiction because it is the ideal of an *arhat* to achieve enlightenment for his own freedom and salvation from this world, the world of *samsara*, the eternal cycle of suffering. But he gives up that ideal once he attains freedom and salvation and turns back into the world again. Siddhartha took this contradiction on himself and went into the world, in the world where the suffering minjung lived.

This behavior of the Buddha—giving aid to others who are also seeking the path to illumination—later became the nexus of the teaching about *Boddhisattvas*. This is in contrast to the *arhat* ideal, which is found in *Theravada* or *Hinayana* Buddhism. The *Boddhisattva* ideal became an integral part of the *Mahayana* Buddhism which was brought to Korea through China. *Boddhisattvas* are enlightened beings who are on their way to, or have arrived at, the state of Buddhahood, but who give up, or postpone voluntarily their own *nirvana* for the sake of others. This is an act of compassion, compassion for others who need and seek freedom and salvation from the suffering of this world. At the center of the *Boddhisattva* ideal are compassion and sacrifice for others. The *Boddhisattva* is a being who has passed beyond all discrimination, has freed himself from all ideas of "I", "mine," "yours," or of any sense of possession.

In the Tibetan language, *Boddhisattva* is translated as Heroic Being. The *Abhidharmakosa* gives a description of the mentality of a *Boddhisattva*:

> For the good of others, because they want to become capable of pulling others out of this great flood of suffering. But what personal benefit do they find in the benefit of others? The benefit of others is their own benefit, because they desire it.[7]

The heroic person is one who does not discriminate between himself and others, who helps all others obtain freedom and salvation. The Mahayanans thus claim that the *Arhat* has not aimed high enough. The ideal man, the aim of the Buddhist effort, is not the rather self-centered, cold and narrow-minded *arhat*, but the all-compassionate *Boddhisattva*, who abandons the world, but not the people, the minjung in it.

Boddhisattva, the heroic being, is a manifestation or an incarnation of Buddha himself. In other words, the Buddha is manifest and incarnate in an infinite number of universes. Buddha comes into the secular world to save the minjung. This is the compassion of Buddha for the world and toward the suffering minjung. While minjung are taught to become *Boddhisattvas*, and to live for others in compassion, they cling to the compassionate Buddha who loves the world and liberates the minjung from suffering and pain. Herein, the *Boddhisattva* is not only an ideal, but an object of worship and prayer for freedom and salvation from this world of suffering. The *Boddhisattva* ideal has thus become the hope of the minjung for liberation and salvation. The Mahayana Buddhism of *Boddhisattva* has become the Buddhism of the minjung in Korea.

Buddhistic ethics are simply this life style of *Boddhisattva*, which is well expressed in the *Boddhisattva* vow. The *Boddhisattva* vow is a commitment to put others before one's self. It is a willingness to give up that which is our own, even our own enlightenment, for the sake of others. And the *Boddhisattva* commitment to others and to the world is based on the recognition of *dukkha*, suffering and pain and confusion of ourselves and others in the world. One who takes the *Boddhisattva* vow commits himself to the effort to alleviate suffering and misery in the world. Chogyam Trungpa, Rinpoche, describes well the life style of the *Boddhisattva*:

> By taking the boddhisattva vow, we open ourselves to many demands. If we are asked for help, we should not refuse; if we are invited to be someone's guest, we should not refuse; if we are invited to be a parent, we should not refuse. In other words, we have to have some kind of interest in taking care of people, some appreciation of the phenomenal world and its occupants. It is not an easy matter. It requires that we not be completely tired and put off by people's heavy-handed neurosis, ego-dirt, ego-puke or ego-diarrhea, but instead that we be appreciative and willing to clean up for them.[8]

An approach to the minjung is clear when you realize that the *Boddhisattva* vow is an expresstion of settling down and making oneself at home in this world. It means self-exposure to the world, openness to a world where there is suffering, where there is the minjung, the oppressed, the sick, the poor, and death itself. This is the highest expression of the compassionate Buddha, who gave up his enlightenment for the liberation of the suffering minjung and the secular world.

Siddhartha's compassionate love and concern for the people in this world has been expressed in an unbroken lineage of *Boddhisattvas*, springing from the great *Boddhisattva Avalokitesvara*, *Vajrapani* and *Manjusri*. It is believed that this unbroken heritage of *Boddhisattvas* continues up to the present day, not as a myth but as a living inspiration in the Buddhist faith of the people. Because of this linkage and heritage connected to the Buddha himself incarnate in the world of suffering for the salvation of man, to become a *Boddhisattva* is regarded as the highest ideal of a Buddhist. A person can become a *Boddhisattva* or Buddha by taking the *Boddhisattva* vow and living according to that vow. Anyone can become a *Boddhisattva*. This is the way to freedom and salvation, to enlightenment. This is a life of compassion, a life lived for others. Furthermore, this line of argument encompasses the fundamental Buddhist assumption that everyone can be, and can become Buddha; more fundamentally, everyone is Buddha. Not only can I become Buddha, but I *am* Buddha.

The *Boddhisattva* is a universalizing concept. Through this faith, Buddhism advocates the equality of man, and inspired the movement in Buddhism to abolish the Hindu caste system. This revolutionary Buddhist movement gave concrete emancipation and social liberation to the minjung of ancient society. Buddhism is open to the minjung, to everyone: high or low, powerful or powerless, rich or poor, oppressors and oppressed alike. For it is the *Boddhisattva* ideal to give freedom and enlightenment to the minjung, to the people, to all people who endure suffering and confusion in the world.

Not only did Buddha advocate abolition of the Hindu caste system. His words were written down in *Pali*, the language of the minjung, the ordinary people, who could not read *Sanskrit*. Buddhism began as the religion of the minjung. This is manifest in its understanding of the suffering of the minjung, in its dedication to the freedom and salvation of the minjung, the people in the suffering world, in its forfeiture of individual enlightenment, the *arhat* ideal, and in its use of the language of the poor and ignorant in the ancient world.

The language of Buddha was the language of the minjung. The teachings of Buddha have been handed down to us not only in the esoteric metaphysical languages. The main body of his teachings have come to us in the form of stories, fairy tales, parables, and myths. As a matter of fact, Buddha was downright anti-metaphysical. And his anti-metaphysical attitude was expressed not in the form of argument, but in the form of stories. In response to metaphysical questions, Buddha likened the questioner to a man who, having been shot wih a poisoned arrow, says, "I will not remove this arrow, call a physician, or heal my wounds until I have ascertained who shot the arrow, what tribe he belonged to, how the arrow was made and so on. Or perhaps to a man in a burning house who declares, "I will not leave the house until I find out who set the fire in the first place, etc."

In the Buddha's view, intellectual exchanges, which are either only theoretical or perhaps pedagogical, are a waste of vital energy for the work of salvation. "Whether the doctrine obtains that the world is eternal or that the world is not eternal, there still remain birth, old age and death, sorrow, lamentations, misery, grief, despair—all the grim facts of human existence—for the extinction of which in the present life I am prescribing ." Buddha was never merely a philosopher. His primary concern was to point the way to liberation—liberation of the minjung from the world of suffering, pain, deprivation and confusion. For this an abstract metaphysical understanding of the world is not necessary. Buddha was anti-intellectual to the extent that his highest ideal is Boddhisattva; he did not produce metaphysics, but spoke in stories and in parables, using the language of the minjung.

The *Boddhisattva* ideal is depicted in a story of a heroic being in the *Prajnaparamita.* The hero went into the forest with his family, and they became lost. As the family became frightened, the hero fearlessly said to them, "Do not be afraid. I will speedily take you out of this great and terrible jungle, and bring you to safety." The *Boddhisattva* ideal is illustrated in this story of a person who would not leave the dangerous jungle by himself, leaving his family behind him.

4. Wonhyo and Korean Minjung

The Silla Kingdom of the sixth century embraced Mahayana Buddhism. And Mahayana Buddhism flourished in the United Silla Kingdom until the end of the tenth century. Silla Buddhism is the highlight of Korean Buddhism. It produced many world-reknown priests and Buddhist scholars. The most prominent among them was Wonhyo, who laid the foundation of both Korean Buddhism and minjung Buddhism.

Wonhyo was born under a chestnut tree in his village in 617, exactly ninety years after Buddhism won official recognition. No one seems to know the date of his initiation into the priesthood, but it must have been during his early boyhood.[9] Anecdotes of Wonhyo, written by Ilyon (1206-1289) in Sam Kuk Yusa (History of Three Kingdoms) tell us about Wonhyo's boyhood:

> As the boy grew into a healthy and handsome youth he proved to be an uncommon person. He did not study with a teacher, but knew everything already. He was a playboy. His companions, his adventures, his wits and his great achievements are all described in detail in the T'ang biographies of the Monks and his autobiography, so here we will include only a few anecdotes from the Biographies of Silla.[10]

At the age of thirty-four, Wonhyo embarked on a tour to T'ang with his priest friend Uisang to study Chinese Buddhism. Toward the end of their trip, they had to spend a night in a field adjacent to a graveyard. During the night Wonhyo woke up with a terrible thirst, and searched for water in the dark. He found water nearby in a container. He drank without checking what he was drinking and from what. The following morning, when he got up he realized that he had quenched his burning thirst the night before by drinking dirty water from a human skull. This experience, according to the story, gave him a great enlightenment. Everything depends on the mind: the mind determines the nature of things ; all depends on how you look at the thing, your knowledge has nothing to do with the nature of things. With this sudden enlightenment, Wonhyo decided to cancel his study trip to China. Wonhyo returned home, and never again left his kingdom.

According to another version of the same story, Wonhyo and his friend had to spend the night in a earthen cave, taking refuge from a severe storm. The following morning they found that place where they had slept was not an earthen cave but an old tomb. They had spent the night among skeletons. That day it rained as before and the two had to spend another night in the same place. After dark they saw many devils moving about. Wonhyo came to realize that when the mind works, various events happen; when the mind does not work, the distinction between an earthen cave and an old tomb disappears. All worldly events spring from one Mind, and all events are of consciouness only. Therefore, one should not seek after truth outside the Mind.[11]

Wonhyo wrote at least eighty-six books (some say some 240 books). In any case he was the most prolific author Silla produced. Among them, only twenty-three are extant, of which fifteen are complete and eight in fragments.

From the time of his enlightenment in the old tomb, the main question Wonhyo grappled with was the difference and dichotomy between the truth and non-truth, knowledge and ignorance, and the sacred and profane. If the mind is everything, and if the mind sees no difference, then in the mind everything is one and the same. There is no difference between the truth and ignorance, and there is no gap between the sacred and the profane. The holy and the secular are the same Mind. Nature is not divided into the holy and the secular. They are part of the same nature, namely, the mind. Thus, the phenomenal world is nothing but reality itself; discrimination is equality; that which is, is that which is not; what is full is emptiness; and the Buddha is all sentient beings and the minjung; life and death are one and the same; and finally, dukkha and nirvana are one and the same. Here we find a "secular theology" in Wonhyo's understanding of Buddhism For the first time in Korean Buddhism, it is realized that the profane world and the secular world of suffering where minjung live are at the same time the world of Buddha which is sacred and holy, the blessed world of *nirvana* itself.

Wonhyo did not see the dialectic of the sacred and the profane. He destroyed the dualism of truth and non-truth, knowledge and ignorance, and *dukkha* and *nirvana*. He saw the *coincidencia oppositorium* in One Mind. One is in the other, and the other in one. This is in the true spirit of Mahayana Buddhism. The *arhat* does not have to leave the world to save himself and others as well. This is the *Boddhisattva* ideal which understands fully that the world is important, and there is salvation in this secular world. As a matter of fact, it is urged that salvation should be obtained in this world, among the minjung and in the minjung.

Wonhyo insisted upon the secularization of Buddhism and practised what he preached by taking off his Buddhist robe and putting on the secular clothing of the ordinary people. He lived among minjung and mixed with them in their drinking places and their gathering places. He met a clown on the street and took a gourd from him. And he sang and danced around the streets with the clown, making music by beating the gourd. In the secular world, with the minjung, he wanted to realize freedom and the *Boddhisattva* ideals. And he wanted to liberate the minjung from their ignorance and suffering. He sang and danced like the minjung themselves. He drank and talked with them in the bars and in their homes and on the streets. His language was vulgar and his acts unheard of.

According to our historian of Koryo, Ilyon:

> One day Wonhyo saw bees and butterflies flitting from flower to flower, and he felt a strong desire for a woman. He walked through the streets of Kyongju singing, "Who will lend me an axe that has lost its handle? I wish to cut a heaven-supporting pole. [13]

According to Ilyon, Wonhyo's song was interpreted by the king (Muryol), that "the love-lorn monk wants to marry a noble lady and have a wise son by her . . . ." The king commented that "if a sage is born, so much the better for the country."[14] Wonhyo 's song was further interpreted by the contemporary commentator as follows:

> Wonhyo 's song alludes to a poem in the Book of Ode, one of the Confucian classics. In this poem the axe-handle symbolizes the male sexual organ, so that an axe without a handle means a widow. Wonhyo is looking for a go-between to find a widow to be his lover, and the King agrees to play this part. This is one more example of Wonhyo's disregard of convention, since

Confucian custom forbade widows to remarry or otherwise have to do with men.[15]

The commentator fails to add that it is also unconventional for a highly regarded Buddhist monk like Wonhyo to sing such a song aloud on the streets of the capital of Kyongju, or to marry a widow and thus break his vow of chastity. The circumstances of his marriage were recorded as follows:

> There was at this time a widowed princess living in Yosuk Palace (now a monastery, Ilyon says). The King told his servants to conduct Wonhyo to that palace, and they found that he had already descended Namsan (South Mountain) and reached Munch'on-gyo, the Mosquito Stream Bridge. Here he deliberately fell into the stream and got his clothes wet. When he reached the palace the princess, already in bridal attire, suffered him to change into a bridegroom's robes, and so they were married and passed the night together.[16]

Wonhyo not only preached and worked in the secular world among the ordinary people as a Buddhist priest to save the minjung; he became a minjung himself. He acted like a minjung, using vulgar language and deceiving others. He enjoyed the life of a minjung, he loved to dance and sing, he drank with the minjung. He gave up his high position in the priesthood. He identified himself with the minjung. He participated in the minjung's joy and sorrow, in their humor and deceit and in their happiness and suffering.

According to the biography of Wonhyo, he made a utensil in the shape of a gourd and called it Mu-ae. "Mu-ae" means in Korean "boundless", namely, both life and death are *nirvana*. Wonhyo composed a song about the gourd for his dance. Wearing a mask and carrying the gourd, he performed his dance in every corner of the country. This was his method of teaching Buddhist enlightenment to the people. Even usurers and poor old bachelors, the most despised sector of the Silla society, were able to understand the meaning of the Buddha. He was a true embodiment of Buddha himself, a *Boddhisatttva*, working for the true liberation of the minjung.

Because Wonhyo was so busy with public affairs, according to his biographer, he was not able to finish his scholarly work of writing commentaries on the Hwa'um scripture. He was not a professional, or a specialist. He was too involved in people and public affairs. He was without political ambition, and cared only for the people suffering from injustice and oppression. For these reasons he never rose above the lowest rank of the monk. Wonhyo took off his priestly robe and put on secular dress, and called himself Sosong Kosa, meaning a little hermit. He lived according to his own name, a hermit of the lowest caste.[17]

The Silla Buddhist monk Wonhyo certainly turned the tradition of Korean Buddhism in the direction of *Boddhisattva* ideal. And his teaching advocated the importance of the secular world. Furthermore, he saw the sacred in the realm of the secular. He found his salvation in the secular world among the minjung. He did not hesitate to give up the life style of a reverend monk and a learned theologian scholar. He lived like a common man with the minjung. Telling stories and singing songs of his own composition, he danced around tthe country. He was the first and foremost model of minjung theologian in the Korean Buddhist religious tradition.

5. Buddhism in the Koryo and Yi Dynasties

The Koryo kingdom which came after the fall of the Silla Kingdom in 933 made Buddhism the national religion. Buddhism in the Koryo period (933-1392) became so popular that it pervaded everyday life, not only of the court and the aristocracy, but of the common people as well. It came to hold an important position in the political, social and economic life of the time. The founding king of Koryo (918-944) was a devout Buddhist, and he believed that the prosperity of his country depended entirely upon the protection of Buddha. As an expression of his faith that Buddhism had the power to defend the nation, he constructed ten large temples in and around the capital, erected a nine-story pagoda in Pyongyang, and repaired another nine-story pagoda at Hwangnyong Temple in Kyongju.

The first King of the Koryo kingdom, Taejo Wang Kun, appointed a Buddhist monk, Do Sun, as chief advisor (or the national priest). The king consolidated the foundation for a state cult of Buddhism by promoting such Buddhist religious festivals as *Palkwan-hoe* and the *Yundeung-hoe,* making them annual national occasions. His plans for the promotion of Buddhism as the national religion were formulated in his "Ten Articles of Will" or "The Ten Commandments." In them he exhorted his descendants to build some 3,800 government subsidized temples, following the orders of the national priest, Do Sun. *Yundeung-hoe* is still in practice in Korea on the birthday of Buddha. On the previous evening, hundreds of thousands of lanterns are lighted on the streets and on the temple grounds, and are carried by the people in a parade to celebrate the birth of the compassionate Buddha. *Palkwan-hoe* is a religious ritual to give prayers and offerings to the mountain gods and water spirits for the protection of the nation.

In the reign of King Kwangjong (950-975), the high point for Korean

Buddhism, a system of government examination for priests came into existence. This examination system established a seven grade hierarchy for the Buddhist order, plus royal tutors and most revered priests. Thus Buddhist monks became involved in the politics of the royal court, acting as both policy advisors and civil servants. Also the number of aristocrats turned Buddhist monks increased in a very short period of time. And this in turn made the Buddhist monks aristocratic and influential in all walks of national and social life. In the meantime, Buddhist temples became the nation's largest real estate holders, and became economically prosperous.

As Buddhists grew in number and in political and economic power and privilege, the powerful among the Buddhist monks began to indulge in a luxurious life, in disregard of their original mission. So the core of Koryo Buddhism was being corrupted. Following the era of King Kwangjong, Buddhism gradually became more inclined to prayer-offering in order to realize prosperity for the state and to avoid all evils and bad effects. Such Buddhism gave rise to shaman-oriented Buddhist priests in the royal court who geared royal Buddhism to prayer offering for the protection of the nation from national calamities. Similarly, Buddhism among the common people was also mixed with shamanistic trends and popular beliefs. These combined to bring about the decline of Buddhism in the Koryo kingdom and ultimately the fall of the monarchy itself.

The moral decline of Koryo Buddhist monks prompted the rapid rise of neo-Confucianism in the country, making the rise of a Confucianist dynasty inevitable by the end of the fourteenth century. In spite of such grand sacrificial efforts as the engraving of the *Tripitaka Koreana* on some 81,258 wooden plates by King Kojong (1214-1259), the whole country was totally devastated by the Mongol invasion of 1231, and the wooden plates burned down by the Mongols. This lent itself to the rise of a new regime in the peninsula.

However, the Koryo kingdom was not without earnest and professional scholar monks. Earlier we mentioned the Buddhist historian Ilyon (1206-1289) who wrote a brief biography of Wonhyo in *Sam Kuk Yusa* (A History of Three Kingdoms). Among the theoreticians, the kingdom of Koryo produced Chinul (1158-1210), who attempted to revive the Buddhist theology of Wonhyo. He emphasized the combination of Sun (Zen) practice and Amita Buddhism, so as to purify the already declining Buddhism of the time.

The Buddhism of the Yi Dynasty fumbled its way into darkness as the dynasty adopted neo-Confucianism as its state ideology. This course of events was in a way natural outcome of the moral corruption of Koryo Buddhism. For five centuries (1392-1910) the Yi Dynasty abided by its anti-Buddhist policy except during the reigns of Kings Sejo, Myungjong and Sunjo, when short-lived attempts were made to revive national Buddhism. The religious activities of Buddhist monks were suppressed, and Buddhist temples were chased out of the city areas and exiled into the remote mountains. In the earlier period of the Yi Dynasty there were some great monks, like Daetong, Powoo, Hyujung (Susan), Yujung (Samyung) and Kaksung. But in the latter half of the period the Buddhist order and various sects declined even further, and endless disputes among Buddhists were such that they had to be satisfied with mere survival.

During the ups and downs of Korean Buddhism under the Koryo and Yi Dynasties, Korean Buddhism has been characterized as Pure Land Buddhism. Pure Land Buddhism has usually been contrasted with the Sun (or Zen) Buddhism of China, Japan and Korea. The major characteristic of the Pure Land Buddhism is a prayer-offering religion, and its prayers are called Yumbul (Nembutsu in Japanese) saying Namiami Tah'bul (Nami-amidabutsu in Japanese). The prayers give homage to the Amita Buddha, the compassionate Kwanum Buddha. And this has been regarded as the Buddhism of the Korean minjung, praying for material blessings as well as earthly success, as they do with shaman prayers to the spirits.

Since the earliest time of Korean Buddhism, a major dispute among the Buddhist scholars has been the apparent difference between Sun (or Zen) and Pure Land Buddhism. Many have attempted to unify the two, or at least see a coherence between them. Nevertheless, in Korean Buddhism, these two "practices" often are combined in one temple and practised by the same monk, sometimes harmoniously, sometimes rather awkwardly. Buddhist scholars like Professor Sung-Bae Park recognize the differences between the two. But Park thinks that "one of the gravest misinterpretations of Buddhist doctrine in the history of Buddhism is to say that ch'an (Zen) is the supreme teaching for the highest level of people, whereas Pure Land is designed for the lower level of people who are incapable of meditation."[18]

Park thinks that the differences between Sun Buddhism and Pure Land Buddhism are only external. Pure Land or Amita Buddhism is an "other power" (or Tariki in Japanese) Buddhism in which the believer depends entirely on the grace of Amitabha Buddha, the lord of Pure Land. Sun Buddhism, which advocates meditation and self-discipline, puts great emphasis on enlightenment by the strenuous effort of an individual, that is by "self-power" (Jiriki in Japanese). Pure Land stresses that faith is an inspiration given by the grace of Amitabha Buddha in her compassion for the ignorant minjung. Sun Buddhism does not rely on the grace or compassion of Buddha, but on self-enlightenment through meditation. Sun concentrates on "the volitional aspects of faith, like resoluteness, conviction, and stedfastness, as well as the cognitive aspects," the belief that one's own mind is Buddha himself.[19]

Pure Land has to do with the purely emotional aspects of faith, and it requires wholehearted love and devotion to Amitabha Buddha. Believers offer earnest prayers to Amita for a better and happier life. The strongest expression of Pure Land as a means to be born into the land of pure (Pure Land), through love and devotion to Amita, was developed by the Japanese saint Shinran (1173-1262). Shinran emphasized the total powerlessness of a person to effect his own salvation, and the complete reliance on Amitabha Buddha's primal vows to save all sentient beings. Shinran went so far as to say that one's faith in Amita is the sole cause of salvation, and that faith is aroused not by one's own willpower, but only through the grace of Amita Buddha. A believer's faith may be aroused when he sincerely and devoutly recites the name of Amitabha, Namiamu-Tabul,Kwanseum-Boh'sal. This is the Yumbul (Nembutsu in Japanese) that can be heard at the Buddhist temples in the most remote mountains in Korea.

A way for the minjung to obtain salvation was provided by the compassionate Amita Buddha herself. It is clearly shown in the *Treatise on Awakening Mahayana Faith*, of which Wonhyo was one of the greatest interpreters:

> Suppose there is a man who learns this teaching for the first time and wishes to seek the correct faith but lacks courage and strength. Because he lives in this world of suffering, he fears that he will not always be able to meet the Buddhas and honor them personally, and that, faith being difficult to perfect, he will be inclined to fall back. He should know that the Tathagatas have an excellent expedient means by which they can protect his faith; that is, through the strength of wholehearted meditation on the Buddha, he will in fulfillment of his wishes be able to be born in the Buddhahood beyond, to see the Buddha always, and to be forever separated from the evil states of existence. It is as the Sutra says: if a man meditates wholly on Amitabha Buddha in the world of the Western Paradise and wishes to be born in that world, directing all the goodness he has cultivated, then he will be born there. [20]

Clearly Amita Buddha is for the minjung who "fears that he will not always be able to meet the Buddhas and honor them personally,"because"he lives in this world of suffering."

6. Amitabha and Maitreya Buddhism

Those who critcize Korean Buddhism from within and advocate reform

Unju Miruk (Maitreya) II, Hong Song-Dam

almost unanimously attack the "secularism" of Pure Land practice which falls back on prayer offerings and meaningless repetition of the Yumbul citation. One of the most representative of them was Han Yong-un (1879-1944) who in 1910 wrote a book entitled *An Essay on the Restoration of Korean Buddhism* in which he criticized severely Pure Land Buddhism in Korea. He even went so far to advocate that the Recitation Hall (Yumbul-dang) in the Pure Land temples should be abolished.

Han Yong-un, who was the only Buddhist who joined the Christian leaders in the signing of the Sam-il (March 1st) declaration of Independence of 1919, has been regarded as the modern seer of the Korean Buddhist reform movement. His criticism of Amita Buddhism in Korea is based upon his strong belief in Sun Buddhism, and he was concerned about the way in which the Korean minjung have been led into the shamanistic-Buddhistic faith. According to Professor Sung-Bae Park, in Korea there has never been a sect *per se* of Pure Land Buddhism. What Park tries to say is that there certainly has been Pure Land practice, but there has been no Pure Land Buddhism sect as such. Park recognizes, though reluctantly, that there is "a strong undercurrent of Pure Land practice," today in Korean Buddhism. He says:

> This undercurrent is still in evidence today. For example, it is a well-known fact that in almost all monasteries and temples in Korea today, the recitation of the name of Amitabha Buddha, which is considered a standard ritual of Buddhist life, is sometimes practised with the sincere desire to be born in the Pure Land. Furthermore, frequently there is a harmonious combination of Sun and Pure Land practice in Korea. For example, if a Sun master were to give a sermon during the course of which was uttered an impressive Sun poem, the audience might respond by reciting in unison the name of Amitabha Buddha in order to create a sublime feeling within the assembly.[21]

Actually, the Pure Land Buddhism practice of reciting devoutly the name of Amita in the murmuring of Yumbul is mixed with shamanistic practice. The Korean minjung come to the Buddhist temple, out of their suffering in life and out of their life of *han*, in order to resolve their *han*-ridden life by murmuring deep inside their psyche the compassionate grace of Buddha himself. When they offer prayers to the Kwanse-um Bosal, they turn their burden over to the compassionate Buddha, whose infinite grace they deeply trust.

The shamanization of Korean Buddhism is most discreet, but it cannot be hidden. A visitor to a Buddhist temple in Korea, large or small, will find three basic buildings in the temple compound. The largest at the center is usually the meditation or recitation hall where Buddha statues and Amita statues are placed. A smaller building adjacent to the main hall (Dae Ung-Jun) is usually the hall for the dead, where the dead are remembered and prayed for. The smallest, almost hidden behind the other buildings in the temple ground, is usually a hall for shaman spirits—the seven-star spirits or the mountain spirits. This smallest building has no Buddha statue to speak of, but it is the most popular place in the entire temple grounds.

A study reveals examples of temples without a main hall, but every temple has a shaman hall where the seven-star spirit was venerated. [22] It is quite usual to find temples without a hall for the dead on the premises. There are mainly three types of religious activities which take place in a Buddhist temple: (1) celebration of Buddha's birthday and other Buddha worship services; (2) family memorial services on the 49th and 100th day of the dead, or funeral services for the dead buried in the temple ground, in accordance with the Buddhist rituals for the dead; and (3) various prayer meetings for childbirth, for wealth, for success and for the general well-being of a family. The people of Korea go to a Buddhist temple for the most part to pray for the good life in this world. The minjung of Korea go to the Buddhist temples to release their *han* in this world of suffering and pain.

In spite of the shamanization of Korean Buddhism, there remains a *Boddhisattva* ideal in traditional Buddhism in which Buddha himself comes to the world to save the sentient beings, including the minjung and the lowest sectors of human society. The Korean minjung cling to this *Boddhisattva* ideal, which is meaningful to the *han*-ridden minjung of Korea.

Along with this *Boddhisattva* ideal of Buddhism, and the Amitabha worship of Pure Land in Korea, there has also existed an undying hope in Maitreya Buddha. According to the story, Maitreya was one of the ten most loved disciples of Buddha who passed away before the master. Maitreya Buddha is revered as the future Buddha, the Buddha of hope, who will come to this world to work for the suffering minjung at the end of salvation history. Maitreya is called the Buddha of love and compassion who was incarnate in the world for suffering mankind.

Since Maitreya died rather young, during Buddha's own lifetime, in statues Maitreya is depicted as young and handsome. He will come again to this world as a vigorous young Buddha to save the suffering people of minjung. At the end of the history of the Buddhist world, Maitreya will lead the future messianic world of *Yong Hwa*, which is the hope of the suffering minjung. Maitreya Buddha is commissioned to save the minjung who have not been included in the salvation of the Buddha himself. Maitreya is thus the Buddha of the end of the times, the future Buddha or eschatological

Buddhahood. Buddha will be completed and the world will be consummated in Maitreya Buddhahood.

According to Wonhyo's fragments on Maitreya, there are three levels of Maitreya worship: (1) the highest level people encounter Maitreya through their deepest meditation; (2) the middle level encounter him either through meditation or through the good works of *karma*; and (3) the lowest level people meet Maitreya through good works and prayer offerings.[23] Maitreya Buddhism, however, has been popular among the lowest level of people through *yumbul* and devout prayer offerings to the Maitreya Buddha. Maitreya Buddhism is minjung Buddhism.

It is interesting to note that contemporary Buddhist monks in Korea are introducing Maitreya as the Buddha of the minjung, an alternative to the Amitabha faith. Mr. Pyo says in his most recent essay that in the past Amitabha Buddhism was imposed upon minjung of Korea by the ruling classes, in order to pacify them and make them satisfied with the present Buddha state, so that they would not revolt against the ruler. But Maitreya has given the people hope for the future, aspiration for a better world, and inspiration for the possibility of the realizing a better world in history.[24] He believes that through the inspiration and ideals of future Buddha of Maitreya, the minjung will become aware of hope for a future world,which will produce revolutionary faith to change the world. Historically, Maitreya Buddhism prevalent in the lost people of Paek'che made it possible for them to rise against the Silla kingdom. This is an historical example in which faith in Maitreya ignited the revolutionary fire against the dominating power of the time.

Kyum Ik, a Paek'che monk who went to India to study Indian Buddhism, initiated and propagated the Maitreya ideal in the nation. For the people of Paek'che under the dominant foreign power of Silla, Maitreya Buddhism was the religious force behind the political independence of the country in the West (of the peninula). A huge Maitreya Buddha statue, standing in the great rice-producing fertile country of what is now Korea's Chulla province, testifies to the aspiration of the Paek'che minjung for independence and national salvation. Faith in Maitreya is not just an individual hope for a future life after death, but a realistic hope and dream for a better world on the horizon of history itself. Hope in Maitreya was a promise for the present, and a critical vision of the future.

Maitreya is not only an object of hope for the minjung in this world for a better world in history. Maitreya is also an image of the minjung themselves. As Maitreya is to be the subject and master of history at the end of history, the minjung is the subject and master of history. As Maitreya statues are scattered around country roadsides, and no one seems to pay any attention to them, the minjung are depicted as the least among people, scattered around the roadside of history, as it were. There is no artistic refinement in the statues of Maitreya. But this Maitreya is the hope of the future. In it lies the messianic hope for the future and a revolutionary vision. Faith in Maitreya is faith in a minjung revolution, a better world. Maitreya is the hope for the future of the minjung in Korea.

A new Buddhism has to come. That is the urgent faith of Maitreya Buddhism. With the coming of Maitreya, the minjung longs for the new world—the new earth and new heaven. For with the coming of the Maitreya, the minjung of Korea would participate in the revolution of the world. In this aspiration, we find the roots of minjung theology in Korea. For the love of minjung, we find the love of Buddha in a thousand forms of *Boddhisattva*. In the *Boddhisattva* ideal of Buddhism, we find the cultural roots of minjung theology. In Amitabha Buddhism and people's devout worship and offering, we find the *han*-ridden minjung of Korea.

Now with Korean Buddhists, Korean Christians could join in saying, "Come O Maitreya!"

In the Fields, Lee Chul-Su

Encounter, Lee Chul-Su

6 MASK DANCE OF LIBERATION[1]

1. CCA Assembly Logo: A Korean Dance Mask

The Preparatory Study Booklet of the CCA Seoul Assembly is covered with a round figure which is striking, strange, and yet attractive and puzzling. The figure is the logo for the 8th Assembly of the CCA. Inside the cover there is this explanation about the figure:

This logo . . . is the work of the Korean artist, Lee Chul Soo. He draws his basic inspiration from the mask of the character *Maltugi* in the popular Korean folk dance *Bongsan Talchum* (masked dance). . . . The artist has superimposed the Cross on the traditional mask motif. . . .

The figure is strange to Koreans, because it is a combination of the cross *and* the dance mask. Koreans have never seen the sign of the cross on the forehead of the *maltugi* mask before. Also, the figure is striking and strange to Christians, because the cross is not very obvious, and it is set in an unfamiliar figure.

The booklet editor explains to us that "even though the boat is not in the picture, the logo is also suggestive of the familiar ecumenical symbol of the Cross on a boat riding on the waves of the sea." This is to say that our logo is brave enough to get rid of the "ecumenical boat," (not because none of you delegates came to Korea on the boat), but because the wave-like lines represent the angry and sad face of the minjung at one time, and the smiling and laughing face of the minjung at another time, depending on how one perceives the mask of *Maltugi.*

2. The Stage

The time of performance is at night. The place of the mask dance is usually in the center of the village, where the market is open during the day, and to which village people and peddlers come, from near and far, for selling and buying. Mask dance performances usually take place around the harvest time, so there is enough food and lots to drink. The village square is lighted with a campfire for warmth and a bonfire for the stage lights. Already the village children are arriving at the invitation of the music—gongs and cymbals.

The people begin to gather around the village center, where they form a big circle to the music and dancing of the actors and actresses. Quickly more people—village *yangban* aristocrats and farmers, women and men, old and young, join in. The actors and actresses are already behind their masks, therefore nobody knows who they are, and nobody should know who they are. Everyone will have great fun. After all, this is a village festival time, this is a part of the festivity. Tonight's dancing team is really great, and some people are already moving their shoulders up and down a little to the rhythms of the dance music.

Presently all the members of the mask dance team are dancing around the big circle of the people, to the loud music. The people are shouting, the dancers' morale is very high, and the stage is set for a play. Well, it is time for a big play. One of the players announces the opening in a loud voice, and the people shout with joy, accompanied by the sound of gongs and cymbals.

3. Act I: Religion and Minjung

The first act is the liberation of a Buddhist religious leader. The people call the first act *Nojang,* "old monk," *ma'dang,* "ground." First, the old monk is brought in by the younger monks. This monk is regarded as pure and well-disciplined, out of this secular world, having lived almost all of his life in the mountain. He is a noble mystic, a highly respected religious figure. His discipline and his otherworldly ascetic life is very evident in his mask: his mask is black, dirty and covered with flies' filthy white spots. The *Nojang,* the old monk, won't respond to the young monks who are making irreverent remarks and joking about his appearance. The young monks loudly sing vulgar songs, but the old monk will not respond. He is impotent and almost dead. So the young monks even sing a requiem mass to arouse his interest, but he is deadly unmoving. He has nothing to do with the people or for the people.

Finally, the young monks decide to bring in a pretty young girl to move our old reverend monk. The pretty young girl is a reputed young shaman, the *mudang* girl, who is a sorceress, a fortune teller, and an exorcist. If the old Buddhist monk is the practitioner of an imported foreign religion, then the young shaman girl is the practitioner of the traditional Korean religion of the people, the minjung.

At the sight of this pretty, white-faced little *mudang* girl, the impotent, otherworldly ascetic reverend monk of ours gets stirred. He moves. He gets up. He walks around the girl. And he starts dancing. Now he has come alive. The old monk seduces the shaman girl to dance with him. They dance together, they dance beautifully and their dance movement becomes dynamic and powerful like the rest of the minjung mask dancers. The old monk gives up his most precious religious property, his beads, to her as a wedding gift. As she accepts the gift, the dance reaches a climax.

The village people now become frantic. They laugh and boo. They laugh at the old monk; they are laughing at the old reverend monk, because it is incongruous for a religious person to be so easily seduced by a little *mudang* girl. What a hypocrite he is! After all, he was acting like a dead person, an ascetic, a mystic, a noble religious personage. But inside him all this time, there was that dark and suppressed desire, the *id,* the life, the possessiveness, the thirst, the *samudaya,* the humanity. In the people's laughter we observe the downfall of the sacred, the reverend monkhood, the priestly authorities and dignities. Some people clap their hands as the old monk and the *mudang* girl dance around the ground as a happy couple. But some people boo, and they seem to show their anger at the breakdown of reverend monkhood, its

No Title, Hong Song-Dam

fall to the ground in front of the people who take religion rather seriously.

The Dead Monk: Irrelevancy

What are we to make of it? Are we to laugh with the people in the crowd, and be happy for the monk? Are we as the Christian people, to be insulted and angry at the bizarre scene of the senile Buddhist monk? Or shall we just leave the scene quietly and not be bothered by it?

A colleague of mine, Professor Hyun Yong-hak, has made the following comments about this scene:

> This Nojang represents a senile spirituality and a metaphysical religion that is separated from this world and thus is unproductive. As such, the value and leadership of this so-called 'higher' religion is the target of jokes, satire, and laughter.[2]

My respectable Christian theologian friend would laugh at the monk with the people. Religion is a big joke; it is powerless, irrelevant, meaningless and unproductive for this world of ours. Like the almost-dead monk, our religions are dead. It would have been better for the old monk to stay in the deep mountain and die quietly without disturbing the world. The people are laughing at the senile monk and booing the scene, because they know the inside of religious people–their hypocrisy, moral corruption, and seduction by evil spirits.

In the laughter and booing of the minjung in the crowd, we hear the angry voice of Jesus as he shouted at the lawyers and Pharisees:

> Alas for you . . . hypocrites! You are like tombs covered with whitewash; they look well from outside, but inside they are full of dead men's bones and all kinds of filth. So it is with you: outside you look like honest men, but inside you are brimfull of hypocrisy and crime (Matt. 23:27-28).

Jesus, with the minjung, pointed out clearly the "brim-fullness of hypocrisy and crime" in our religion. The lawyers and Pharisees, they are clean—they wash when they walk into a house. They wash their hands immaculately. They never touch unclean food. They observe the Sabbath faithfully, to the letter of the law. They are clean and righteous in appearance and in terms of the law. But inside, they are filthy and they smell like the inside of a tomb, like a dead person's grave. Their legalism has trapped them. Washing hands becomes more important in legalistic religion than dirtying your hands to help your neighbors in trouble. Ascetic practice becomes more important in legalistic religious ethics than moving your live body as you work in the world to bring about the kingdom of God. Observing the Sabbath becomes more and more important in the legalistic religion—more than saving the trapped sheep, or feeding the hungry people.

The minjung in the crowd watching the old monk in the Korean masked dance are making fun of a dead religion which is irrelevant and meaningless to the world and to them. At the time of the late 18th century and early 19th century of Korea, when a village-to-village market economy was slowly emerging to form a "modern" society, and when the consciousness of the minjung was slowly rising in a feudalistic society, through the plays of masked dances, the Korean minjung came out to pronounce the death of the old monk, the meaninglessness of the old religion. Perhaps we have already announced the irrelevancy of our old traditional religions in Asia when we adopted the new religion from the West. But can we claim that our new religion is vital and powerful and meaningful and relevant in our Asian world? Or can we say with confidence that it may be true that Christianity is dying out and irrelevant in the West and in the first world, but that is not the case in the East and in the third world? Our Christianity is only one hundred years old, and therefore, do we have the right to say that our Christianity is young and vital?

The young martyr theologian, Dietrich Bonhoeffer, announced from his Nazi prison cell the passing of religion in a world that had come of age. We are now wondering how he could be so naively faithful and optimistic about the world as he faced his own death and the destruction of the world from the war. It is rather ironical to hear the announcement of the passing of religion in Asia in a new light–the world come of age through "economic development." It is not the case that—since Asia is developing economically and technologically—God is no more needed and religion is not that impor- tant. Nor is it the case that religions in Asia are powerless in helping and pushing the nations' economic and technological development. Rather we look powerlesss against the force of "development ideologies," and we cannot cope with the problems of the world.

Will our religious spirituality feed the hungry people in Asia? Can we deal with the problems of child labor and low wage earners in the multina- tional corporation factories? Can we deal with the police brutality against the peaceful demonstrators? Can we cope with the nuclear armaments which are scattered around Asia to protect peace in the first world? Can we put dreams and visions of the kingdom of God in the minds and eyes of the Asian youth, concretely, in terms of politics and in terms of socio-economic systems? The young monks in our masked dance drag out the old monk to respond and do something for the world.

Life in the World

This scene of the old Monk being dragged out into the world has an historical precedent. This scene is not just to laugh at, nor merely to mock and judge the priesthood of a Buddhist monk. It is to depict the secularization of a religion, a meditative religion coming into the world, the real world where there are sins, temptations, agonies, moral conflicts and social struggles. This scene of the old monk being dragged out into the world reminds us of the famous Korean Buddhist monk, Wonhyo, the greatest Korean Buddhist scholar-monk the ancient Silla kingdom (57 BC-AD 778) ever produced. I suspect that the old monk scene in the mask dance is a dramatization of his life. I have already discussed him at length in the preceding chapter. But it is important to reiterate here that Wonhyo saw no difference between the sacred and the profane. The holy and the secular are the same mind; the Buddha is all sentient beings and the minjung; life and death are one and the same; and *dukkha* and *nirvana* are one and the same. For the first time in Korean Buddhism, it is realized that the profane world and the secular world of suffering where the minjung live, are at the same time the world of Buddha which is sacred and holy, the blessed world of *nirvana* itself.

Wonhyo insisted upon the secularization of Buddhism, and practised what he preached by taking off his Buddhist robe and putting on the secular clothing of the ordinary people. He dragged himself to the secular world. He took off his beads, and he lived among the minjung and mixed with them in their drinking places and their gathering places. He met a clown on the street and took a gourd from him. And he sang and danced around the streets with the clown, making music by beating the gourd.

In the secular world with the minjung, he wanted to realize freedom and the *Boddhisattva* ideals. And he wanted to liberate minjung from their ignorance and suffering. He sang and danced like the minjung themselves. He drank and talked with them in the minjung bars and in their homes and on the streets. His language was vulgar and his acts unheard of for a respectable monk.

We can imagine how people gossipped about him, and how they laughed about his actions, and how many people would have been indignant about his way of practicing religion, as in our mask dance scene of the old monk. Wonhyo married a widow and thus broke his vow of chastity, as our old monk in the mask dance married a pretty little shaman girl. Are we to laugh at the monk? Or are we to boo at our old monks Nojang and Wonhyo? Are we passing judgment on Wonhyo and our Nojang in the mask dance, because both of them broke their vows of chastity? Are we to shout at them because they were hypocrites? In our laughter, are we not welcoming our Nojang's coming into the world, coming alive like a human being with life, joy and all that there is to life with a young shaman girl?

To Break Down the Idols

Irrelevancy of religion is ironically connected with a form of idolatry. In order to make something relevant, one tries to make that an idol. It is human tendency to make an unimportant thing absolute, and to try to dwell in it and feel secure and comfortable. The more one tries to make a thing relevant and legitimate, the more one tends to make it an idol. We human beings are idol-makers and thus we are called *homo religios*.

However, at the center of Christian religion there is this strong denial of idols. The first and second commandments demand the complete denial of all images and all idols, "or any likeness of anything that is in heaven above, or that is in the earth beneath, of that is in the water under the earth" (Exodus 20:4, *RSV*). As Paul Tillich understands, the cross is the iconoclastic sign; it is to destroy anything and anyone that absolutizes itself before God. The Cross is to destroy anything–any earthly power or even religion that claims to be absolute, standing over the heads of the people.

Matthew reports to us very vividly that when Jesus on the Cross gave a loud cry, and breathed his last, "at that moment the curtain of the temple was torn in two from top to bottom" (Matt.27:50-51, *NEB*). When Jesus was forced to bow down before the devil of the political power, he declared decisively, "You shall do homage to the Lord your God and worship him alone" (Matt. 4:10, *NEB*). Jesus was through and through iconoclastic: he did not wash his hands before he ate; he defended humanitarian works on the Sabbath; he was the friend of sinners, tax collectors and prostitutes; he talked with unclean women and sinful women; and even more unpardonably, he announced that he would destroy the holy temple of Jerusalem.

The boos and laughter of our minjung in the Korean mask dance ring with this iconoclasm. The minjung are tearing down the religion that has been lording it over their minds and spirit. Our minjung crowd in the mask dance is experiencing the destruction of the religious idols. They feel now their own sense of freedom as they ridicule their religious master–the old monk who is falling down in the arms of a pretty little shaman girl.

We must recognize that one of the most serious religious problems of our time in Asia is idol-making and idol-worshipping. Certainly, missionary Christianity in Asia was, and has been from the beginning, a powerful idol-breaker. The Christian missionaries urged the natives in Asia to destroy whatever devils, gods, and spirits we have had. Koreans burned down the precious ancestor tablets to be obedient to the commandments, and as a consequence, they themselves were burned and beheaded by the Confucian authorities. Korean Christians burned down shaman shrines and "spirit decorations" in and out of the house, only to be chased out of the family and become alienated from the traditional society. Korean Christianity has grown up, so to speak, on the debris of the broken idols of Old Korea. We are deeply proud of this iconoclastic tradition in Asian Christianity.

But at the same time, we are wondering if we are now making Christian idols. Are we not still hanging on to the good old religion that the missionaries brought to us some centuries ago? Are we not making their way of life, their songs, their music, their liturgy, their church life, their preaching, and their ideologically biased theology, our idols? Do we not worship our missionary gods? Our missionaries enforced their gods with the authority of the Bible. As we accepted the missionary gods as our idols we also made the Bible an idol.

Sallie MacFague, a feminist theologian, sharply pointed out that the basic problem of the crisis in religious language is its idolatry. She says:

> The Bible, says this movement (of religious conservatism), *is* the Word of God; the Bible is inerrant or divinely inspired, the words and images of the Bible are the authoritative and appropriate words and images for God. The Bible is a sacred text, different from all other texts, and not relative and pluralistic as are all other human products. The Bible becomes an idol: the fallible, human words of Scripture are understood as referring correctly and literally to God. Even where these sentiments are not expressed clearly or in such extreme fashion, religious literalism remains a powerful current in our society. [3]

In our Asian culture and Asian Christian culture, we certainly destroyed primitive shaman artifacts and idols, but we have replaced them with the gold-trimmed, leather-bound Bible. Although we have done away with the rote memorization of the Confucian letters and Buddhist sutras, now we cling to the letters and the proof texts of the Bible. We do not read the Bible open-heartedly with the inspiring Spirit of the Lord, but we do obey and worship the printed letters and translated and (sometimes mistranslated) words in the Bible. As the Bible became an idol, it is no wonder that women look still inferior, morally and spiritually, to men; that women are seen as the ones who brought sin into this world and history, and therefore, believed unfit to speak up in the church or to be ordained.

We have made ourselves so absolute, standing over against other religious idols of Asia, that we cannot speak to other religions of Asia. As we have destroyed other religious idols of Asia, we must now destroy our own idols in the Christian religion, in order for us to talk with our genuine religious traditions in Asia. As we try to transform ourselves in Asian religious and cultural soil and in our contemporary Asian social and political situation, we must come down from the seats of Christian idols and talk with other religions and work with Asian religious friends side by side.

To Free the Gold-Crowned Jesus

The now-famous Korean poet Kim Chi Ha has depicted our Christian idol-making in his poetic play, *The Gold-Crowned Jesus.* In the play the statue of Jesus in concrete, with a gold crown on his head, pleads in tears to the beggar, the helpless leper and the prostitute:

> I have been closed up in this stone for a long,
> long time, . . . entombed in this dark, lonely,
> suffocating prison. I have longed to talk with
> you, the kind and poor people like yourself, and
> share your sufferings.

The leper asks the gold-crowned Jesus: "Who put you in prison? Tell me who they are."

> Jesus: You know them well. They are like the Pharisees.
> They locked me in a shrine for their own gain. They
> pray, using my name in a way that prevents my reaching
> out to poor people like yourself. In my name, they
> nailed me down to the cross again.
>
> They boast about being my disciples, but they are
> egotistical, they cannot trust each other, they do
> not suffer loneliness, and they are without wisdom,
> like those who first crucified me . . .
>
> It is the same with those without courage who are
> unwilling to resist such evildoers as dictators and
> other tyrants who inflict great suffering on the weak
> and poor. Prayer alone is not enough; it is necessary

also to act.

Only those, though very poor and suffering like
yourself, who are generous in spirit and seek to
help the poor and the wretched, can give me life
again. You have helped give me life again.

You removed the gold crown from my head and so freed
my lips to speak. People like you will be my
liberators.

The leper is honest : ". . . I am helpless (pointing to his crippled body).
I cannot even take care of myself. How then can I help you?"

But Jesus insists:

It is for that exact reason that you *can* help me. You
are the *only* one who can do it . . . It is your poverty,
your wisdom, your generous spirit and, even more, your
courageous resistance against injustice that makes
all this possible . . . .

The gold-crowned idol Jesus shouts at the minjung—the beggar,the leper
and the prostitute—to set him free. "Come closer, come closer and liberate
now my body. . . . Remove this prison of cement . . . . Be of courage. Remove
the cement quickly. Hurry, or I will suffocate. I already feel constricted.
Hurry, so that I may overcome this feeling, and present myself before the
people, refreshed and resuscitated. . . Hurry, Hurry!"[4]
Jesus was liberated by the poor and oppressed in this play, and Jesus was
locked up in the cement block by the rich and powerful. The minjung set
Jesus free to serve the minjung. Only the minjung could liberate the gold-
crowned Jesus, so that he could come to live with the minjung and work
among the minjung in this world, in this secular world. This is a challenging
message to us Christians in Asia to be liberated from our own idol-making.
We have been challenged to come out of the gold-crowned church buildings,
and we are called to destroy the shining gold crosses on which we have nailed
Jesus so that he can not move and can not speak. The Apostle Paul declares
that the cross he glorifies is "the Cross of our Lord Jesus Christ, by which the
world has been crucified to me, and I to the world" (Galatians 6:14). Indeed,
the Cross of our Lord Jesus Christ urges us to die to the world. If we are to

die to the world as disciples of Christ Jesus, we will be free in Christ Jesus to serve the world. The direction of freedom and service is to come down from our *status quo* and statues and church towers. It is to come out of the holy of holies. It is to take off the gold crown. It is to die to the world and to serve the minjung.

4. Act II: Maltugi, the Hero

Our hero Maltugi shows up in the second scene of our mask dance play. The second scene is sometimes called the Yangban or village landlord scene, but the actual hero of the scene is our Maltugi. "Yangban" in Korean means the highest social class with the highest education. The members of the Yangban are supposed to have passed the state civil examinations in the difficult and respectable Chinese letters, not in the vulgar Korean language. They are the ones who receive land free from the king, and by inheritance they are the largest landowners. The magistrate of a village comes from this class. They do not have to work. They are the masters of the nation and the landlords in the village. They are the political rulers. In short, they are the most powerful people.

Maltugi, the servant of the three Yangban brothers, leads them onto the stage. Maltugi announces the arrival of the Yangban brothers, who look noble with their white robes on.

> Maltugi: "Hear, hear, the Yangban are here. But don't think these Yangban are real scholars or great statesmen. They are nothing . . . .
> Yangban: "What did you say?"
> Maltugi: "Oh, I only said that the most respected brothers of the great statesmen are here . . . .

Maltugi ridicules the yangban brothers, who pretend to be dignified. When the yangban brothers cannot hear, or pretend not to have heard Maltugi's ridicule, the crowd at the mask dance laugh loudly. In the mask dance, the people in the crowd are ready to take sides with Maltugi and ready to laugh at the "false" dignity of their ruling masters.

Maltugi's ridicule and the yangban brothers' reprimand are repeated, first on the false (but correct) introduction of the yangban brothers by Maltugi. And then Maltugi shouts at the people in the crowd to make themselves at home, to smoke their long stemmed pipes and be merry. But smoking and making noise before the yangban are forbidden to the low-class people. Maltugi speaks out as he wants with the people, but in front of his masters, he has to say what his masters order him to say. Maltugi's language is vulgar and mocking.

The yangban brothers ask Maltugi where he has been. Maltugi's answer is that he has been to the Seoul house of the yangban brothers. In those days, some of the less able yangban were sent out to the countryside, to less important government positions, to work and live even without their wives or families. Maltugi's Seoul trip is to show that these yangban brothers are lesser officials, so that they want all the more to show their false dignity to the people. But Maltugi answers the yangban brothers "Where have *you* been, brothers? I was looking for you all over the world. So I went to your Seoul house and found your wife all alone. I did it many times. As I was leaving after a hearty feast, your wife gave me a penis as a gift." The yangban brothers protest and beat him. But Maltugi corrects himself: "No, no, your wife gave me a stick of dried fish."

Then the yangban brothers order Maltugi to provide a place for them to have fun. The yangban brothers are totally dependent upon the slave Maltugi. And Maltugi has to provide the place to stay, and food for them to eat but these things have to come from the people. Maltugi has to exploit his fellow minjung to make living for the yangban brothers. When the yangban brothers order him to provide a place for them to have fun, Maltugi answers, making a big circle in the sky with his whip: "I have this beautiful house that has a huge window open to heaven." This is another way of saying that there is no place and no decent shelter for them.

Maltugi is sick and tired of the yangban brothers. He is resisting them. In the mask dance, the first reaction of Maltugi towards the yangban brothers is resistance, disobedience, and if not hostility, then mockery or vulgar language. The people in the audience laugh at the yangban brothers' false dignity and actual impotence, but with Maltugi their feeling of resistance against their landlords and oppressive masters is burning deep inside their guts. Now Maltugi and his minjung audience become one in expressing their deep-seated *han*, the unresolved angry feeling of injustice and hunger, deeply stored in their hearts and stomachs.

This is the moment they become critical of the existing order and social system. As they shout with Maltugi in the mask dance, they let out their *han*, their frustration, and their desire for resistance. Professor Cho Dong Il, one of the Korean mask dance critics, observes:

> The yangban with their status oppress the minjung, but the minjung want

to be liberated from oppression. Although the minjung could not deny completely the *status quo* of the yangban, the minjung work for their final victory. This theme of resistance in the mask dance is in a sense a historical reflection of 19th century Korea. The yangban lose the battle at the end because of their greedy attachment to their empty dignity and power.[5]

There is this *han* that is expressed in tears and in sobbing and weeping. But Maltugi's *han* expressed in the mask dance is shouting, laughing, mocking, telling lies and resisting. *Han*, the deep feeling turned inside, is coming out into the open. The minjung in the audience join with Maltugi in shouting for a fight, the fight against injustice and oppression. In the mask dance play, Maltugi is no longer a subservient slave boy; he is an independent fighter ready to resist and to cut the vicious circle of oppression. In the laughter and shouts of the minjung audience, we hear the voice of the minjung for liberation; we sense a storm coming.

No wonder, under the Japanese colonial rule, that village mask dance performances were prohibited. No wonder that even the Korean authorities stopped our student mask dance performances, for the reason that the mask dance performance would lead to anti-government demonstrations. The Maltugi performance is a dangerous political play. Maltugi could become a resistance leader in a farm rebellion. The authorities today know what the mask dance-performing students are doing, and they know that it is dangerous because it criticizes the *status quo*, and conscientizes the people. For as Professor Cho recognizes: "Mask dances point to the reality as reality critically, and the audience does not act just as onlookers, but they join in as critical participants."[6]

5. CCA Assembly Logo Again: The Cross on the Mask of Maltugi

In his theological reflection on the Korean mask dance, C.S. Song once said:

> A mysterious hand seems bringing together the mask and the cross. The cross transcends its particular space and time to become present in the mask. The mask too seems to break out of its spatial and temporal framework to get transposed into the cross.[7]

But our Korean artist brought the mask of Maltugi and the cross together in his theological imagination, and in his deep faith and hope. Our CCA Assembly logo mask is a unique one, for it bears the cross. It is not that we have converted Maltugi to become Christian. But in our theological imagination, we see Jesus dancing a mask dance with Maltugi mask on. Jesus has put on the mask of the minjung, of Maltugi the slave. And Jesus cannot hide his identity; his Maltugi mask bears the sign of the cross. As C.S. Song has seen--through his participation in the Korean mask dance–that God is dancing the mask dance in the life drama of Jesus. Now we see that Jesus himself is dancing the Maltugi dance, wearing the Maltugi mask.[8]

Our Maltugi has no gold crown on his head. Our Maltugi bears the cross on his head. Our Maltugi is bearing the burdens of the slaves. Our Maltugi is the victim of the system. He is the only one who works for his masters. He has to look after the yangban brothers. He has to look around for the whereabouts of the yangban brothers. He has to provide a place for them to enjoy their life. In short, he has to work like a dog. Yet he is poor, dirty, unlearned and powerless, vulgar and despised. But he is beaten up by his masters whenever he raises his voice against them. Our Maltugi is a suffering servant. It is theologically appropriate that our Maltugi has the cross on his forehead. He is bearing the Cross, and he himself is the cross.

The cross on the mask of Maltugi reminds us of Isaiah 53:

> . . . He had no beauty, no majesty to draw our eyes,
> no grace to make us delight in him;
> his form, disfigured, lost all the likeness of a man
> his beauty changed beyond human resemblance (v.2).

Certainly, the Maltugi mask is no beauty to speak of. And there is no grace in the dancing Maltugi, nor in his speeches, neither in his dealings with the masters. Indeed our Maltugi mask is disfigured and has lost all the likeness of a human being. Maltugi's mask is a suffering face of the cross.

The suffering servant in Isaiah 53 may have been a slave-servant prisoner of Babylon. He was beaten up and tortured by the Babylonian police on the charge that he spread a false rumor that the Babylonian empire would be destroyed by the Persian Empire, and that the time of liberation was imminent. This was a crime against the state. No wonder he was put into prison. But he carried the hope of Israel, of the prisoners and slaves of the Babylonian Empire. He suffered for the people:

> He was afflicted, he submitted to be struck down

> and did not open his mouth;
> he was led like a sheep to the slaughter,
> like a ewe that is dumb before the shearers (v.7).

Our Maltugi is beaten up by the masters because he is accused of spreading false rumors that the yangban brothers are no good and ignorant and powerless and immoral, and that their days are numbered.

But in the dance of Maltugi the audience shout for joy and liberation, because Maltugi finally wins. In the final act of Maltugi, he liberates a wanted criminal, the *Chewbari*. And at the end of the Maltugi scene all five of them, Maltugi, Chewbari, and the three yangban brothers, dance together. The dance is a lively one, a dance of liberation. There is no distinction between the Yangbans and the slave–servants. They are equal now, and all are liberated in dancing.

Jesus Christ with our Maltugi mask liberates us and liberates the minjung, the suffering minjung of Asia and in the world. The suffering Maltugi as the slave-servant with the cross on his forehead will free us, the suffering minjung of the third world. We hear the clear voice of Maltugi with his cross on his forehead, shouting:

> Prepare the way of the Lord,
> make his path straight.

> Every valley shall be filled,
> and every mountain and hill shall be brought low,
> and the crooked shall be made straight,
> and the rough ways shall be made smooth;
> and all flesh shall see the liberation of God (Lk 3:4-6).

Here, Be With Us, Lee Chul-Su

Gong Sound Rejoicing Reunification, Lee Chul-Su

7 THEOLOGY OF REUNIFICATION*

1. Hanshik and Wandering Spirits

Hanshik is a national holiday in Korea. Officially, this day is set aside for people to plant trees over the barren hills. However, only government officials seem to engage in planting trees while the common people use this day to visit the grave sites of their ancestors. This is a day when the people pay tribute to their ancestors by offering them food and drink, planting new flowers and trees in the area surrounding the graves and generally tending to the grass and foliage in the area. There is another memorial holiday which occurs in the first week of June. But this day, unlike *Hanshik*, is in memory of soldiers and other important government figures, but the common people of Korea do not place as much significance on this day as they do on *Hanshik*.

In Chinese characters, the word "hanshik" refers to cold food, or eating cold food. According to Chinese folklore, rainstorms on this particular day were so harsh and strong that they would blow out the cooking fires, and thus the people had to forego cooking the food they ate. So on this day, it is customary to eat cold food. My father used to tell me that the reason cold

---

*A Korean Theology of the Cross and Resurrection

foods are eaten on this day is because you had to work around the grave sites all day long and so you had no time to cook a warm meal.

Eating cold food is no longer a problem for most of us. But millions of people are still unable to visit their ancestors grave yards on the day of *Hanshik* because of the division of the country. There are millions of lost souls still wandering the hills, rivers, valleys, and mountains as *han* -ridden spirits, unable to rest because they lack a place to rest in peace. There are no Confucian or *mudang* priests to care for the wandering spirits who died in the Korean War between 1950 to 1953; killed in the crossfire during the run for refuge, kidnapped or fallen dead on the road to their unknown destiny; or blown up by bombs and scattered all over the countryside. For nearly forty lunar years, forty *Hanshiks* and August lunar holidays of *Chusuk*, no religion has cared for the wandering spirits of these *han*-ridden souls. No priest of *han* is forthcoming on the horizon of Korean history neither to offer food and drinks nor to provide a final resting place in a free and united Korea to these lost souls.

Since *Hanshik* falls on our Christian Easter season, as we contemplate on the death of Jesus Christ on the cross and his Resurrection, we are also compelled to reflect on the death and resurrection of the lost souls who died during the process of national division which has lasted now for four decades. In addition, since *Hanshik* falls on the month of April with the blossoming of azaleas and dog-berries, we think about the student martyrs of the April 19, 1960 Student Revolution as well as the other lives who died throughout the 70's and 80's in order to nurture the blooming of the spring flowers of democracy and freedom. On the arbor day of *Hanshik*, as we plant trees in our small yards, we reflect on the millions of wandering souls all over the hills of Korea. And as we do, we cannot help but think about the cross they had to bear and the cross that we are all bearing—the cross of division imposed on the Korean people. On the Korean holiday of *Hanshik* and the Christian Easter season, during this cruelest month of April, we think of the death and resurrection of the divided people of Korea.

2. The Cross of Division

The cross of division was imposed on the Korean people by the victorious superpowers at the end of the Second World War. The "liberation" of Korea was the beginning of our division. The end of WWII marked the beginning of the Korea War. It is understandable why Germany, an aggressor nation, might be divided after the Second World War. On the other hand, no one seems to know why a victim of the war, like Korea, was divided rather than Japan, the aggressor nation? Opinions regarding the division differ: some contend the division was created because of an ignorance of history; some say that the line of demarcation was drawn in order to disarm the Japanese soldiers; some claim the action was part of U.S. 's imperialistic policy of expansion; and still others assert that division reflects Soviet aggression in the Far East. What is clear, however, is that Koreans did not participate in the decision-making process; the cross of division was imposed on the Korean people by the superpowers. Moreover, the Korean people were innocent of the cross; that is, Koreans received the cross despite the fact that they were innocent of any crimes committed against the world or the superpowers. Thus, the cross of the division is a cross of *han*. (*Han* is a Korean word which describes a deeply imbedded feeling of anger, frustration, and resentment which lies in the deepest subconsciousness of the Korean psyche.)

The millions of people who lost their lives during the Korean War died unfair deaths. Russian lives were not lost defending communism in Russia; but tens of thousands of American lives were sacrificed on the Korean soil in defense of freedom and democracy and millions of Chinese lives were likewise sacrificed in defense of communism. Koreans also fought in the war under the rhetoric of defending freedom and democracy in the south; and in the north to defend communism and the threat of foreign invasion. But, in effect, the war planted the roots of division even further into the soil; partitioning off the north from the south and the south from the north. The war was not faithful to its original intentions of national unification, but rather created a division among the people which was wider and deeper than when the war first began in 1950.

Today, in order to keep this line of division tight and secure, nearly two million soldiers armed with the most deadly, contemporary, and sophisticated weapons systems have besieged the peninsula. In order to maintain this force, we must provide them with the comforts of expensive food, clothing, and housing. We have to purchase the most expensive weapons systems, keep the tanks oiled, repair the trucks and cranes, and keep the guns and artilleries in tiptop shape. We are forced to send our brightest and strongest sons to first-rate military academies only to have them trained in the most advanced forms of technical warfare. The cross of national security and national defense has been imposed on the Korean people of both north and south. Exorbitant defense spending is the greatest barrier to the development of north Korean economy, and one-third of the south's national budget goes annually to defense spending.

Tremendous natural and human resources are being poured into maintaining this line of division. And as if this weren't enough, the people of both north and south Korea live under the constant threat of nuclear weapons which could annihilate the peninsula from the face of the earth. The cross of the division has been forced on innocent travellers aboard airliners carrying the Korean flag. A Korean Air's flight was shot down by the Soviet Air Force in 1983, killing 269 passengers. Then again in November 1987, another Korean airliner was blown up by north Korean terrorists which resulted in the deaths of 115 lives. Wherever we go, we Koreans have to carry the cross of division. Under constant threats of being bombed or kidnapped, we are in fear for our lives.

Another cross of the division borne by south and north Koreans alike is the loss and separation of close family members. When tens of thousands of north Koreans left their homes to begin lives in the south, most left family members behind with only a few words of optimism expressing the hope that they might meet again in a month or two. That month or two has turned into some 500 months. The Korean War forced families to separate and many still do not know the whereabouts of missing family members. Almost everyday, a missing cousin, brother, or sister reunited with family members are seen on television crying tears of joy and anguish. It is even conceivable for a missing father presumed to be dead to suddenly appear during *Hanshik* and disrupt not only the rituals of the ancestor memorial ceremony but the normal routines of life as well. Some 10 million people still live with this kind of uncertainty in their lives separated from family members by the line of division.

In order to maintain the division, north Korea has become one of the most closed totalitarian countries in the world. No letters from south Korea can enter into north Korea and vice versa. No television or broadcast frequencies of the south or north can be picked up on either side of the demarcation line without serious ramifications. No papers, magazines, jokes, not even comic books can be exchanged across this fortified line. Only gunshots, propaganda, curses, and nasty remarks are exchanged between the two sides. Any opening in this eye of the needle across the line of demarcation between the sides for dialogue or personal exchange would only end up being interpreted as a "peace offensive" or result in gross verbal attacks and all-out propaganda warfare by both sides. Nonetheless, the Korean people have not given up hope for widening that eye of the needle and continue to hope that they might perhaps be able to freely cross this line in their lifetime.

Korean democracy itself has been nailed on the cross of division for more than thirty years. A "logic of division" has been created and is now pervasive in all walks of Korean life. The logic of division is used to suppress freedom and democracy. The logic behind tight press control is the division. The reason for the military dictatorships in politics is to make sure national security remains protected and division is kept intact. The justifications for suppressing the labor movement are prevention of north Korean infiltration and preservation of national security. The reasons behind keeping taps on what ministers preach in their churches are again division and national security. The weight of the arguments behind maintaining the national security and anti-communist laws rests on the division. Because of this logic of division, Korean students have been prohibited from reading books on sociological analyses and original texts of Karl Marx. The study of the liberation theologies of Latin America is prohibited except when taught for the sake of criticism. Gutierrez's classic *Liberation Theology* has been banned from university bookstores.

The Korean people, nailed to the cross of division, have been robbed of freedom, justice, and basic human rights. With the red light of division, all creative and critical actions were put to a halt. With the red flag of division, frank intellectual discussions about the division, democracy, human rights, justice, due process, and human dignity were all put to a stop. With the red sign of division, everyone was silenced--even in front of horrendous corruptions and at the cruelest violations of human rights. We have been told that as long as we are nailed to the cross of division, there can be no resurrection of freedom, democracy, and human rights. We are left to die nailed on the cross of division forever.

With clear Christian consciences, we hear the agonizing cry on the cross of division, *Eli, Eli, lama sabachthani?* This cry of *han* is a cry to God from the forsaken people on the cross of division. Has God forsaken the Korean people on the cross of division? When we hear the cries of the cross of division, we feel numb and powerless. We are lost, we do not know how to respond to these cries. We have no theology to help us with the pain and we have no miracles to perform to take down the suffering people from their cross of division. Nor do we possess the spirituality to endure the long years of suffering on the cross of division. Just as the disciples of Christ ran away from the agonizing cry on the cross, so have we been running away from the cries of the Korean people on the cross of the division.

3. Resurrection and the Rice Community

On the traditional Korean holiday of *Hanshik* which comes to us in the cruelest month of April during Easter season, we think of death and resurrection for the dead and the living. If resurrection has only to do with the immortality of the soul, then it has nothing to do with the death of our people on the cross of division. By the same token, it has nothing to do with the death of Jesus Christ on the cross. And if resurrection is something about the occurrence of a life after death and death after life, that is, history in cycle, then it is nothing more than mere vanity, for nothing under the sun will ever be new. Christian resurrection has to do with the resurrection of Jesus Christ and we believe, it has to do with the cross of Jesus. Resurrection opposed death on the cross. In the same way, it is resistance against death on the cross of division. It is the argument against the death on the cross imposed upon us by our oppressors. Resurrection is understood as the rising up against the principalities of death on the cross of division.

A more theological understanding of the resurrection in the context of recent Korean historical developments came from a female undergraduate student. She wrote in one of her school newspapers the following:

> It may seem as if our history is nothing but a continuous series of suffering on the cross without the hope of resurrection . . . But Jesus who died on the cross resurrected to push away the heavy tombstone to create the space for glory and salvation. Resurrection without suffering is as meaningless as death without resurrection. Likewise, the history of death and suffering of this land, this peninsula, is ready for resurrection . . . As we see the deep wounds of the young Jesus which are the suffering of the people on the streets, in the labor situation, at school and in prison, and as we see their wounds become deeper still, we are sure of the dawn of Easter with the battle cry for freedom . . . . (*Idae Hak Bo*, April 4, 1988).

Our students do not give up hope in the midst of the cruelest month of April, because they believe that death and suffering within the struggle for democracy is not altogether meaningless. Right in the middle of their death and suffering, they are able to meet with the risen Lord of the resurrection. In the cries of the people's suffering on the cross of division, we await the dawn of resurrection of the Korean people, and we possess a hope, a desperate hope for overcoming the division.

As long as we, the suffering people of this divided land, view the cross in this historical context, we cannot help but hope for resurrection in our historical future. We cannot stop at the idea that the resurrection of Christ was his own miraculous doing. Nor can we stop at the idea that Christ's resurrection is nothing more than wishful thinking and the memories of His disciples, or even the collective memory of the earliest Christian communities. We have to go beyond the metaphysical idea that resurrection has to do with simply the eternal life of individual souls. Resurrection is the hope of the community of the table; it is the search for people coming together at the Lord's table as a community. Resurrection is eating and drinking together at the same table with the Lord in a community.

Jesus, the risen Lord, meets with two men on the road to Emmaus and shares a conversation with them and breaks bread with them (Lk 24: 13-32). The resurrected Jesus again showed himself by the Sea of Tiberias, when he fed his disciples with fish laid on a charcoal fire (Jn 21: 9-13). The risen Lord showed the scars of the nails on his hands to Thomas (Jn 21: 24-29). And the angels told the apostles to go to the Land of Galilee, the land of suffering and oppression, to meet with the risen Lord (Mk 15:7). The resurrection is to be the memory of the disciples in the community of breaking bread together, and in touching the wounds of Jesus in the world of the suffering Galilee. As the disciples of Jesus Christ, our risen Lord, Korean Christians believe in the resurrection in the hope of bringing together scattered people to the table of the Lord in peace, in justice, and in community. We believe in the resurrection of the divided people from the cross of division, in overcoming division and obtaining resurrection through the reunification of Korea–its land and its people. We believe in the resurrection as the reclaiming of the community. In the resurrected body of Christ, we struggle for the community, the unity and commonwealth of peace with justice.

We would like to see separated families reunite not only on the television shows but in their homes, sharing rice and kimchi at the same table in the north and south. I would like to go back to Pyongyang myself by driving through a newly built Seoul-Pyongyang freeway, then my family and I could visit my father's grave site, and I would offer drinks to my father by pouring Korean rice wine over the grave mound, although my Puritan father wouldn't approve of the idea of pouring rice wine over his grave.

We would like to join with north Korean Christians in an open place for worship and break bread together to celebrate the resurrected body of Christ in our common Eucharist. We were overwhelmed at the news of official north Christian delegates and south Korean ecumenical leaders coming together in Switzerland to celebrate the Lord's Supper together. We experienced the resurrection of the body of Christ in that community of Christians who broke bread together in one faith even in a place so far away from home. Now, we would like the chance to taste the wine we might drink together in the name of our risen Lord in the history of the divided and suffering land of Korea. We would like to celebrate our traditional holiday of *Hanshik* (arbor day) and Liberation Day of August 15 as well as *Chusuk* (the autumn festival) together at our ancestors' burial sites sharing the best of our own food with each other, among both the living and dead. This, we believe, would truly be a celebration of the resurrection of the dead and the living alike.

Again, we believe in the resurrection in the Messanic Kingdom. As Paul says, "Then comes the end, when he delivers up the Kingdom of God the Father, after abolishing every kind of domination, authority, and power" (I Cor 15: 24). The resurrection we believe in is a socio-political one. In terms of the divided Korean people, resurrection means overcoming the state of division and achieving reunification with an eschatological vision of the Messianic Kingdom. Yes, we are theologically obsessed with the resurrection of the divided, dead nation of Korea in the eschatological Messianic Kingdom. Without this eschatological vision for the reunification of Korea, Korean Christianity would lack power in its theology and its mission within this divided and war-torn world of ours. The eschatological vision of resurrection exists in the vision of a New Earth and a New Heaven– "Now at last God has his dwelling among men. He will dwell among them and they shall be his people, and God himself will be with them. He will wipe every tear from their eyes; there shall be an end to death, and to mourning and pain; for the old order has passed away" (Rev 21: 3-4).

4. Resurrection and Eschatological Visions of Reunification

The more we become committed to overcoming our division and realizing the reunification of Korea, the more we think and believe in the reality of the faith of resurrection. Simply and clearly, overcoming the division and realizing the reunification of Korea is the resurrection and the coming of the eschatological Kingdom of the Lord within the particular history of this land of ours.

Our eschatological vision of the resurrection is theologically connected, *firstly*, with the year of Jubilee, the favorable year of the Lord. The February 1988 general assembly of NCCK adopted a declaration in which the Korean Christian churches revealed intentions to carry out a movement for a Jubilee Year for Peace and Reunification in 1995. The year 1995 will be the fiftieth anniversary of Liberation and at the same time the fiftieth year of the division of Korea. As in the declaration of the Jubilee by Jesus Himself, Korean Christians will be empowered by the Holy Spirit to be liberated from the yoke of division to see the oppressed and prisoners of the division return home and join their reunited families. The declaration of the Jubilee year embodies the history of salvation of the people of God. No dynasty or king has actually declared the Jubilee and seen it acted upon as promised. But it is the promise of God in history, and with faith in this promise, the people of God have struggled, died and suffered on the cross.

We do not know whether God would allow us to celebrate the Jubilee year in the year 1995, or if Christians and separated families of the north and south would be able to join together to share common meals at the table of the Lord. We do not know whether the year 1995 will bring the end of hatred and conflict between brothers and sisters in the north and south. But, what we do know for certain is that in our faith and conscience, we cannot go beyond the fiftieth year of division and separation, and remain silent about the suffering of our people on the cross of division.

However, as soon as the NCCK's declaration of the year of Jubilee was reported in the Korean press, a Christian ethicist openly criticized the declaration, stating that if the Jubilee year is actualized, it would mean the realization of socialism, and therefore the NCCK cannot escape the criticisms that it endorses socialist ideology. This has been a typical way of attacking the Bible as communist literature by true believers in the Bible. There is no mistake about it. The declaration of the Jubilee for Peace and Reunification of Korea is a movement toward the second liberation of the Korean people from the yokes of division, hatred, terrorism, murder and the deepest sins of mutual annihilation, Therefore, internally, the movement for the Jubilee in Korea is a movement for penitence, a theologico-ethical movement which is a faith preparation for the coming of the kingdom of God. Without a full-fledged movement of religious repentance, confessing the sins we have committed in the eyes of God—the sins of division, mutual hatred, mutual annihilation and mistrust—we will not be able to come together with our own brothers and sisters to the table of our rice community.

Immediately following the NCCK's February 1988 declaration, Christian colleagues began to criticize the movement, from mild and friendly advices and suggestions to pretty much open attacks such as examples mentioned earlier. But, what is basically lacking in these criticisms is an articulation of their faith and theological grounds for their opposition to the movement for the Jubilee year of peace and reunification. One cannot help but question where these critics stand on the issues of reconciliation, love, justice, and repentance for their deep-seated hatred, let alone their reasons for opposing responsible Christian responses to the task of overcoming the division of Korea and realizing peace in Asia as well as the world.

Our eschatological vision of resurrection, *secondly*, is connected with shalom, the peace of God which has been envisioned in the Messianic Kingdom in a New Heaven and New Earth. No present day Christian in

Korea, I believe, would oppose peaceful means of overcoming the division. And this concept of peace—yes, it is still a word and only a concept in our time—has become a dangerous word. If "the other side" proposes peace, then it is believed as a dangerous "peace offensive." And if this side proposes peace, then it is interpreted as a "sign of weakness." And when and if Christians talk about peace, we are criticized as either religious fanatics or as being the agents of "the other side."

Despite the danger, suspicion, and disbelief, Christian efforts for peace-making on this land are imperative, and we believe it is a commandment of God. In practical terms, peacemaking begins with the Christian mission of raising our voices against military build-up and intensifying tension across the line of division. Furthermore, with clear conscience, no one, neither Christian nor non-Christian of this land, could possibly advocate the use of nuclear weapons against each other. And no people of a sovereign and independent nation would welcome the perennial presence of foreign troops on their land, no matter how friendly or helpful they might be.

However, the Korean Christians' "peace proposals" in the NCCK Declaration have been criticized as "threats to peace." And we are still waiting for alternative peace proposals from our critical friends. We believe that as long as the present level of military confrontation is maintained, there can be no hope for national efforts to search for and reunite separated families, and no hope for the road to reunification of the land. Some argue that given this present state of tension, peaceful co-existence might be an alternative. This is a fantastic illusion. First of all, present levels of military build-up preclude the possibility of peaceful co-existence which requires mutual trust and respect. In order to maintain the present level of military balance, one side always has to out-do the other side in all respects. And the rhetoric does not promote peaceful co-existence, but military deterrence which always presupposes aggression from the other side.

Our critical Christian friends would ultimately not even accept the idea of peaceful co-existence for they strongly advocate eventual unification of the peninsula. Our friends neither accept our peace proposals nor the co-existence formula. Given this, the remarks made by the Korean Association of Evangelical Theologians in response to the NCCK's proposal are interesting as well as significant. They state that 1) they agree to the proposal (of NCCK) to widen the participation of the people in policy discussions on reunification; 2) they agree to the free exchanange of non-political visits across the demarcation line; and 3) they propose prayers and mission work to achieve reunification through the grace of God. These positions are asserted in spite of the fact that they oppose the NCCK's peace proposals and peaceful co-existence. They propose wide discussions on the issue of unification yet they offer only prayers.

In principle, our movement for peacemaking on the Korean peninsula and our proposals for peaceful co-existence only aim for the ultimate reunification of the people and the building of a new national community. We have no idea how to separate the issue of peace from reunification within the particular context of Korea as a people and as a nation. In Korea, division of the people and land opposes peace or peaceful co-existence. Reunification is the only road to peace not only on the Korean peninsula but the surrounding areas as well. For nearly half a century, we have been thrashed about between the two horns of the Korean dilemma – a fragile peace or reunification. We now have the courage and the understanding to realize that "fragile peace" is no peace, and fragile peace without positive efforts for unification is again, no peace at all. Peace on the Korean peninsula is an end in itself in the light of reunification and reunification is also in itself an end in the light of peacemaking.

We believe that working for peace on the Korean peninsula is working for international justice and the task of achieving unification is a task for achieving international justice. The division of Korea was a historical accident and an unfair solution. The division which was supposed to be the solution only raised more problems, to say the least. Therefore, the dialectical argument that peace must forego justice or that justice must assume an absence of peace cannot apply to the Korea case. Some latter-day Niebuhrian in Korea has made the comment that NCCK has not dealt with the justice issue in light of a balance of power. I myself had thought that this kind of argument went out with the American pull-out from the jungles of Vietnam. When you talk about justice from the point of peace, military strength is not necessarily being advocated. We have learned the hard way that the cost of building military strength is taking rice away from hungry children. Maintaining international justice through military power would bring about neither peace nor justice. Justice implies forgiveness rather than retaliation; and justice is reconciliation, not mutual accusation. Justice is needed because of the sinfulness of human nature. And justice is possible because of the righteousness of the human conscience. Justice cannot be maintained through hatred and mistrust, but by trust and goodwill within the human community. Peace is opposed to justice only when the peace is unjust. The peace in Korea cannot be true peace as long as nearly two million soldiers confront each other at gun point across the dividing line. We must agree on a simple point regarding peace and justice in Korea, namely, that we have come to realize more and more that without peace and unification, there can be no justice, freedom, respect for human dignity, or national integrity.

Our *third* vision of the eschatological nature of our belief in the resurrection of a divided people on the cross of national suffering has been the subject of many questions. People ask what kind of blueprint or ideological vision do we have for the united Korea. I am puzzled about the priorities that a person who asks such questions has. Do we have to have some kind of a detailed blueprint about the kingdom of God when we talk about our dreams and hopes besides what we have in the Gospel? Are we disqualified from talking about the future of a united Korea simply because we have an open and unprogrammed computer disk? The picture of our united Korea will become clearer as we begin to work step by step toward building peace on and around the Korean peninsula and implement various political, economical, cultural as well as scholarly and humanitarian exchanges. And as these programmes become frequent and varied, a slow but steady and certain process will be developed to achieve a political solution for unification. Then and only then, will the question of what kind of ideology present itself as an issue. As we take steps to building peace and an atmosphere for wide participation by the people on the reunification issue, the question of ideology is not the most urgent problem. But when this question is raised, it is clear that the people will have to draw this ideological blueprint. For now, our blueprint is based on a dream of the kingdom of God where space exists for the people of Korea to freely choose their own system of government as well as ideology for their own united nation. Our immediate hope is for freedom of the people in both the north and south to discuss the issues of peace and unification. This freedom will allow Koreans to live with dignity as persons and as the subjective forces within their nation and history.

Now we hear the voice of the suffering people in the divided land of Korea–

Prepare the way for the Lord,
make his path straight.
    Every valley of barbed wire shall be filled with flowers,
and every mountain and hill of nuclear mines shall
be brought low ;
and the crooked will be straightened,
and the divided line of the DMZ shall be demolished
and erased from the map;
and the rough ways on the bridge of no return shall be
made smooth and wide for the free traffic of people;
and all flesh shall see the salvation and liberation of God
(Lk 3:4-6, *Paraphrased*).

Re-commitment, Lee Chul-Su

Harvest, Lee Chul-Su

Notes

1: Faith, Praxis and Theology.

1. My father insisted I should go to the Japanese schools in Manchuria, because they give the best education to their own children.

2. W.L. Swallen, *Sunday School Lessons on the Book of Exodus* (Seoul: Religious Tract Society, 1907), p. 4.

3. George L. Paik, *The History of Protestant Missions in Korea, 1832-1901* (Seoul, Yonsei University Press, 1970, first published in 1929 by Christian Union College, P'yongyang), p. 97. But Paik records that "on July 28, 1884, the Mission Board appointed Rev. H.G. Underwood as the first clerical missionary to Korea," *ibid.*, p. 109. There is a question on this date of Allen's arrival. Some believe that Allen arrived in Korea earlier. See Sim Il-sup, "The First Protestant Missionary Work in Korea," *Korean Christianity and the Third World* (in Korean), (Seoul: Pul-Bit, 1981), p. 74. This is an excellent study based exclusively on the work of Dr. Allen. Also, Kang, We-Jo, "Horace Newton Allen's Contribution to Korea, 1884-1905," a Master of Arts degree thesis, Department of History, The University of Chicago, 1962., F.H. Harrington, *God, Mammon and the Japanese: Dr. Horace N. Allen and Korean-American Relations, 1884-1905* (Madison, Wisconsin:

The University of Wisconsin Press, 1966). Probably the best material on Allen would be his own work, *Things Korean* (New York: Flemming H. Revell Co., 1908) and his papers deposited in the New York Public Library.

4. We notice Mollendorff's name in the 19th century diplomatic history of Korea in various connections with the first missionary endeavors. For a general account of his diplomatic involvement in Korea, see Martina Deuchler, *Confucian Gentlemen and Barbarian Envoys: The Opening of Korea, 1875-1885* (Seattle: University of Washington Press, 1977). Also, Koh, Byong-ik, "P.G. von Mollendorff, His Employment by the Korean Government," *The Chin-tan Hakpo, the 30th Anniversary Volume for December 1964,* pp. 225-244.

5. Allen's letter to F.F. Ellingwood from Seoul dated October 8, 1884, quoted by Paik, *ibid.*, p. 97.

6. Arthur Brown, *Mastery of the Far East* (New York: Charles Scribner, 1919), p. 517.

7. William Blair, *The Korean Pentecost* (Edinburgh: The Banner of Truth Trust, 1977), p. 42.

8. A full account of the 1907 revival movement of Korea by an American eyewitness is in Blair, *op. cit.*

9. Allen D. Clark, *A History of the Church in Korea* (Seoul: CLS, 1971), p. 166.

10. *Ibid.*

11. James H. Cone, *God of the Oppressed* (New York: The Seabury Press, 1975), p. 29.

12. See Kim Yong Bock, ed., *Minjung Theology* (Singapore: The Christian Conference of Asia, 1981), Particularly my chapter, "Minjung and Theology in Korea," pp. 17-42.

13. *Documents on the Struggle for Democracy* (Tokyo: Shinkyo Shuppansha, 1975), p. 43.

14. Paik, *The History of Protestant Missions in Korea,* p. 202.

15. Clark, *A History of the Church in Korea,* pp. 112-113.

16. Paik, *op. cit,* p. 127.

17. *Ibid.*

18. Helen Kim, *Grace Sufficient* (Nashville: The Upper Room, 1964), p. 30.

19. Paik, *op. cit,* p. 230.

20. *Ibid.,* p. 130.

21. *Ibid.,* pp. 203-204.

22. *Ibid.,* p. 58.

23. "Han" is a Korean word difficult to translate. But it may be translated "a feeling of unresolved resentment against unjustifiable suffering."

24. Paik Nak-chun, "The Persecution of the Korean Church" (in Korean), *Sinhak Nondan*, Vol.6, (October, 1962), p. 19.

25. *Ibid.*, p.7. Translation and quotation by Kim Yong Bock, *Historical Transformation, People's Movement and Messianic Koinonia*, unpublished doctoral dissertation, Princeton Theological Seminary, 1976, p. 320.

26. A full account by a missionary in Korea is Federal Council of Boards of Foreign Mission, U.S.A., *Korean Situation: Conspiracy Case*, 1912.

27. Also by F.A. McKenzie, "Torture a la Mode" in *Korea's Fight for Freedom* (New York: Fleming H. Revell company, 1920).

28. *Ibid.*, p. 251.

29. *Ibid.*

30. *Ibid.*, pp. 251-252.

31. *Ibid.*, p. 252.

32. *Ibid.*, p. 244.

33. Quoted by McKenzie, *ibid.*, p. 243.

34. *Ibid.*

35. *Ibid.*, p. 246.

36. *Ibid.*, p. 247.

37. *Ibid.*, p. 249.

38. *Ibid.*

39. *Ibid.*, p. 247.

40. Song Kun Ho, "The March First Independence Movement and Christianity," *Korean Christianity and the Third World* (in Korean), (Seoul: Pul-Bit, 1981), p. 78.

41. *Ibid.*, p. 79.

42. Lee, Man Ryul, "The March First Independence Movement and Christianity," *Korean Christianity and Historical Consciousness* (in Korean) (Seoul: Jisiksanup-Sa, 1981), p. 70.

43. McKenzie, *op. cit*, p. 11.

2: The Minjung Movement

1. Choo Chai-yong, "A Brief Sketch of Korean Christian History from the Minjung Perspective," *Minjung Theology* (Singapore: The Christian Conference of Asia, 1981), pp. 69ff.

2. Song Kun Ho, "Korea under Japanese Imperialism and Christianity," *Nationalism and Christianity* (in Korean) (Seoul: Minjung-Sa, 1981), p. 81.

3. Kim Yang Sun, "History of Korean Christianity," *The Cultural History of Korea* (in Korean) (Seoul: Korea University Press, 1970), p. 629.
4. Song, *op.cit.*, p. 83.
5. *Ibid.*, p. 84
6. Kuma Kenichi, *The Problem of Chosen Farmers*, pp. 45-46, quoted by Song, *op.cit.*, p. 84.
7. Illuminating studies on the period: Kang Dong Jin, *A History of Japanese Policies in Korea* (in Korean) (Seoul: Hangil-Sa, 1980); Kang We Jo, *Religions and Politics of Korea During the Japanese Occupation* (in Korean) (Seoul: CLS, 1977).
8. Song, *op.cit.*, p. 85.
9. Lee Yong Hun, *History of Korean Church* (Seoul: CLS, 1975), p. 174.
10. Kim, *Grace Sufficient* (Nashville: The Upper Room, 1964), p. 87.
11. A full account of Lee's mysticism is in Min Kyong Bae, *The Church and the Nation* (Seoul: CLS, 1981), pp. 280ff.
12. Letters of Lee Yong Do, edited by Pyun Chong Ho, 1934, quoted by Min Kyong Bae, *Korean Church History* (in Korean) (Seoul : CLS, 1968), p. 288. My translation.
13. Lee Yong Do, *op. cit.*, p. 173. My translation.
14. *Ibid.*, p. 188. My translation.
15. A full account of "Fundamentalism Debate of 1934" is given by Kim Yang Sun, *Ten Years of the Korean Church since the Liberation* (in Korean) (Seoul: Presbyterian Press, 1956), pp. 173-185.
16. Allen D. Clark, *A History of the Church in Korea* (Seoul: CLS, 1971), p. 223. Also, Harry A. Rhodes and Archbald Campbell, *History of the Korea Mission, Presbyterian Church in the U.S.A., Vol. II. (1935-1959)* (New York: Commission on Ecumenical Mission and Relations, UPUSA, 1964), pp. 7-16
17. Min, *Korean Church History*, p. 322.
18. Rhodes and Campbell, *op. cit.*, pp. 17-26.
19. Minutes of the 27th General Assembly, Min, *Korean Church History*, p. 324. My translation.
20. Min, *loc. cit.*
21. Kim Yang Sun, *op. cit*, pp. 233-234.
22. George L. Paik, *The History of Protestant Missions in Korea, 1832-1910* (Seoul: Yonsei University Press,1970), pp. 215-216.
23. Kim Yang Sun, *op. cit.*, p. 272.
24. An excellent survey on the Korean theological development in the 1960's by Han Chul Ha, "Trends of Korean Protestant Theology," in *Korean Christian Almanac, 1970* (in Korean) (Seoul: KNCC, 1970)

pp. 44-72.

25. The title of my dissertation: "The Problem of Cognitivity in Religious Speech Acts."

26. For English texts of Park's emergency decrees, see *Documents on the Struggle for Democracy in Korea* (Tokyo: Shinkyo Shuppansha, 1975).

27. *Ibid.,* p. 123.

28. *Ibid.,* pp. 124-125.

29. George Ogle, "Development and the Labor Struggle in South Korea," *Human Rights,* edited by Dong Soo Kim and Byong-suh Kim (Montclair, N.J.: Association of Korean Christian Scholars in North America, 1979), p. 179.

30. Cho Seun Hyuk, *Realization of Urban Industrial Mission* (in Korean) (Seoul: Minjung-Sa, 1981), p. 112.

31. *Ibid.*

32. Harvey Cox, *The Seduction of the Spirit* (New York: A Touchstone Book, Simon and Schuster, 1973), pp. 262ff.

33. In Kim Chi Ha's poem *Whang To* (1970), translated by Suh Nam Dong, in *Minjung Theology,* p. 57.

34. *Documents., op. cit.,* pp. 215-221.

35. *Ibid.*

36. Jurgen Moltmann, "Toward a Political Hermeneutics of the Gospel, "USQR Vol. XXIII, (Summer, 1968), and "Political Theology," *Theology Today.*

37. *Documents, loc. cit.*

3: Shamanism : The Religion of Han

1. "Han" is a sense of unresolved resentment against injustice suffered, a sense of helplessness because of overwhelming odds against, a feeling of acute pain or sorrow.

2. Ryu, Dongshik, *Hankuk Mukyoeu Yuksa wa Kujo* (History and Structure of Korean Shamanism) (Seoul: Yonsei University Press, 1975). p. 274.

3. Kim, Teagon, *Hankuk Musok Yonku* (A study of Korean Shamanism) (Seoul: Jipmun-Dang, 1981), p. 194f.

4. Laurel M. Kendall's excellent doctoral dissertation on Korean Shamanism based on her intensive field work in Korea, *Restless Spirits : Shaman and Housewife in Korean Ritual Life* (Unpublished Doctoral Dissertation from Columbia University, 1979), p. 241.

5. *Ibid.,* pp. 241-242.

6. *Ibid.*, p. 242.
7. Kim, Teagon, *op. cit.*, p. 11.
8. *Ibid.*
9. Sohn, Jin Tae, *Chosen Minjok Munhwa eu Yunku* (a Study on the Culture of the Korean People) (Seoul: Eulyu MunhwaSa, 1948), Also, Lee Jung-young, "Concerning the Origin and Formation of Korean Shamanism, "*International Review for the History of Religions* (Vol. XX, Fasc. 2, August 1973), pp. 135-159. Lee quotes Mircea Eliade, "It is difficult to determine the 'origin' of Korean Shamanism" and agrees with Eliade by saying that "the origin of Korean Shamanism is uncertain." Mircea Eliade, *Shamanism: Archaic Techniques of Ecstacy* (New York: Bollingen Foundation, 1964), p. 462.
10. Yim, Suk-jae, "Introduction to Shamanism, " *Korea Journal* (Vol. IV, No.2, 1972), p. 15.
11. Charles A. Clark, *Religions of Old Korea* (Seoul: Christian Literature Society of Korea, 1961), p. 194. First lectured in 1929 on the subject.
12. In Korean, Jishin Balp'ki.
13. Ryu, *ibid.*, p. 250.
14. *Ibid.*, p. 256.
15. Kendall, *ibid.*, p. 86.
16. Clark, *op. cit.*, p. 204.
17. *Ibid.*, p. 206.
18. Ryu, *op. cit.*, p. 314. My translation.
19. *Ibid.*, p. 315. My translation.
20. Michael Saso, Professor of Religion, University of Hawaii, May, 1982.
21. Homer B. Hulbert, *The Passing of Korea* (Seoul: Yonsei University Press, 1969, first published in 1906), pp. 403-404.
22. I am indebted to Michael Saso's interpretation on the psychological aspects of *Kut* ritual in his short but significant paper; "Korean Shaman: A Preliminary Report," July, 1981. Also, Kim Kwang-iel, "Psychoanalytic Considerations of the Korean Shaman," in *Korean Neuro-psychiatric Association Journal* (Vol. II, No.2, 1972), pp. 121ff.
23. Michael Saso, in his report, p. 14.
24. Hulbert, *op. cit.*, p. 404.
25. Gale, *Korea in Transition*, p. 78.
26. Clark, *op. cit.*, p. 195.
27. *Ibid.*, p. 196.
28. Underwood, *Religions of Eastern Asia*, p. 110.
29. *Ibid.*
30. Clark, *op. cit.*, p. 196.

31. Ryu, *op. cit.*, pp. 288ff.
32. I am indebted to Youngsook Kim Harvey, *Six Korean Women: The Sociali- zation of Shamans* (St. Paul, Minnesota: West Publishing Co., 1979), a study based on her extensive interviews with Korean shamans and field work in Korea.
33. *Ibid.*
34. *Ibid.*, p. 208.

4: Minjung and Spirituality

1. The chapter was originally prepared for a workshop on spiritual formation sponsored by the PTE/WCC at Iona, Scotland on April 26, 1987.
2. The Mud Flower Collective (Katie G. Cannon and six others), *God's Fierce Whimsy: Christian Feminism and Theological Education* (New York: The Pilgrim Press, 1985) pp. 164 f.
3. *Ibid.*
4. *Ibid.*
5. Juan Luis Segundo, *The Liberation of Theology* (Maryknoll, N.Y. : Orbis Books, 1982).

5: Minjung and Buddhism in Korea

1. Edward Conze, *Buddhist Scriptures* (New York: Penguin Books, 1979) p. 39.
2. *Ibid.*, p. 40.
3. Walpola Rahula, *What the Buddha Taught* (London : Gordon Fraser, 1978), pp. 19f.
4. *Ibid.*
5. *Ibid.*, p. 29
6. Quoted by Nancy Wilson Ross, *Buddhism: A Way of Life and Thought* (New York: Alfred A. Knopf, 1980), p. 186.
7. Edward Conze, *Buddhism: Essence and Development* (New York: Harper and Row, 1959), p. 126.
8. "The Boddhisattva Vow" from *Garuda V Transcending Hesitation* (Boulder, Colorado, Vajradhatu, 1977), p. 44.
9. Ko Ik-Chin, "Wonhyo and the Foundation of Korean Buddhism," *Korea Journal*, Vol. 21, No. 8 (August, 1981), p. 4.
10. *Sam Kuk Yusa* (Seoul: Yonsei University Press, 1972), p. 306.
11. Quoted by Ko, *loc. cit.*, *Sang Kaoseng Chuan*, Vol. 4, "Sok Uisang."

12. Cho Myung-Ki, "Prominent Buddhist Leaders and Their Doctrines," *Korea Journal,* Vol. 4, No. 5 (May, 1964), p. 17.
13. Sam Kuk Yusa, *op. cit.,* p. 306.
14. *Ibid.*
15. *Ibid.*
16. *Ibid.,* p. 307.
17. *Ibid.,* pp. 307-308.
18. Park Sung-bae, *Buddhist Faith and Sudden Enlightenment* (to be published by New York State University Press, Stony Brook, 1982), p. 114.
19. *Ibid.,* p. 117.
20. Yoshito Hakeda, *The Awakening of Faith* (New York : Columbia University Press, 1967), p. 102.
21. Park: "Sun (Zen) and Pure Land in Korea" (an unpublished manuscript, 1975).
22. Ryu Dongshik, *Hankuk Mukyoeu Yuksa wa Kujo* (History and Structure of Korean Shamanism) (Seoul : Yonsei University Press, 1975), pp. 260ff.
23. Pyo Il-Cho, "An Introduction to Korean Minjung Buddhism, "*Korean Minjung Buddhism* (Seoul: Hankil-Sa, 1980), p. 343.
24. *Ibid.,* p. 347.

6: Mask Dance of Liberation

1. This chapter was originally written for the D.T. Niles Memorial Lecture at the 8th CCA Assembly in Seoul, Korea, June 26 to July 2, 1985.
2. Commission on Theological Concerns of the Christian Conference of Asia, *Minjung Theology: People as Subjects of History* (Maryknoll, N. Y. : Orbis Books, 1983), p. 48.
3. Sallie McFague, *Metaphorical Theology* (Philadelphia: Fortress Press, 1982), p. 4.
4. Kim Chi Ha, *The Gold-Crowned Jesus and Other Writings,* Chong Sun-Kim and Shelly Killen, eds. (Maryknoll, N. Y.: Orbis Books, 1978), pp. 121-125.
5. Cho Dong Il, "An Analysis of Bong San Mask Dance," *History and Principle of Mask Dance,* [Korean] (Seoul : Hong Sung Sa, 1979), p. 203.
6. *Ibid.,* p. 206
7. C.S. Song, Unpublished paper, no date.
8. *Ibid.*